## Also by Lee Wulff

*Salmon on a Fly*
*Leaping Silver*
*The Atlantic Salmon*
*Handbook of Freshwater Fishing*
*Lee Wulff on Flies*
*Trout on a Fly*
*Fishing with Lee Wulff*
*The Compleat Lee Wulff*

# Bush Pilot
# Angler

# Bush Pilot
# Angler

## A MEMOIR

*by*
*Lee Wulff*

Down East Books

Down East Books
P.O. Box 679
Camden, ME 04843
BOOK ORDERS: 1-800-685-7962

Library of Congress Cataloging-in-Publication Data

Wulff, Lee.
    Bush pilot angler : a memoir / by Lee Wulff.
        p. cm.
    ISBN 0-89272-480-3 (hc)
    1. Fishing—Newfoundland—Anecdotes. 2. Bush
flying—Newfoundland—Anecdotes. 3. Wulff, Lee.  I. Title.
    SH572.N6 W86 2000
    799.1'09718--dc21
                                                    00-056962

# Contents

# Introduction

Twelve hundred miles northeast of New York City lies the Canadian province of Newfoundland/Labrador. Today it is a destination for tourists visiting Gros Morne National Park and the L'Anse-aux-Meadows Viking settlement. In the late 1930s, however, Newfoundland was little more than a remote, isolated, fog-bound island stretching across the mouth of the St. Lawrence River. Labrador was a place on the map, nothing more.

The region's timber and fishery resources were bountiful: the cod fishery off the Grand Banks supplied much of the North Atlantic and Caribbean with food, and logging for the pulp mills was in its infancy but growing steadily. Because Newfoundland lacked a road network, goods and people traveled by the single, narrow-gauge rail line that ran from the southwest corner of the province, at Port-aux-Basques, to the capital, St. John's, on the Avalon peninsula. The only other means of transport was coastal steamers and pick-up schooners that plied the waters to the outport towns in the summer. The steamers departed from Corner Brook, on the west coast, at the mouth of the Humber River, and from St. John's.

Communication was indubitably slow—a linear telegraph line along the coast of the northwestern peninsula served as the principal information link to most communities. The majority of settlements lacked electricity, but battery-operated radios tuned to St. John's gave focus and great pride to Newfoundlanders. Messages to and from the many boats at sea were read on the six o'clock news.

The people were independent and resourceful, necessary traits for living in these remote areas. Fishing for cod occupied the summer months, and work in the forests cutting trees for the paper mills kept the locals busy in the winter months. In between, household chores were crammed into a few short weeks. Women were strong and capable of sawing and splitting the wood needed to keep the fires going, and men were good cooks of basic staples. Their love of the land and the hardscrabble culture ran strong.

To the north, on the continent, lay Labrador, with its stunted trees and bogs underpinned by the broad Canadian shield. Few people from the outside ventured into this wilderness. But World War II changed everything. Newfoundland became important because it was a place that German U-boats frequented. In 1941, the Nazis torpedoed and sank the S.S. *Caribou,* the link across the Cabot Strait between Sydney, Nova Scotia, and Port-aux-Basque. This was the principal ship bringing basic supplies to the island. To this day, many Newfoundland homes have a framed photo of the *Caribou* with its crew and their lost relatives.

Pristine salmon rivers abounded throughout Newfoundland. It was these waters and their Atlantic salmon that attracted Lee Wulff to the province in the late 1930s, after he found a career in civil engineering and graphic arts unfulfilling. Born and raised until age eleven in Valdez, Alaska, Lee had the boreal forest in his bones, and salmon fishing was his passion. He was as close to these fish as most of us are to our kin. When he wasn't trying to catch salmon, he was thinking and writing about them; tying flies and making doodles of salmon consumed his spare moments.

Portland Creek, midway down the northwestern peninsula of Newfoundland, was his favorite river—a short flow, quiet except for the continuous splashing of leaping salmon. Lee wanted to share its beauty with other anglers. He wanted others to enjoy what he found to be the ultimate fishing experience. Thus, he embarked upon establishing a series of fishing and hunting camps. Lee was able to mobilize many of the residents of Portland Creek, the River of Ponds, and Daniel's Harbour to work for him. The Newfound-landers admired him and, out of respect, gave him the title of the "old fella" at the relatively young age of forty-five.

After World War II, in the prime of his life, Lee took up flying as a necessity: to transport his guests to remote fishing rivers and their rich bounty. He made his first flight to Newfoundland in a sixty-five-horsepower, J3 Piper Cub soon after receiving his pilot's license, and this trip was the beginning of a second love. Quickly, flying became a passion to parallel salmon fishing. Lee was as born to fly as he was to fish. His marriage of flying and fishing would continue for another forty-five years until his death of a heart attack while flying his Super Cub, *Lima Whiskey*, at age eighty-six. He loved the feel of the Cub; it was light and agile, a plane he was at one with. Late in life, he once commented that were he starting over, he would do it in an ultralight aircraft.

Through the years and with a number of planes, he explored Newfoundland's northwestern rivers into the 1950s. Beginning in the middle of that decade, he watched the decline of the fishing as roads were built in an effort to bring the province's outport towns into the twentieth century. Soon he was flying "down" to Labrador, where he knew the roads would be decades behind him. Here again, he found rivers teeming with salmon and big brook trout.

My father always found salmon fishing to be a challenge. He championed the sport throughout his life and shared his knowledge with all who would listen. And so, here is the story of Lee Wulff, drifting flies to Atlantic salmon in Newfoundland/Labrador and exploring the bush in his flying machine.

Barry Wulff
Philomath, Oregon
June 2000

# THE CROSSING

## JUNE 5, 1947

∼

T he night was black around me save for the pinpoints of light in the cluster of houses on the far side of the brackish-water pond. Even they were blinking out, one by one. My Piper Cub, *Yellow Bird*, was pulled up beside me on the gravel, tail in. The waves of Cabot Strait hissed in and out over the beach on the far side of the thin strip of land that separated Dingwall Pond from the open sea. The lagoon itself was quiet, with only the faintest lapping of waves at the water's edge.

I lay on the gravel, fully clothed, with a blanket wrapped around me. I rested with one hand stretched out toward the water so that the rising tide in the pond would wake me in time to shift the plane farther back and higher on the beach. As a further precaution, I had wrapped a light rope around me and had tied its far end to a wing strut in case I still slept while the rising water floated the plane free.

Behind me lay a long, tiring day of hippity-hop flying from Eastport, Maine, to St. John, New Brunswick, and then to New Glasgow and Sydney, both in Nova Scotia. I was now at the province's northeastern tip, where there was nothing but a hundred miles of open water between me and Newfoundland, where my fishing camps awaited me.

At each stop on my route north from my home at Shushan, New York, I'd had to land where I could taxi the plane in to a low pier or beach so that I could get gas and carry it back to refill my tanks. The regular tank, just behind the firewall and ahead of where I sat, held twelve gallons. Overhead was a five-gallon auxiliary tank, and on the single seat in front of mine there sat a five-gallon tank from which I could transfer gas to the main tank with a hand pump. Fully fueled at Sydney, only an hour behind me, I had more than enough gas for the crossing.

The days were long and getting longer as the latitude grew greater and the June sun moved higher in the sky. It would be a short night.

I dozed until the cold water reached my hand, then rose and went to the tail of the plane, lifting and sliding the Cub higher on the beach. Four times I woke to shift the *Yellow Bird,* and on the last there was a faint glow in the east. The pond, which had been quiet, was sending small but steadily increasing waves up onto the beach, where they beat a rhythm against the aluminum sheeting of my floats. The wind was rising, and soon I could make out clouds above me moving swiftly to the northeast.

The wind was freshening. Whitecaps were showing up downwind and out to sea. What had my flight instructor, Lew Lavery, said about the wind? "If you don't fly in more than fifteen miles of wind, it won't bother you." But the wind was already up to twenty miles an hour or more, and it was gusty from the hills it had just come over. Out over the open water, though, it would be smooth and . . . it was going my way.

I pushed the plane off the beach until it was barely afloat, then turned it toward the pond. Stepping up onto a float, I primed the engine and gave the prop four turns to lubricate the cylinders and get some gas into them. I walked back on the float to turn on the switch, then forward again to swing the prop. When the motor caught, I got into the back seat to taxi slowly for a while and let the motor warm up. I checked out the magnetos at 1,500 revolutions.

Half a mile away, the little village of Dingwall was still sleeping. No ribbon of smoke lifted from any house. Finally, the needle of the oil-temperature gauge began to move up. It was time. I pushed the throttle full forward and lifted off the pond, into the wind. At two hundred feet, I turned downwind and climbed slowly, staying a little under my normal cruising speed of sixty-five-miles an hour, heading northeast, out over the lead-gray sea.

There is time to think when you fly over long stretches of water. All pilots know that at such times, airplane motors develop mysterious sounds that they never make over the safety of the land. They seem to run rough and emit little surges and knocks you've never noticed before. But I was heartened by the words of a little man I'd met in Sydney when I stopped there for gas. He'd introduced himself as Billy Bishop and said he'd been a flight instructor in England all during the war.

"Don't worry about that motor," he'd said. "As long as your oil gauge shows pressure and you still have gas, it will run forever." So what was there to worry about? Plenty.

Suppose I crossed the hundred miles of water and there was fog right down to the waves? If the fog was just over the water and I was just over the wave tops, there was no way I could make a fast turn. Would I see the shore before I banged into it? If it fogged in before I was halfway across, should I turn back and fight a wind that was more than half as fast as I was flying and might increase? What had Lew Lavery said? "It takes a good pilot to stay within twenty degrees of a given compass heading."

I felt sure I'd hit Newfoundland somewhere within a hundred-mile stretch of coastline, even allowing for the drift the wind might give to my course. My small compass pointed to the magnetic pole, which was almost thirty degrees off true north by my map. But, if I had to turn back, there was a lot of empty water on either side of that narrow eastern point of Nova Scotia. I flew sixty degrees, magnetic, as well as I could. The strong wind was behind me, and my bird was flying faster over the roughening sea than it had ever traveled before.

An hour is a long time to think, and when I wasn't mesmerized by the white-crested waves a thousand feet below me my mind drifted back to things behind me. The letter had come from Jake Miller, sales manager for Piper Aircraft. He would agree to my suggestion, he wrote, and Piper would exchange a J3 Cub on floats for a thirty minute, 16mm color-sound film that would show how valuable the airplane could be in taking me, its pilot, to fabulous wilderness fishing available in no other way. Piper would teach me to fly at Round Lake, New York, not far from my home. The film would have to be ready by February 1, 1948.

There was some question as to the advisability of the venture. My friend H. G. Tapply, editor of *Outdoors* magazine, for which I wrote a fishing column, had talked with Bill Turgeon, chief pilot for Maine's Fish and Game Department. Bill had said, "The guy's crazy. There's too much wind for a little plane like that in Newfoundland. He'll be blown apart in the gales they have down there."

Dave Harbour, a wartime pilot, who also wrote for *Outdoors,* had called me up when he heard of my proposed trip and said, "It's pretty risky. Remember to keep your nose down. Don't risk a stall. Fly right into the ground if you have to make a forced landing."

Not one of the experienced pilots I knew had given me the least encouragement. There were no light planes in Newfoundland, no private aircraft. There were only military planes that came and went from Canada, including one or two heavy bush planes like the Norseman. The U.S. Navy had brought two J3 Cubs down to Argentia on one of their freighters, but none of the pilots at that base wanted to fly them there, though many had trained in Cubs. The planes were never taken out of the crates and went back after VE day, just as they'd been shipped. I'd be breaking new ground, but because I knew and loved the country I'd be flying over, I felt sure I could manage. If I were forced down on land, no matter where in Newfoundland, I could walk to some habitation. I had no fear of the "bush." I was a woodsman and knew how to survive.

On the negative side I was forty-two, old to become a pilot, and I had to rush through my training period in a recklessly short time—less than three weeks—because the plane was delivered late. Ten days after I got my license, with scant time for practice flying, I had taken off for the camps. I was green and I knew it. Now and then, as I flew, I would repeat to myself, "There are old pilots and bold pilots but there are no old, bold pilots." Flying was new and wonderful, but I had an awful lot to learn.

Forty-five minutes out of Dingwall. Ceiling less than one thousand and lowering. Wind growing stronger to judge by the white curls of the waves.

I was closer to the sea now, but there was no sign of fog ahead. All I could see was graying distance over a dull carpet of endless crests foaming in the wind. I strained my eyes. Nothing. Was this how Lindbergh felt? Or Coli and Nungesser whom perhaps the waves reached up and took as they tried to make the first east-to-west crossing of the Atlantic? Or did they reach some as yet undiscovered stretch of Newfoundland or Labrador, only to crash and die there?

Ella Manvel, my bride of half a year, would be waiting at Lomond. She'd driven down with my small sons, Allan and Barry, and her own two boys, Jonathan and Tony. Lacking a radio in my plane, I'd sent a wire from Sydney but hadn't known then that I was going to fly by way of Dingwall or when or where I'd try to fly across Cabot Strait. If I went down, who'd know where I'd be in the wide stretch of water between the Atlantic and the Gulf of St. Lawrence? But that was only a fleeting thought. Hadn't Billy Bruce said these motors ran forever . . . and hadn't I leaned from a good instructor?

The motor was running rough again. It was hard to remember just how it used to sound when there was land below me and I took its more or less steady roar for granted. The clouds were still coming down. I was flying just under them at five hundred feet.

A dark line stretched across the horizon like a heavy cloud. Then it was gone. A moment later it was back again. It came on swiftly and grew to be waves pounding on rocks, with the dark green of spruce and fir lifting from the waves to dissolve into the clouds.

I'd made the crossing.

I turned left at the shore, and as I flew north the sky grew lighter. Fifteen minutes more and I could see sunshine ahead, shining on the broad expanse of St. George's Bay. I'd come back to the evergreen forests, the deep, blue bays, and the flashing trout and salmon rivers I loved.

Now I was flying over the railroad. Below me was Crabb's

River. It was almost as if my legs were deep in that beautiful salmon pool below where I'd landed a fifteen-pounder. I could feel the current. I could smell the scent as the dark and sober evergreen tips took on the look of bursting buds—like pale green flowers. I could hear, in my mind, the rustle of the river and the sound of the birds, freshly north, bursting into love songs.

I was home.

# THE BEGINNINGS

❦

My fishing began long before I knew that Newfoundland existed. When I was two, my Norwegian-born mother took me to the little brook behind our house in Valdez, Alaska. My tackle was a bent pin on a string, tied to a willow switch and baited with a piece of bacon to catch small trout. Later on she told me, "Son, you were born to fish."

I was the fishing prodigy in our small town, where every family put down at least one barrel of salted salmon or trout every winter. In Valdez, there were hundreds of sled dogs, and all of them had to be fed during the summer—when they weren't useful—on the cheapest possible food, which was fish. Slop Jake, who was clean-up man at the two major saloons, had the job of feeding the dogs. At age eight, I was his right-hand man. We covered the salmon and trout runs, and we caught fish by spearing, snaring, gaffing, and snagging.

Spearing was the most fun. It was challenging to judge a fish's speed and take into account the index of refraction when striking while the salmon were swimming past at fifteen or twenty miles an hour. When they were lying quietly in deep, clear water, you could reach down with your soft wire snare on the end of a long pole and slip it over a fish's head, tightening the noose between his head and front fins and lifting him out onto the bank. With gaffs—big 14/0 hooks fastened to the end of long, light bamboo poles—we could reach out and hook the fish in the back when they were visible. Or, when the streams were cloudy with glacial runoff, we could just rake the water where we knew the salmon would lie.

When the fish were lying beyond the reach of gaffs and snares, we would use a long bamboo pole with an equal length of line tied to it and a big treble hook attached. We'd throw it out and let it sink and drift to a point just beyond a big trout or salmon, then we'd yank and set the hook in his side and play him to the shore. Again, when the streams were cloudy, we would just cast the treble and drift it into the eddies or runs where we knew the fish should be lying and yank when we thought it was in the right position. There were so many fish that even with blind snagging we were very successful. It is hard to imagine how many thousands of salmon and trout crowded into our small streams and rivers.

In my ninth year, "Rosy" Roseen, an Englishman, came to town and got a job as a jail guard. He worked mostly nights and was free to fish in the daytime, and he was a dedicated fly fisherman. He fished for the residual trout in the streams, the fish that were always there. They were smaller than the fish that came in from the sea in periodic waves—and they were much harder to catch, particularly on flies. But whenever there was no run of fish from the sea in any of the streams, I went out with Rosy and he taught me to fly-fish. My father bought me a simple fly-casting outfit, and from then on fly fishing was my favorite way of taking trout and salmon.

Later on, when I was finishing high school in San Diego and going offshore to fish, I went through a period of seasickness where I'd be catching tuna or yellowtail and throwing up at the same time. In time, I got over it because I wanted nothing to stop me from savoring and understanding every kind of sportfishing that existed. I wanted to become the All-American Angler, even though I knew such a classification could never be recognized because angling is not a sport where scores can determine without question which contestant is best at any particular moment. As time went on, my strategy for trying to be the best was to concentrate on the most difficult fish. I decided that if I could really learn the ways of these species, then understanding the rest would be easy.

One of the two most difficult fish, I concluded, was the Atlantic salmon, for to catch him, an angler has to reach his mind, rather than his stomach. When the salmon returns to his native rivers he simply cannot digest any food. Only mammals can recognize their own young, and because salmon are great predators, they would soon eat up the young fish of earlier spawnings and destroy their own species. Nature sends the Atlantic salmon back to their native rivers so supercharged with energy that they need not feed to have strength enough to spawn and, hopefully, get back to the sea to recuperate for another run the next year.

The second fish, the giant bluefin tuna, is the toughest in the angling world. It is stronger and often bigger than any of the other fish in the sea and requires the greatest skill and heaviest tackle to subdue. In time I was able to concentrate on those two species. Strangely, it was a tuna that enabled me to get to know the Atlantic salmon as few anglers have known him.

# THE TOURNAMENT

❧

There it was in the *New York Times,* a picture of the biggest fish taken at Wedgeport in the world's first great angling tournament, a three-day competition between the Americans and the Canadians. Standing beside that great 569-pound bluefin was a smiling angler, and I was that man. Catching this fish meant success and, literally, the kind of fame Irving Berlin had written about in his Easter bonnet song, "you'll find that you're in the rotogravure." It was a long way to come for a kid who had wanted—more than anything else—to be a great fisherman.

There had been some lucky breaks. I'd come to Wedgeport in 1937 to watch and, perhaps, to write and sell a magazine story on the match. Just before the tournament, a vicious September storm had struck, and one of the British team members who wasn't a good sailor had backed out on the morning the contest started. They needed a replacement. I was the only one around who had ever caught a tuna and was asked to take his place.

"But I'm not a Canadian," I said.

"You've spent a lot of time here and you caught a tuna up at St. Ann's Bay in a little open boat," came the reply. "That will qualify you as a Canadian,"

There were two teams of five men each, and the Americans were leading two to one going into the third and final day. There were no strikes on either side until, just before noon, a tuna took my bait. That was my second hook-up of the contest and, as in all the others, the fish was a small one, a bluefin of between two hundred and three hundred pounds. Like the others, it came in without difficulty except that, just as we were ready to boat the fish, the engine stalled. Edouard Ritchie, the captain, and Emil, the mate, had to work on it for ten minutes to get it running again. Had this happened earlier, while the tuna was at full strength, we might have lost him. But the tackle held him in close, the mate reached the wire leader, and the fish was gaffed and brought aboard.

About three o'clock that afternoon, a big blue shadow materialized behind our boat, only to hang there and take the cut-up bits of herring we were constantly throwing over the stern. He stayed well behind us, taking the free chunks of bait but refusing the whole herring we drifted back with a hook in it. Next we tried bits of herring on the hook and then half a herring as well as the whole herring, but to no avail. This fish must have been hooked before and escaped, for he was wary. After fifteen minutes, he dropped out of sight. Neither of our teammates, who had moved in on either side of us, had him come into their wakes.

Ten minutes later, that same fish—or one just like him—showed up behind us. Again our baits were ignored while the chum we drifted back was taken readily. Finally, I hooked two fat herring through the lips on a single hook and dropped it astern. Greed got the better of the tuna's judgment, and he took the bait. The 130-pound-test line streamed off the reel, and our boat turned to follow the fish.

The fear of a more permanent motor stoppage hung over us. Twice in the long struggle the engine did conk out, but each time, Edouard and Emil revived it before my reel spool was empty. After an hour and a quarter, the tuna was still strong, and my hopes were dim that the engine would run much longer. Ten minutes later, we were closing on the tired fish when he swam into a great area of kelp on the surface. When we followed him, some kelp stems caught in the prop, and with a pathetic cough the engine died again.

The silence was eerie. I set up the drag as heavy as I could and supplemented it by applying pressure to the line on the spool with my fingers, which were by that time poking through holes I'd already worn in my gloves. The sound of the drag was rising and falling spasmodically as it stopped the spool's turning momentarily and then broke free with another scream of agony as it gave up its lock on the spool under the driving fish's pressure.

Slowly the line went out, measured by those cries of agony from the reel. I pressed until my fingers bled from the roughness of the line. The salt water on the twisted linen made them burn. I strained back against the harness to hold the rod higher and, so, increase the drag a little. The only sounds I heard were those of the reel and my heavy breathing and, faintly in the background, the cries of circling gulls and the curses of the crew as they worked on the dead engine.

The six hundred yards of line originally on the spool was dwindling. Slowly, inexorably, the fish moved farther and farther into that great patch of kelp. I could see the bare metal of the spool's arbor showing at one edge. A few more seconds to go! Pressing against the barely covered spool with all the strength my fingers could manage, I waited for the reel's last groans and then the snap of the breaking line.

The sound never came. The line stopped moving out of the guides. In a moment I was able to begin to pump, lowering the rod and reeling between lifts. I felt some pressure on the line but assumed it was some kelp that had become entangled either with the line or the hook. Sweat ran down my face. I was tired and filled with deep despair. Mechanically, I pumped and wound the line back onto the reel, bringing it in about six feet with each lowering and lifting of the rod. I stared, mesmerized as the twisted linen piled up slowly on the reel spool. Looking up and out at the spreading kelp, I saw a flash of silver just under the brown strands some fifty feet away.

I hadn't been reeling in some captured kelp after all. The pressure was my tuna. He was still there.

The bluefin came in without resistance. The crew crowded in beside me as I drew him and a mess of kelp strands to the stern of the boat. Captain Edouard let out a low whistle. Emil said, "Damn! He's a good one."

He was big. And he was beautiful. And he was dead. He'd

fought his heart out till he could fight no more, and he'd almost broken mine. Had he lived ten seconds longer, my life would have been far different.

Two weeks later a letter came. It was from the members of the Tourist Board on the small British island colony of Newfoundland. They had read some of my magazine stories and had heard of my film lectures. They had seen my picture in the *Times* and knew I was a good tuna fisherman. They believed they had an abundance of bluefin around their island in the late summer and needed someone to explore and open up their tuna fishing and to promote their fine Atlantic salmon fishing. Was I interested?

# NEWFOUNDLAND

❧

Newfoundland was Great Britain's first Dominion, predating Canada and India. She had fought France for it and had won the island and its valuable fisheries on the Grand Banks.

With the depression of the early thirties, however, Newfoundland's economy collapsed and Britain reduced her status from Dominion to "Britain's Oldest Colony." Hence, the island became a Dominion in suspension, a colony in hock to the motherland. A commission of six was set up to rule her. Three commissioners were Newfoundlanders. They had the portfolios of Health, Education, and Justice. The important portfolios—of Natural Resources, Public Works, and Commerce—were held by Englishmen. It was England that ran the little country, and she ran it for trade.

The island of Newfoundland is approximately forty-two thousand square miles in area, about the size of the state of Pennsylvania. In the 1930s, almost two hundred salmon rivers flowed into the sea along its deeply indented, six-thousand-mile-long coastline. Some of the runs had been badly treated by overnetting on the high seas and by poaching with spears and nets in the rivers themselves. But most, away from the settlements, were a salmon fisherman's dream. Part of my work for the Newfoundland Tourist Development Board was to evaluate those rivers for their tourist possibilities and to give lectures and write magazine stories that publicized them, along with the island's other hunting and fishing assets.

Since the tuna would not show up off Newfoundland's shores

until August, early July 1938 saw me at Big Falls on the upper Humber River. My photographic assistant, a Newfoundlander named Plus Parsons, had predicted that it would be the most dramatic salmon fishing on the island. He was right. It made the angling I'd enjoyed in Nova Scotia over the past half-decade pale by comparison. The salmon pool below Big Falls, I thought, might be the most dramatic in all the world.

We had taken a full day to come up the river thirty miles in poled canoes to reach it. The river was high and, while in a normal flow the fish could jump the twelve-foot barrier presented by Big Falls without trouble, the incoming run of salmon was now held up in the pool below until the water dropped to a more reasonable flow. There I saw a most extraordinary circus of leaping salmon. At least one fish was in the air at all times, and sometimes a dozen or more would burst from the foam and try to leap the solid wall of falling water that stretched two hundred feet or more across the river.

They leaped in a spray of silver bellies and dark blue backs, then fell back—save for an occasional fish—into the foam at the foot of the falls. In the five-hundred-yard stretch of river below, there were thousands of salmon, waiting for the spate of rain to run off and the river to drop to its accustomed spring level. Little did I dream that the controlling paper company would soon blast a pathway through that wall of rock to make it easier to drive pulp logs over the barrier. In the process, of course, it became easier for most of the salmon to swim up through the break, and the fantastic leaping spectacle that had been so wonderful to see was almost eliminated.

I had never seen or heard about such salmon fishing before, nor have I since. One day, starting out after breakfast, I caught thirty salmon—large and small—by noon. Though it was time to go in to the camp for lunch, those salmon were taking my flies as I had never had salmon take them before. It was like a dream, and living through it was the peak of exhilaration. I thought, "This is unbelievable. I'll stay out here until I can make five consecutive casts without hooking a salmon."

I stayed and stayed, covering the water cast after cast and hooking fish that leaped with wild abandon. My rod was a nine-footer designed for trout. I played the salmon hard and learned just how tight I could hold them with the ten-pound strength of my gut leaders. I lost a few but in the end had learned how to speed up my playing techniques until I could bring them in at well under a minute to the pound. Toward the evening of that long June day, I decided that number seventy-five would be enough.

The number came and, with eager salmon still waiting, I climbed the steep bank to the camp. I carried with me the first salmon I had caught, the only one I had killed and kept, which was all that was needed at the camp for food.

Why would anyone want to catch so many fish? Is it like a child riding a carousel, taking a ring each time around to prove that he can do it or, perhaps, to get the gold ring for another, free ride? Is it like a kitten that chases a bit of yarn at the end of a string until it is thoroughly tired, playing so hard in order to develop or keep sharp the skills it will need to survive if ever left on its own? Is it like the predatory fox that kills every chicken in the hen house or the weasel that kills every rabbit in the warren, practicing so that when hard times come it will be skilled enough to survive while those less able will starve?

There is an urge within all predators, of which man is the fiercest and most successful, to develop and maintain their skills. The hunting and fishing instinct is older than we are. Since man began to evolve he has been a hunter. Everyone alive lives because his ancestors were good hunters, good killers. If they weren't, they and their families starved and we wouldn't exist. Man only began to farm and live without wild meat some ten thousand years ago.

The basic hunting instincts are still deep within many of us, even though the needs that created them are disappearing. I think we, who have inherited them, take pleasure in our angling as a lion cub does in learning to catch its prey or an adult lion in maintaining its skills. Out of man's growing dignity has come the catching and releasing of something we have captured but need not kill. It is said of anglers that at first they want to catch all the fish. As they gain experience they want to catch the largest fish. Finally, in the mature stage, they want to catch the most difficult, the most challenging fish.

Unfortunately, this evolution is not universal.

About two weeks after my incredible salmon fishing experience at Big Falls, I read in the *Western Star,* the Corner Brook newspaper, that Sir Humphrey Walwyn and his small party had just returned to Corner Brook from the Big Falls of the upper Humber with a total of two hundred salmon for their two days fishing.

At the time, I was in St. John's, the capitol of Newfoundland, and was to make a speech before the most important society on the island, the Rotary Club. I pointed out that if such catches were allowed there'd soon be no salmon left in the upper Humber. There was support for preserving the run, and an eight-fish limit was set for the following year.

I had begun my involvement in the conservation of Newfoundland's fish and game.

# THE FIRST TUNA

⌒∾⌒

There were, in fact, tuna in the waters off Newfoundland. Although some of my informants confused them with porpoises and dolphins, the knowledgeable fishermen, who knew them as horse mackerel, told of these great blue-and-silver fish tearing up their nets and sometimes even dying there, tangled in the mesh. They were known to frequent Conception Bay, only a few miles from St. John's, the capital, and some of the other big bays around the north shore of the island. Since the tuna had no commercial value at the time and because nobody wanted to eat them, little attention had ever been paid to these fish except at Bonne Bay, on the west coast of the island.

There a man named Bryant Harding had, until ten years earlier used these horse mackerel for food on his fox farms. His crew had harpooned them, year after year. The bluefin were around, it was reported, from August on through September, summer after summer. It was decided that I'd make my first tuna try at Bonne Bay.

At that time, Newfoundland was like a feudal state. The merchants of St. John's controlled the economy, buying the cod and other fish and selling them abroad at a considerable profit. They imported the food and drugs and all the things the island needed or could afford. And they exacted a good percentage of gain. Whenever anyone anywhere in Newfoundland bought a box of cornflakes or a bottle of aspirin, someone in St. John's got a little richer. Similarly, each village had its own merchant who, though a step below his counterparts in St. John's, controlled the business in his little domain. Bryant Harding was the merchant of Norris Point, the major settlement in Bonne Bay.

The bay turned out to be a magnificent, fjord-like harbor. The salt water of the Gulf of St. Lawrence stretched inland between towering mountains, some of them still carrying patches of snow in August when the tuna arrived. The bay split into two long arms, and three small settlements clung to its shores. Two were fishing villages, and the third was a small logging company's town, dying now because of the depression that had ruined Newfoundland's economy and lingered to leave poverty on all sides. When you needed a man to work, he'd be happy with one dollar a day.

The water in that steep basin was usually as still as an inland lake. Fourteen miles inland at its farthest point the water's depth was over 120 fathoms. Into this narrow bay came great whales, porpoises, and tuna to feed on the herring, mackerel, and squid that were there abundantly during their annual runs.

Bryant Harding was a very well-read, well-traveled gentleman whom I liked immensely. When his fisherman father was a small, unprepossessing lad of seventeen, he had rushed aboard the first British battleship to drop anchor in the bay and had convinced the supply officer that he could furnish whatever bread, meat, fish, and other staples the ship might need. The elder Harding never learned to read or write or count in arithmetical numbers. Bryant showed me some of his father's old ledger books, where the records appeared as strange squiggles and signs that even Bryant did not fully understand.

It was Bryant's boat from which I was to fish for tuna. Forty feet long with a big Graymarine engine, it was built for sunshine and pleasure. It had a broad, low, open foredeck and a cabin in which a tall man had to stoop low to reach the engine or to take cover from a rainstorm. The open cockpit in the rear was small but big enough for me to build a well, a steep-sided "dish" of lumber against which an angler could place his feet and brace his legs, turning in any direction to fight the fish he played from the chair

Pursuing tuna in Bonne Bay was a far cry from doing it at Wedgeport, where we fished in a four-mile-an-hour flow of tide that ran over a rocky reef on its way from the open Atlantic to the Bay of Fundy and back again. There, the tuna swam past our boats with little heed, but in Bonne Bay the bluefin were shy.

This may have been because of the decades of harpooning. These giant tuna ranged from fifteen to twenty years of age and, I believe, had long memories. Or, perhaps it was because the killer whales sometimes invaded the bay and fed on the tuna like pickerel on minnows. Unlike the fish in Wedgeport, these tuna fed below the surface, and we rarely saw them breaking water. They did surface, however, when well fed and lazy. Then they'd swim along slowly in schools, often with their stiff dorsals and tails showing above the surface. It was when they were "schooling" like this that they had been harpooned for Bryant in past years.

The milling fish, however, showed no interest in our offerings. They were spooky and would sink down every time they felt the ripple of our wake as we strove to get a trolled bait in front of them.

We trolled unless we saw fish schooling. I rigged my mackerel and herring baits carefully, taking out a section of the backbone to make them limber, sewing the mouth closed, and hiding the hook inside the fish's body in such a manner that the bait would ride upright and appear to swim naturally as we pulled it through the water. Finally, I hooked one great tuna as we trolled past the Lomond wharf. The watchers saw the big fish take the bait and barely get started on its first run when another tuna from the school raced up alongside to strike at the silver bubbles of air made by the big swivel between the end of the line and the wire leader, cutting the line and freeing my fish.

It was time for a different strategy. I devised a handheld board with pegs on which I could wrap line in such a way that when I threw a mackerel bait the line would flow out as from a modern spinning reel. If a fish took it, I could set the hook with a yank on the line then move to the reel to bring in any slack through the guides and be ready to play the fish.

At the end of a week of frustration, we were able to get ahead of a school that was moving slowly along a mirror-like surface. Once in position, we stopped, our motor quiet. Often when we did that, the tuna would veer to one side or the other since they seemed to swim aimlessly, as if half asleep. This time we lay right in their path. As they approached within range, I threw the rigged mackerel. It landed just ahead of the oncoming school and as they scattered, one tuna raced up and took the bait. I set the hook, reeled up the slack, and got into the fighting chair. The battle was on.

I had worried a lot about the great depth of the water in Bonne Bay. I knew it was over a hundred fathoms and was concerned that if a fish went deep, I'd never be able to bring him up to the surface again. I needn't have worried. The water not far below the surface was so cold that tuna could not function in it. I was to find that tuna never dive deep in those cold arctic waters.

The tuna made the usual surface runs, counting on his speed and endurance to gain his freedom. But in a little over an hour, the fish came to the side of the boat and was gaffed. We towed it to Bryant's dock, where we took pictures and hung it on a special set of scales I'd brought with me. It weighed 480 pounds. When "Uncle Bob," the man who had for years harpooned the big bluefin for Harding's fox farms, saw it he laughed and said, "That's the littlest one I ever saw—a young one, foolish enough to take a bait."

In the eyes of the ordinary tuna fisherman, though, it was a good-sized fish. I had fulfilled my mission. I'd caught a rod-and-reel tuna in Newfoundland to show that it could be done and, of course, I wrote a story about it. The piece appeared in *Yachting* magazine.

Later, fishing in Conception Bay, I caught two much bigger fish in a single day. But the tuna fishing was not to develop as we had hoped. In 1941 the squid, which had come perennially to the shores of Newfoundland in August and September, failed to show up. Perhaps for lack of their favorite food, the tuna stayed away, too. (Both the tuna and the squid were absent for more than a decade before arriving in Newfoundland waters again more plentifully than anywhere else on the Atlantic Coast.) Tuna, then, were temporarily off my list.

Salmon, however, were to become more and more important.

# CONSERVATION

T hat winter I wrote and lectured back in the United States, using the films I'd made on my fishing for trout, tuna, and salmon, and my hunting for moose and ptarmigan.

My film work and explorations had taken me all over the island. I had hiked into the most remote places and was learning to know Newfoundland as perhaps no one else would. It was an untouched countryside, for all the settlements were either along the railroad or the seacoast. Only a few trappers or hunters ventured inland, and they usually knew only one particular remote area. I traveled into the respective "country" of each of the relatively few professional guides—sometimes for movies, more often for stories.

My publicizing the sporting opportunities in Newfoundland would bring tourists to its fishing and hunting grounds, and conservation measures were essential if the quality of these sports was to be maintained. Even without an influx of new people, the opening up of the wild areas by roads—which was slowly beginning—would be accompanied by increasing hunting and fishing pressure. Without good management all my work would be wasted.

Returning to St. John's in June, flushed with my success in spearheading the establishment of an eight-fish daily limit on salmon, I went to the Colonial Building one morning to see the acting secretary for natural resources. He was a small man with a rather large, balding head and curly, reddish hair about his ears. He looked up as I came into the room and frowned. I took the chair he offered and waited a minute or two while he finished reading a short paper. He looked up, unsmiling.

"It's about the salmon," I said. "I believe you've read my report to the Tourist Board, and I'd like to recommend that the salmon nets near the rivers be lifted on Sundays, as is done in Canada, to give the fish some chance to get into their rivers and spawn."

"I've read it," he replied. "But our commercial netters say that the salmon run into our rivers only over a two-week period, so they cannot afford to miss a single day. Fisheries incomes are down, you know."

"But, sir!" I replied, "Please look at it from the salmon's point of view. They have only two weeks to get into their rivers to spawn. If you don't give them even one day, what chance do they have to survive?" He lifted his head to look at me with a cold stare. "The commercial fishermen tell us they need every day." He dropped his head again to the papers he had been reading. I was dismissed.

If I'd won one battle on the daily limit for salmon, I'd certainly lost a second, even bigger struggle.

Even so, my work for the Tourist Board continued with considerable success. Occasionally, Jack Meehand or one of the other board members would come with me. Jack was a wonderful companion, and we became fast friends. On one trip together into a hard-to-reach potential salmon-fishing area we stopped by Jim Tompkins's Afton Farm Lodge on the Little Codroy River. That was the first river the railroad crossed on its way from Port-Aux-Basques (where the ferry from Nova Scotia landed) to Saint John's, on the far corner of the island. For many years Jim had taken in salmon anglers—some from Corner Brook and St. John's, but most of them from the United States.

It was to Jim's place that I had come on my first trip to Newfoundland back in 1935. That had been a great fishing experience and, although I hadn't caught anything weighing more than ten pounds, my companion had taken a twenty-six-pounder on a big white dry fly I'd made up for him. And I had seen an angler named Daniels, from Corner Brook, bring a forty-two-pounder to the shore beside the Widow's Pool. That had been a fine experience, and I looked forward to a day of fishing on those magnificent pools.

Jim Tompkins was a big man, tall and broad. His face, too, was wide, with a high crowned nose. His hands were rough from the hard work of running his farm with its vegetables, oats, chickens, sheep, and cows. He was a quiet man, courteous but never garrulous. He loved his land and his river, and he loved to fish—though only when he had no sports at the lodge.

We arrived in time for supper and after greetings and fishing talk with the other anglers, Jack and I sat up long after everyone else had gone to bed. We talked of many things but mostly of the steady deterioration of the salmon rivers I had known. It seemed that there was no stopping the poaching, the continuous overkills. There were too many fishermen and too many nets taking too many fish, both inland and at sea.

Newfoundland had many rivers that Jack knew and I had not yet seen. We talked of all these waters, wondering how we could reach the politicians who controlled them and were failing to provide adequate protection. Jack and I thought we were talking softly, but apparently Jim could hear us from his bed in the next room. We were winding up our discussion when he appeared, an apparition in a long nightshirt, and sat down beside us. Jim told us, then, of his river and its slow but certain failing.

There was poaching he dared not talk about lest his sports hear of it and refuse to return. There was a diminishing of the salmon runs and of the individual size of the fish. At times, there were nets too close to the river mouth, inside the caution boards. The lodge's sports hadn't taken a single salmon over twenty-five pounds since that big one Peter Daniels had caught. As Jim talked, his voice dwindled to a whisper. At the end, there was a soft little sob, and I looked up to see teardrops on his rugged face. Abruptly, he stood up and left the room.

I had never seen a grown man cry, but as I turned to Jack there was a deep sadness in his face, too. "There is a job to do," he said, "and I guess it is our job—the Tourist Board's. I hope we can do it. The Department of Natural Resources wants to be popular with the commercial fishermen and doesn't seem to care about the future."

From Jim's lodge we went on to our main objective, the Fox Island River. Jack said that it was water with good potential, but the river was isolated and didn't have a camp on it. Perhaps we could get someone to establish one there. To reach it, we traveled by train to Stephenville, then drove by car (on one of the few stretches of road in Newfoundland) for fifteen miles to the little fishing station of Port-au-Port, where there were a store and half a dozen houses.

From Port-au-Port, we headed for the river, ten miles northward on the shore, in a small, open fishing boat driven by a loud one-cylinder Acadia engine. There were two small houses located at the mouth of the river in an open cove where the boats could be beached and then pulled well back on the gravel, beyond the storm tides. Jack, my photography assistant Ralph, and I shared a room in one of the houses, boarding with the family that owned it. They were poor and welcomed us and our three dollars a day each with open arms.

The Fox Island River was a small one as salmon water goes. One of the few northern rivers that ran gin clear, it originated in the Lewis Hills, which rose steeply from the shore and reached over three thousand feet, one of the highest points in all of Newfoundland. The river was known for both big salmon and a run of extremely large sea trout that followed a heavy run of smelt in from the ocean. Later, the fish went back to salt water until spawning time or the next year's smelt run.

Every fish in the pools was easily visible. Salmon of over thirty pounds had been caught there, but we saw no such monsters. In the first two days, we did, however, take several in the twelve- to fifteen-pound category, which was very good fishing. Added to that, we caught over a dozen sea-run brook trout of more than five pounds, which was even more exciting. These trout, living in the sea, had taken on the natural protective coloring of most saltwater game fish. Their sides and bellies were a shining silver, so that they were light and inconspicuous when viewed from below. And they were dark blue-green on the back, so that they blended with the color of the sea when seen from above by predatory birds. This was the sort of fishing trout anglers dream about and very rarely find. The pictures I took and the story I would write would bring anglers from the States to enjoy this very special experience.

And then it rained—not a gentle rain but walls of water driving in on strong gusts of wind. We stayed in the house and talked of many things. Our hosts were unhappy because, although we'd brought the salmon home for them to cook for us and use themselves, we'd only kept two trout, and they certainly could have used the rest. I learned then that their "use" was to feed the fish to their dogs. All the families in such Newfoundland "outports" had sled dogs to to provide transportation in the winter, when the sea froze over.

The thought of feeding trophy sea-run brook trout to these dogs was horrifying. I knew anglers who would give a month's salary just to catch one such fish. I had the feeling our host regularly used the simple outfit he showed us—a long spruce pole with a heavy line and a cod hook on it—to take as many as he could. And, I surmised that if the trout wouldn't bite, he'd substitute a big treble hook for the cod hook and snag them. Somehow, we had to sell this angling abundance to tourist fishermen who would provide our host a good living through guiding and keep him from wasting the resource on his dogs.

When the rain clouds cleared away, we saw a raging river—over its banks and a rare chocolate brown in color. It was unfishable, but I had cabin fever and was restless. I put on my waders to wade along the beach and cast into the surf in the hope that some of the trout would be working along the shore, anxiously waiting for the river to drop and let them in.

The fish were there all right, in great schools. Never, since Alaska, had I seen trout in such quantities. It was like an impossible dream—a strike at almost every cast. At fifty fish, I stopped counting but kept on catching big trout and releasing them, hoping that one of them might be a world's record. I know I caught more than a hundred while my host, wringing his hands, watched me put them back. Seven of the fish, I was sure, weighed more than seven pounds but there was no great monster of twice that weight to break the record. In mid-afternoon, weary and happy, I gave up and went back to the warmth of the house and the ever-available hot tea.

That was the second week of June 1940. It was the week my first book on the Atlantic salmon was due to come off the presses. It was the week France fell to the Germans. On our drive back from Port-au-Port to the railroad at Stephenville Crossing, we saw a small, twin-engined flying boat, painted in military camouflage, anchored off Stephenville. The gossip was that the Americans were going to build an airport in western Newfoundland and that Stephenville was the chosen site.

I thought of that beautiful Fox Island River, like a wild aquarium with its tremendous fish. Then I pictured an air base with hundreds of construction workers and thousands of military personnel, both stationed there and passing through. I knew what would happen. The river would soon be devastated unless very strict rules on taking fish were established and rigidly enforced.

The statement I'd made in an earlier book, "A good game fish is too valuable to be caught only once" had found at least a little sympathy at home. In Newfoundland, however, it drew only ridicule. If you fished to catch fish, why would you ever be stupid enough to throw one back? The next line in the book, "The finest gift one angler can give another is a fine game fish to catch," left them cold as well. The point that no one fishes a river that holds no fish—and provides no angling pleasure—had no significance. Everyone thought like a commercial fisherman: There are fish in the sea. Sometimes they come within range, and when they do you'd better catch all you can because they may not stay long. The idea of limiting catches was laughed at. No one worried where the fish came from, nor did the Newfoundlanders think like farmers, who know there must be seed before there can be crops.

They could not conceive of catch-and-release because they wanted to believe—and did believe—that once a fish has been caught he is sure to die from his exertion. My argument was that if simple exertion could kill an animal, then every horse that put his heart into the race would drop dead at the finish line or shortly thereafter. Such reasoning was brushed aside because "fish aren't horses."

Undaunted, I sent to the Department of Natural Resources a suggestion that a one-salmon and two-trout limit be established to preserve the sport. At the DNR there was ridicule for this "loony" who believed that trout and salmon belonged in the streams instead of in the bellies of men . . . and dogs. Five years later, however, all that big breeding stock had been caught and killed. By then, a one-pound fish was as big a trout as anyone could find. Forty-five years later, the DNR would enact a catch-and-release rule for the island's larger salmon, but in 1940 such a program didn't have a chance.

# THE WAR

World War II came quietly though not unexpectedly to Newfoundland. In 1938, which had been my first year on the job, one of my assignments was to photograph the visit of the king and queen to St. John's. During the coverage, one of my helpers, Bob Stick, who had been an infantry captain in World War I, said, "Mark my words, Lee, we'll be at war within a year. They only visit the Colonies and Dominions when they're going to need our help." Bob was wrong about the timing but not by much. The royal visit was in June. The Germans marched into Poland on the first of September, just a little over a year later.

I was eventually called in for a conference with Sir Wilfred Woods, K.C.M.G. (Knight Commander, St. Michael and St. George) the commissioner for public works and the man under whose direction the Tourist Board fell. The war was here, he explained, but things would go on as close to usual as possible. We would win, he was sure, because the Americans, as in 1918, would join the British side. A bill would soon be coming up in the U.S. Congress to exchange some "overage" destroyers for bases in Newfoundland and other British Territories.

U.S. troops would be coming to Newfoundland, and many of them, from generals to privates, would be anglers. They'd need to relax, and Sir Wilfred wanted to be hospitable. I could help the Americans on that score and, because I knew the island well, I might assist them, too, with the planning of roads and such things. And, said Sir Wilfred, "I've already had a request to release you to them for the making of a film on the eight-million-dollar telephone line they are going to run all the way across the island. It will extend from a site on the west coast to St. John's and, perhaps, Placentia Bay. Can you help us out there?"

Things went on more or less as normally for a while. Stephenville, on the west coast of the island, was in fact chosen for the major air base. Supplemental bases would be at Gander, already in operation by the Newfoundlanders; at Torbay, near St. John's; and at a big naval base at Argentia, not far from the city in Placentia Bay.

St. John's began to change. There had been a few millionaires here before the war, but with the coming of the U.S. troops there were dozens more. The going rate for a secretary or sales girl jumped from the old pay scale of $6 per week to $35 a week. Country girls learned to type. Destitute men for whom a dollar a day had been the standard wage rushed to work on the ever-expanding projects. The gathering of spruce and fir poles for the phone line began, and I made the long-line film for the Signal Corps.

There was one wartime day I'll always remember. That June morning slowly spread its dull gray dawn and blotted out the landing lights of the newly constructed Harmon Field at Stephenville. The water to the west stretched away to the horizon like a plate of tarnished silver, ending abruptly at the hard line that separated it from the leaden underbelly of the clouds. We heard the slushy splash of tires passing through puddles as a truck went by. There'd been a reddish glare under the gray of the brightening east, and there was a soggy feeling to the air itself. I knew the signs: There would be more rain before long, and the rivers were already running full to their banks with more than a week's worth of downpours.

The commanding officer of the base, Colonel H. H. Maxwell, had phoned me the day before to say, "I've got a couple of men coming through here tomorrow who'd like to do a bit of fishin'. How about coming over to join us?" That was all. I'd been back in Newfoundland just a week and had yet to put my waders on. I was due to travel out that way in a day or two, anyway. "Sure," I told him. "I'll be there."

Maxwell's assistant, Captain Spruill, phoned half an hour early to be sure I'd be ready, and we rode across the soggy ground to the Transient Mess, where I could surround a good breakfast before joining the others. I sat down at a table with some operations officers and a navy lieutenant who wanted to fish and was asking for information. Said the man on my right, "Fishing's pretty punk right now. There are some coming down the Harrys River, but it's so high you pretty near have to cast from the bushes."

I ate and listened and watched as the lieutenant passed over his fly box for the scrutiny of the men on my side of the table. When we finished breakfast, I took the officer out to my gear bag in the car and gave him a couple of flies with more sting in them for salmon. His own collection had consisted primarily of trout and bass flies.

We drove over to the tracks where the railcar was waiting. The sun was up, but its glow filtered down weakly through the heavy clouds. The spruce and fir trees were more gray than green in its light. The wind was from the east, just a breath now and then. Fishing was going to be tough. The water was too high, the wind was wrong, and I wasn't familiar with the river to which we were going. I climbed aboard and stowed my stuff. Spruill came back with Jim Sullivan, a Newfoundlander who was employed on the base but worked, ate, drank, and slept only to go salmon fishing. We stood outside the railcar waiting for the others.

They came in two cars, Colonel Maxwell; another colonel; General Lawrence Kuter, whom I recognized; two two-star generals; and two others on whom there was no need to search for stars. Jim, standing beside me, whistled under his breath. The next moment he was being introduced to the chief of staff of the U.S. Army and the chief of staff of the U.S. Army Air Force. The thought flashed through my mind that it was a wonder they both flew over in the same plane. For either one of them to be lost in a crash would have been catastrophe enough.

Colonel Maxwell, who—just for fun—drove or flew everything mechanical to be found on the base, settled himself at the controls of the self-propelled railroad car, and the rest of us spread around while we headed out the spur on the narrow-gauge tracks, toward the main line of the Newfoundland Railway. General Marshall, General Arnold, Jim, and I occupied one double seat.

The party had left Italy the afternoon before and flown the hop across the Atlantic from the Azores that night to reach the base for an early breakfast. They'd decided that half a day's fishing would probably give them more relaxation than anything else in this brief respite between their checking up on the actual fighting on the two European fronts and their returning to the planning and overall direction of the war back in Washington. We spoke of many things on the way to the river—the war in the Pacific, the mud in Italy—but we talked mostly about salmon and rigged up tackle and looked at salmon flies. All the while I kept thinking that our chances for good fishing were slim and asking myself why, oh why, they couldn't have come when conditions were better.

Someone had dug out the best outfits on the base for the party, but the wartime tackle situation had hit the army as well as the rest of us. I loaned General Arnold my special five-ounce, two-piece, five-strip, Longacre-impregnated rod with a Hardy St. George reel and 150 yards of backing. To General Marshall I gave another of my three-star rod outfits. For myself, I rigged up my two-and-a-half-ounce, seven-foot rod, which was going to be pretty light for the conditions. We got out of the railcar at a high bank by the bridge and made final adjustments to our tackle after we'd descended to the level of the deep pool that lay directly under the span.

Fishells River is a small one, and the salmon enter it early in the season. There was no question but that the fish were in the river, as a party from the base had struck good fishing there a few days earlier, when the water first started to rise. But salmon travel quickly when the rivers are high. Two or three days might have caused a radical change in the fishing.

The mist was growing heavy, and the bare limestone face that rose perpendicularly on the far side of the pool made the water take on a milky look, with just a tinge of green from the surrounding spruces. As I watched, the first drops of rain came down and made a fluttering pattern on the velvet smoothness of the river's flow. We spread out along the fifty-yard length of the pool and began casting.

General Marshall, fishing at the head of the pool, broke the ice within two minutes of our arrival. His rod arched and a bright grilse (a small salmon of only one year's feeding at sea) fought his way four or five feet into the air and showered the surface with a circle of spray. The fish then swept downstream with the current and worked in close to the cliff to leap again. He ranged back into the main flow and bored down to the rocky river bed. But he'd met a skillful angler, and not long afterward the chief of staff beached the grilse gently on the pebbly shore. Colonel Maxwell put him on the keep-em-alive stringer and anchored it to a log at the water's edge. We went back to our casting with a new hope. This, I thought, will be a day to remember.

The fly lines drifted out lazily through the air and, straightening out, fell to the water. Our small wet flies swam back across the current in graceful arcs time and time again. The rain came down more heavily, and we began to check up on those small crevasses at our necks where the water might seep through. Jim, who had come away without a raincoat, turned up the collar of his leather jacket. The rods worked rhythmically . . . but the salmon paid no heed.

When about twenty minutes had passed, General Arnold headed downstream, saying that the pool was crowded. Jim was busily casting at the head of the pool. I left off watching and followed General Arnold, thinking that Jim should have been going downstream instead of me. I had fished the pool at the bridge and one or two pools above it on one occasion several years before. But, I'd never been on the section of the river for which General Arnold was headed, and those who understand Atlantic salmon will tell you that a knowledge of the pools and where the salmon lie in them is the real key to success. Now, with the river so high that much of the river was just heavy rapids, I was going to have difficulty finding the salmon lies, especially since I didn't have Jim's knowledge of the pools in normal flow.

Half a mile downstream, we struck a place that looked as if it might hold a few fish. We cast there for half an hour without success before moving on to try another spot below. Here the river was wide, twisting and swirling around big boulders in its bed. It looked fishy all right. But neither the General's Jock Scott nor my Silver Gray brought forth a rise. I knew there were three good pools in the four-mile stretch between the bridge and the salt water. Perhaps they were still farther downstream? Leaving General Arnold, I followed the river to a point where it struck against a solid rock wall and slid off into deep water at a seventy-five-degree angle. I cast through that pool twice without a rise.

Had the fishing gone completely dead after its auspicious start? Or were the others making good catches at the bridge while we were downstream fishing water that held few, if any, salmon? I rejoined the general, and we worked over the pool again with smaller flies, then with larger ones . . . then with bright ones and dark ones. We had no success. More than two hours had passed since we'd reached the river, and our fishing time was half gone. A little bitterly, I thought: When you want them most they're the hardest to get. It's always the same.

Then I saw figures coming down the river from the bend up above. One by one they appeared until all the others were in view. I knew then that the fish had turned contrary and weren't rising. Otherwise, at least one or two of the anglers would have stayed on at the pool up above. I knew before we heard them say it that they hadn't had a rise since we'd left.

Turning to General Arnold I said, "Let's hike back to the upper pool. No one's fishing it now. We have to get back there to meet the railcar anyway, and I know that pool and where the salmon should lie in it. At least I can be certain that we'll be passing our flies over some fish." He nodded, and we started back.

General Arnold worked over the spot where General Marshall's fish had risen and continued on down through the easy flowing water. I worked along behind him with a #8 Silver Gray. He passed under the bridge, and his cast reached out to the quickening water just ahead of the rapids below. Suddenly there was a boil behind the general's fly. Two casts later there was another boil, and this time it was followed by a quick bending of his rod. The spell was broken. The general felt the surge of the salmon's run quiver into the flexed bamboo. The water was heavy, and I hoped the fish would stay in the pool.

He did, but not entirely because he wanted to. Twice the general coaxed him back from the very edge of the rough, high waves that the rocks threw up in the stream below us. Once the salmon threatened to wind the line around a long log that angled up from the streambed near the far shore and at the last minute swung back around it the way he'd come up. Five times he flashed out of the water into the rain-filled air above it. Finally the leader tip showed at the guides, and I readied the tailer. The fish seemed docile enough to let me slip the noose over the broad, firm tail that fanned wearily in the shallow flow. I moved up beside the general and waited.

Beware the false weariness of the fresh-run salmon. One minute his long, blue-backed, silvery body was that of a beaten fish; the next he was racing for deep water at top speed, taking a Jock Scott with him for a souvenir. "I guess," said General Arnold with a wry grin, "that fish deserved to get away." And I saw no trace of anger in his face—nothing but the pleasure he'd had in playing the salmon.

In the next few minutes, I connected with two grilse and added them to the first one, still alive, on the stringer. When the others came back, empty handed, General Arnold was in the act of beaching a grilse that had come up out of the dark, deep waters at the head of the pool to take his fly.

When the water in a river rises rapidly in a heavy rain, salmon will often take a fly avidly at a certain point in the rise, though scorning it before that moment and afterward. Fish were showing all along the line as the members of our party spread themselves out. Jim fought a salmon at the head of the pool, while a two-star general snapped his rod at the first ferrule on an eight-pounder that had been lying almost at his feet, in very shallow water near the tail of the pool. Played on the butt joint with the rest of the rod seesawing back and forth in the current, that salmon finally came in close enough for me to slip the tailer on him and tighten its noose.

As quickly as it had started the action stopped. The rain beat down even more heavily than before. The river began to run muddy with the red of a clay bank upstream. The moment had passed, and the fishing was over. As a group we huddled under the bridge with its scant covering of well-spaced ties. There were no complaints, no cussing—just the good-natured banter that goes with men who are used to taking the weather as it comes.

At two o'clock the railcar came back for us, and we relaxed in the warmth of hot coffee and sandwiches. Again we talked of many things as the car swayed along—of other rivers in Newfoundland and the right time to fish them, of the marvels of air travel on a planet that was growing smaller overnight. This was a world in which one could leave Italy one afternoon, be in the U.S. capital the next night, and still have time for a morning's salmon fishing on the way! After an hour's ride we were back at the base, and the generals were soon on their way to Washington, only six hours away, carrying with them salmon from a Newfoundland river.

What were they like, these men who headed our army and air force? They were the sort of people you'd like and enjoy as friends. They were real and sincere. They might well have been completely preoccupied with the enormity of the responsibility that was theirs. Instead, they brought a rich interest and warmth to their conversations with Jim and me, unimportant civilians in a world at war. They were men who knew and understood the outdoors and believed that a morning's fishing, even in a downpour, was the right sort of break in what must have been a time of almost continuous tension and strain for them.

In the days that followed, there were many times when the salmon were eager to take the fly, and I was lucky enough to be wading a stream with the sun laying its golden glint both on the moving water and on the lush green mountains that held it to its course. At such moments, I often thought of the rain falling on drenched anglers who had expressed a hope of coming back for a longer trip when conditions were right. I recalled a sharp mental image of General Marshall, knee deep in the river, casting with an intentness that belied his having left a bloodstained Italy only hours before. I remember, too, General Arnold's subdued grin as he watched that salmon spurt off with his Jock Scott.

I'll be forever grateful that I was with these men that morning on the river in the rain.

# THE LAST RESORT

W hen the war ended, there was more disappointment on the conservation front. Newfoundland's new commissioner for natural resources was interested in the possible discovery of million-dollar mines, and he thought that sportfishing was more of a kid's game than something tourists would pay money for. The plans I'd made were rejected out of hand.

Even the Tourist Board had changed. Some of the stalwarts who had vigorously supported my ideas for resource conservation and the development of the outdoor sports on the island—men like Jack Meehan, Sid Bennett, and Cyril Duley—had been replaced by people who thought in terms of big hotels and seaside resorts. My cause was all but lost, and I could see only one way to save it. My last hope was to actually demonstrate to the doubting politicians that salmon fishing could bring tourists to the country and be a benefit to particular areas and to the economy as a whole.

I didn't know much about running a fishing camp, but I'd stayed in plenty of them and figured I could make one a success. My biggest problem would be competition from local fishermen, since no sports could hold their own on a river with the Newfoundlanders, who knew every rock and salmon lie in the pools. If we were to have happy anglers, they'd need rested pools and unharrassed salmon to fish for.

There was one place on the island that offered this possibility—Portland Creek. It was part of a land block that remained under the control of the Reid Company, which had built the railroad. There was a thirty-three-foot right-of-way for travel along its banks, but I could buy the land on both sides. Portland Creek was a fantastic salmon river, only one mile long with one fine pool after another. It flowed from a big lake (the Newfoundlanders called it Portland Pond) into the Gulf of St. Lawrence on the island's northwest coast.

The river met the sea on a "straight shore," meaning that there was no harbor to protect its mouth. Had there been one, deadly commercial salmon nets could have been set in protected waters at the outlet. Instead, on the open shore, storms would destroy any such gear and, as a result, most of the salmon of the Portland Creek run were sure to get into the river. This situation was also true of the nearby River of Ponds and Western Brook, where I hoped to set up subsidiary camps.

Buying the land took all the money I had, but by owning it I knew no one else could set up an operation close to the river and offer competitive fishing. And no one could camp on the river and monopolize its pools. Portland Creek was a long way from any harbor or populous settlement and, of course, that was why the fishing was still excellent. It could only be reached by the occasional coastal boat during the summer months, when the sea was not frozen over. My problem would be getting my sports into and out of the camp from the railway that ran farther south. To do that, I planned to charter a forty-foot boat for the sixty-mile trip from Bonne Bay. It was a boat from which I'd fished for tuna and had made earlier trips to reach various rivers on that long, lonesome coast in my explorations for the Tourist Board. The skipper was Norm Parsons, an old salt who knew these waters well.

Norm had been the mate on my first tuna catch, working happily for two bucks a day. And, I'd helped him out when he was broke. A friend of mine had wanted to come down to fish tuna in Bonne Bay. There were no boats available, so he agreed to pay to have one built and to take it out in charters. I recommended Norm, and my friend sent down a forty-horse Redwing motor.

The Newfoundlander then built the boat with the help of some men he knew. They went into the woods to find the "moors," roots of just the right shape and size to make the ribs and head up the keel. They cut the logs of spruce and worked them through a local sawmill.

Besides Norm's place in the forward cuddy, the design included four bunks, so that if he had to duck into some small cove along the way on a trip, his passengers would have some comfort. He built the boat on the beach in front of his house and had it ready for the tuna season. But that was the year the tuna failed to show up in Bonne Bay for the first time in a century. It was tough on my kind friend, Alexander, but the new boat made Norman a skipper of consequence in Bonne Bay.

I knew weather would be a problem at Portland Creek. Because there was no safe harbor, Norm would need smooth seas to slip his boat over the bar and into the tidal pool at the mouth of the river. There'd be times when the sports would have to come in through the breakers in a dory. There would be occasions, too, when the seas would be too rough for Norm to even make the trip, and he'd have to wait out the storms. I hoped the excellence of the salmon fishing would make up for the inevitable problems in getting to and from the camps.

My first visit to Portland Creek, in 1941, had all but convinced me that it would. I'd come down alone in Norm Parson's boat and lived aboard it, anchored in the tidal pool, for three days of fishing. What a river it was—a broad flow, studded with great boulders. One could almost see the whole length of it looking from the sea pool to the running out of the lake.

We'd no sooner dropped anchor and were slipping the dory into the water to go ashore when we had a hail from the bank. A tall, skinny man with a long, narrow face shouted, "Be ye fishermen? I can guide yez." We rowed ashore and then, as it started to sprinkle, rowed back out to the boat again.

The first few big drops became a downpour before we had shipped the oars, tied the dory to the stern, and hopped down into the cabin. Norm went to the stove to start a fire, for the sudden storm had brought a chill and it was not too far from time for supper. Our fly fishing tackle was in plain view. Our visitor said, "I'm

Arthur Perry. I lives just in the cove here, summers, and I salmon fishes and guides."

Norm put on the kettle to heat water for tea. We talked about the fish and the flies that seemed to work. Arthur obviously knew a bit about salmon fishing. He mentioned that he had a Hardy rod and a Hardy reel, which a British naval officer had given him after a few days of successful fishing some years before. When I suggested he might have some supper with us—ham and potatoes and bread and jam—he just said, "Do ye like lobsters? I can get some." At my vigorous nod he jumped up, looked out at the sky to find that the rain had settled down to a light drizzle, then clambered into the dory and was off for shore.

Talk of the river and salmon fishing continued after the supper was over and the lobsters were reduced to empty shells. Our bottle of 150-proof Hudson's Bay rum came out, and Arthur's eyes lit up with an alcoholic glow. Norm and I sipped ours over many minutes. Arthur's went down in a single gulp. Amused, I poured another couple of ounces for him. It disappeared in another swift gulp. Then I decided to let well enough alone.

The interesting thing about the river, Arthur said, was that you had to use a "rivveling itch" on the fly if you wanted to catch a salmon.

"What do you mean a 'rivveling itch?'" I asked.

His words were confusing, and I wondered if this was just the liquor talking. I got out a salmon fly and a gut tippet for him to demonstrate. Of course, he had to chew on the end of the gut tippet to soften it enough that it could be tied in a knot. I watched as he chewed, the alcohol apparently helping his saliva. When the gut had softened sufficiently, he passed the end of the leader through the eye of the fly, tied a conventional turle knot, then took two half hitches behind the head of the fly, making it hang off the leader end at an odd angle. "That 'itch,' sir, makes it rivvel across the top of the water, and that's what our salmon likes."

Morning found us at the Low Rock Pool, the one just above the tidal pool where our boat, the *Red Wing,* was anchored. I couldn't believe that tying a fly on at a grotesque angle was the only way to tempt the local Atlantic salmon to take a fly. So I put on the most traditional pattern I had, a Jock Scott, and fished through the pool. No luck.

I then put on a Silver Gray and worked through the pool with that. Still no rise from a salmon. Arthur stood beside me muttering a bit, and from time to time I could make out something like, "Won't do a damn bit of good!" and then, in a louder voice, "There's salmon there sir, right where you're casting, but they won't rise without the itch."

A breeze came up, and soon wind squalls were racing across the pool. The wind caught my line on a long cast and whipped it across the surface, dragging the leader to the top of the water so that the knot made a tiny V on the surface. Immediately, a salmon slashed up at it. Arthur said, "You've got to rivvel your fly like that, sir. Then ye'll catch a salmon."

Reluctantly, I passed my Silver Gray over to him. He took his two half hitches just behind the head of the fly and said, "Now, sir, if ye'll make the same cast as before ye'll have a fish." And he was right!

The salmon came ashore in good time, a fourteen-pound male whose acrobatics kept me busy for almost fifteen minutes. I began to fish again with the hitched Silver Gray. Three casts later, I hooked a female of about the same size and played the fish out, saving it so that I could give Arthur a fish and still have one for our trip back to Bonne Bay in the boat. Then we headed upstream to explore the river. It was everything I had hoped for.

Establishing the camp at Portland Creek, however, brought problems I hadn't anticipated. There was a lot of resentment among the local anglers, who felt that bringing in sports would take fishing away from them. There was bitterness that I had "bought a river" and a feeling that my intrusion was the beginning of a trend that would limit every Newfoundlander's God-given right to fish wherever he pleased. Apparently the customs officials felt resentment, too, for they charged me 60 percent duty on the beds and other things I ordered shipped in.

In contrast, the Bowater Paper Company, a start-up operation like mine, was allowed to bring in all its equipment duty free. My appeals fell on deaf ears. The Tourist Board made a cursory effort on my behalf but quickly abandoned the cause. I guess I should have given up then, too, but I'd already put so much effort into trying to save the extraordinary salmon fishing—both for the Newfoundlanders and for the rest of the world—that I felt I had to push on.

# Getting Started

❧

Before my first fishing party arrived at Portland Creek, I set up tents with six-foot walls and board floors on the high bank overlooking the Low Rock Pool. We had the necessary cook tent and outhouses. There were iron cots equipped with sleeping bags and flannel sheets. We had ice, cut from the lake the winter before, to keep our groceries fresh, and we had plenty of simple food shipped to us from Corner Brook through Angus Bennett, the local merchant in the little community of Daniel's Harbour, five miles farther north along the shore. Here a slight indentation in the coastline gave small boats some shelter from most storms, and they could be hauled up beyond the tides in case of a bad blow. Supplies had to be rowed from Angus's store to us in a dory.

All was in readiness for our sports but, on the appointed day, Norman's boat didn't show up. Fortunately, Daniel's Harbor was on the telegraph line that ran along the coast, and word came through that my anglers had been delayed but would be along in good time.

This initial group was made up of three brothers—Herman, Ben, and Caesar Cone—and a friend, Marion Heiss. They were from Greensboro, North Carolina. Their trip to the camp wasn't an easy one. They flew Northeast's lone DC3 from New York to Sydney, Nova Scotia. Then, because there was no air service closer than Gander, in the center of Newfoundland, they'd elected to take the Canadian National Ferry across the strait to Port-aux-Basques and let the Newfoundland railway carry them from there to Deer Lake, our pick-up point.

Of course, their flight was late and they missed the ferry. Rather than wait two days for the next one, they chartered a sixty-foot coal boat to make a night crossing. There were no bunks on the collier, and the ride was pretty uncomfortable. The Cone party reached Deer Lake the next afternoon, then traveled by car to the lodge at Lomond, on Bonne Bay, where they overnighted during the bad weather. Fortunately, the next day was a good one. Norm picked them up and brought them to the camp in mid-afternoon.

I expected to greet four angry, grumbling, unhappy sports. Knowing that when things don't go smoothly at a fishing camp it's essential that the food be good to help make up for the problems, I had our cook prepare a hot fish chowder and had lobsters all ready to drop into the pots the moment the water boiled. The fishermen were annoyed at the delay, but that was all. They said, "To heck with the food. Let's go fishing."

And fish they did. The salmon run was just in, and the river was filled with bright fish weighing from ten to twenty-five pounds. All members of the party caught fish, and it was not until nine o'clock that evening, with the sun still well up in the sky, that the lobsters hit the boiling water and my sports sat down to eat and talk about the fish they'd caught or lost. I'd had a break in both the people and the fishing, and I was off to a good start. But I knew that more obstacles lay ahead, and one of them was finding competent guides who could put my sports into fish consistently.

Arthur Perry was the only accomplished salmon fisherman and guide among the people who lived in the few houses at Portland Cove, two miles south of the river mouth, or in the settlement at Daniel's Harbour. They were of a hardy stock that came over long ago from the fishing villages of the west coast of England. They spoke Elizabethan English, and their accent was much like that I'd heard among the settlers of the outer banks of North Carolina. Tide was "toide." A fir tree was a "var." Riffling was "rivveling." A dredge was a "drudge." A bird didn't fly over, he "flid" over. And he didn't land in a tree, he "pitched" there. An eagle was a "heagle," and an ax was a "haxe." The sound of small waves beating against a dock or the side of a boat was a "flobber." What we called a lake was a "pond," and what we'd call a river was a "creek."

Only a very few of the settlers could read or write, but they were very capable at the tasks that faced them: fishing for lobsters, cod, halibut, and the like; butting logs that they sawed and shipped to Corner Brook by coastal steamer; and trapping fox, lynx, beaver, and otter. Still, they had to be trained in the niceties of guiding for salmon, where fishing with a fly was the only allowable method. But most of my sports, like the Cone party, were accomplished anglers and needed only to be shown where the salmon usually chose to lie and how to handle the nets, tailers, and gaffs that were needed to secure and bring a tired fish to shore.

I chose trappers to be guides whenever I could because they had learned to be alert to the signs of all the wildlife in the woods, and they had a knowledge of the ways of fish and animals that ordinary folk did not. Moreover, they could tell stories of that wild country and thus add interest to a fisherman's trip. My guides were great. That was a big plus. It was rare to have a complaint of any sort.

My second party—made up of Harold Lyons, Bob Coulson, and Al Coss of Buffalo, New York—was just as happy as the first. They were all accomplished fishermen. Bob was an outdoor writer, and Harold was in the fishing-tackle business. They caught salmon by the dozens. At that time, the river seemed endlessly full of fish. There was one spot where salmon were jumping so constantly that Al, with his movie camera, would have only a few empty frames between jumps and more time with fish in the air than not. But these particular sports were *so* eager they gave me a problem.

They were up at the crack of dawn, which in early July in Portland Creek was about 3:30 A.M. They fished until dark, and that meant almost 11:00 P.M. At the end of the week, they were happy but tired and went home to rest. My guides, however, didn't have the same opportunity to catch up on their sleep. For future parties, I had to set up a schedule where the guides started work after the 7:30 breakfast, were free for rest or chores in the afternoon after the 12:00-to-1:00 lunch break, and guided again after the 5:30 supper until dusk. Then there'd be hot tea, coffee, or chocolate; hot soup; sandwiches; and cookies as a snack before bedtime.

Any sport out on the river before breakfast fished alone, and he fished his assigned pool only. After breakfast, he and his guide went back to that pool for any further fishing. Assigning pools for the mornings like this was necessary to ensure that every sport had first whack at a rested pool each day. Otherwise, one angler might take the cream from several pools, leaving his fellow sports only fished-over water. In the afternoons, anglers could fish anywhere someone else wasn't fishing, and they were free to move around the rivers at will.

The fishing camp was off to a good start. My rates were $25 a day, $7 of which—along with meals—went to the guide. With this arrangement, I could make a profit and was generating business for Norm and his boat, the railroad, and a lot of other people along the way.

# THE LOCALS

❧

Old Hebbert Caines had come down with his wife from Bonne Bay to Portland Cove some forty years before, when there was nothing but an open beach with untouched forest behind it. He'd built a house and put in a hand winch to drag his small boat up to safety, beyond the reach of the waves and tides. He'd survived by fishing and cutting timber, growing vegetables in his garden, cutting wild hay for his cow, killing caribou for meat, and picking great baskets of berries when they ripened in the fall. He was a loner and didn't want to move in with the other few families that established themselves at Daniel's Harbour.

His eldest son, Hebbert "Eb" Junior, was thirty-eight years old. Like almost everyone else along the coast, he could neither read nor write. However, he was a very clever man and the best boatbuilder on the shore. He could find the best curving roots to fit the varying shapes of the ribs for the hulls he designed. He could determine the hull shapes that would slip most swiftly through the water yet be stable in a stormy sea. He could tune a motor so it ran its very best and made the sweetest sound across the water.

When I first came down to Portland Creek by boat, set up my tents, and brought in the initial parties of sports, it was Eb who proved to be the most helpful of the men I had hired. "Eb," I told him, "if you'll learn to read and write, I'll make you my foreman next year."

He had impressed me with his wisdom when, in that first season, he had guided a woman angler, a beginner who was inexperi-

48

enced with salmon tackle. She had never played any fish larger than a small trout. Heeding Eb's advice she'd hooked a good salmon, which hadn't jumped right away. Eb had seen the fish and didn't want to unnerve her because of its size. He told her that she'd only hooked one of the many trout that were in the river and that she should play it gently because it was small. Five minutes later, when it jumped, he faked surprise. When his angler started to freeze up, he convinced her that all she had to do was to continue playing the fish as if it were a trout and eventually it would tire. She did as he suggested. In time, the salmon grew weary and proved to be a larger fish than any that her husband—an experienced fisher-man—caught all week.

Later, Eb helped me select the guides for the Portland Creek operation. To give the local people a real interest in the camps, I hired a guide for every angler, although that was not common practice at the time.

Eb knew pretty well which locals could cook and bake the best bread. Oddly enough, practically all the men along the shore could turn out a loaf of bread. When they went into the woods for log-ging or trapping, or when they lived in a little shack on a lonely shore to tend their lobster traps, they were their own cooks. That was a blessing because sometimes there'd be a need for one or two of my anglers to camp overnight or even for several days in order to take advantage of especially good trout or salmon fishing in some hard-to-reach spot. I didn't want to send a full-time cook to such a camp unless there were at least four in the group. One or two of the regular guides could do very well in such circumstances if they could cook a little.

The men and women of that area were a rugged people. I came to know them well, not only as guides and workers but as friends. The men fished, going out in their dories or trap skiffs to net salmon, jig cod, or trap lobsters as soon as the ice was off the sea in May. It was cold work, and there was always danger.

These people could live simply and comfortably. When the fish were plentiful, the rewards were good. In the winter, the trappers usually went back into the mountains, each one jealously guarding his own special territory. Being alone for weeks—with no one to talk to and no one to call for help if you were sick or injured—called for intestinal fortitude.

They were supremely independent. Any man could sit on his porch with his legs on the railing, looking out over the sea for weeks at a time if he so chose. There were dried cod slabs if he didn't want to spend an hour catching a fish for dinner. There were things from the garden, fresh or canned. There was caribou meat bottled on the shelves from last winter's hunt. His wife would cut the stove wood, keep the fire going, tend the kids, and keep the house in order. She'd carry water from the well and do the necessities, while he sat comfortably and listened to Gerald S. Doyle deliver the news from St. John's or to other programs that came over the battery-powered radio. His work was more dangerous, but it was now and then. Her work was always.

I was sure it would be educational for my youngsters, when they visited the following year, to see and compare these Newfoundlanders with the anglers who came to the camps. They were from two different worlds. Although the sports had the special education of our society and were quite well off, some were quite worried about losing their jobs. I hoped the kids would see that the local people were not inferior, because they had all the special skills their work demanded and because their work was always there, just beyond that porch railing.

# SPREADING WINGS

⌘

S almon fishing tapers off as the season progresses. The fish lose much of their eagerness to take a fly as they become reaccustomed to living in a freshwater stream. Because they are fasting, they lose some of their strength, too. Their color changes from a bright blue and silver to a darker brownish that is more protective in the stream environment. By August, the salmon have become sulky and hard to catch unless the water is suddenly freshened and its oxygen content renewed by a good rainfall.

My last few parties of that first season were not as happy as the rest. The fish were still there, but the sports caught few of them. Besides, storms had held up two groups, and on one occasion, Norm had been forced to put into St. Paul's Inlet, where a party was delayed for one more day by strong winds. Another group was stranded at Lomond and was two days late in reaching camp. They'd had excellent trout fishing while they waited there, but they felt they had been gypped and wouldn't pay for the two days of salmon fishing they missed.

All in all, though, it had been a fair season and I'd been lucky with the weather. Normally there'd have been a lot more wind and rain. I knew that during an average season, almost half my parties would lose at least one day of the six they expected to have at the camps. I thought of chartering a bigger, faster boat out of Corner Brook but found the cost prohibitive. I knew the potential was there, and I wanted desperately to make a go of the camps, expanding them to other nearby rivers. If only I had a seaplane!

Back in the early thirties, when I was a freelance artist in New York City, I'd listened to the Piper Aircraft ads on the radio saying, "Send in your statement of why you want to learn to fly in twenty-five words or less and win a Piper Cub and free flying lessons." I had tried three times, but my letters hadn't been successful. I hadn't heard ads like that in a long time and I doubted that I'd be any more successful than before. But I had another idea. I had something to trade. I decided to get in touch with Piper.

It was months before I received a response, and by the time my proposal to trade a promotional film for a float plane was finally accepted, the second season at the camps on Portland Creek was rapidly approaching. Waiting at my home in upstate New York for word that the J3 Cub was ready tested my patience to the limit.

On the morning of May 2, 1947, the phone call came through. My brand-new Piper Cub was at the Round Lake Seaplane Base. I left immediately for the thirty-minute drive, my lunch only half finished. I had to learn to fly and be ready to take off for Newfoundland in just five weeks. There wasn't a minute to waste.

There had been delays all along the line. For one thing, there was a change in the Edo floats designed for the Cub. The new 1400 series would replace the old 1320s, offering more flotation and greater surface area when they rode the water or provided lift in the air. Mine would bear serial number 1400-2, the second set to come off the line, right after the test pair.

Instructor Lewis Lavery walked beside me from his office to the lake. There she was, tied up at the floating pier—a brand new Piper Cub J3. It was a warm, bright yellow because old man Piper thought that was the most conspicuous color an airplane could have—the easiest to find, I guess, when you're looking for a wreck in green trees, on water, on snow, or against the brown earth of fall. Naturally, we would name her *Yellow Bird*.

Empty, the Cub weighed 725 pounds. Except for her metal cowling, she had dope-covered linen fabric over a framework of light steel tubing. Her wings stretched out for a span of thirty-six feet, and she rode on a set of floats that would support 1,400 pounds.

She was beautiful because she could fly. And she was mine, or she would be when I finished the film I now owed the Piper Aircraft Company. She had one door, on the right side, and it was divided in the middle, so that the upper half could swing up and lie flat against the underside of the wing. There were two seats, fore and aft, and dual controls. Lew climbed into the front seat and motioned me to the one in the rear. That was the position in which a pilot, flying alone, would normally sit.

Lew Lavery was a small man of perhaps a hundred and thirty pounds, which, I was to learn, is a great advantage in flying light seaplanes. Here, every pound counts and the lighter the load, the quicker the plane can build up speed and take off, the faster it can climb, and the more joyfully it seems to fly.

As we taxied out and I heard and felt the small waves lapping against the floats, my first impression was one of fragility. The whole airplane quivered violently from the continuing series of little wave shocks. The motor roared. The nose lifted then leveled off, and the shocks diminished as we gained speed. So smooth was the liftoff that I saw, rather than felt, the moment we left the water. I was in my own airplane and learning to fly!

Lew turned from his position in the front seat to tell me to put my feet on the set of rudder pedals on the floor and my hand on the stick that rose up between my knees. I'd been in airplanes before but had never taken the controls. I touched them lightly in an effort to read the movement Lew was giving them. I saw a lone gull flying between us and the water. Now I, too, was like a bird. Soon I'd be flying north, on my own, to familiar lakes and streams that I could look down on from the sky. I'd fly to places no other man had flown. I'd land and wade where no other man had ever waded and cast where no fish had ever before seen an angler's fly.

Bush flying was practically nonexistent in Newfoundland. The Colony took in not only the 42,000 square miles of the island itself but also the 110,000 square miles of Labrador to the north. The only airplanes that came through before the war were the early transatlantic fliers, a Fairchild or two to make aerial photos for the paper companies, or the occasional military plane on government business. With the war over, Newfoundland would be open for development. Its aviation laws were non-existent. I would be lucky to be there at the very beginning, with the first private plane to be based there.

*NC6194H log: May 10, 1947*

The Cub's nose pointed up and up . . . and up. The engine labored. The plane quivered and, with a shudder, the nose fell away. Now, instead of looking up at the high, bright sky, I was looking right down at the green earth and falling toward it. Lew let the motor idle. We picked up speed, diving, then leveled off. Lew said later that leveling came when we stopped falling and started flying again. We'd fallen through the open stall for about three hundred feet. Part of my stomach was still up above; the rest was up in my throat.

"Climb back to two thousand feet," Lew shouted over the drone of the motor, "and this time, you do it."

Obediently I climbed to two thousand and poked the nose up into the sky until the plane shuddered. As if the string holding it up suddenly snapped, the nose fell through the horizon and we started to fall. I had left a little power on, so we dove a little farther and faster than we had in Lew's demonstration stall before we were leveling out and flying once more. Again, my stomach was up in my throat.

After two more stalls, each one better than the first, Lew was satisfied. "Now," he said, "it's time for spins."

This day had been a little different from the others: we'd strapped on parachutes. They were attached by belts and shoulder straps and, because they hung low, we sat on them as we flew. This time, as we reached the high-nosed point of stalling, Lew pushed hard on the right rudder. Instantly, we twisted into a turn and plunged toward the ground, nose first and spinning. My stomach came up into my throat halfway around the first turn. My eyes seemed to glaze over, and the turning earth below me was blurred and indistinct. At the end of the second turn, Lew pushed the stick forward and gave the plane opposite rudder to straighten us out. As in our stalls, we picked up speed and the flow of air over the wings reached a point where we started flying again.

Lew signaled to me, "Your turn."

Dutifully I climbed back to three thousand feet. I'd been reasonably cool when we came out, but now I was sweating and weak. It took all my concentration to pull the stick back hard and shove the nose up into a stall, then push hard on the right rudder. The airplane twisted and fell. In a dim haze I managed to push the stick forward and bring the rudder back to center after what I hoped was two turns. That brought us out of the spin and back to flying again.

I was swallowing hard, ready to throw up, and it seemed a miracle that I didn't. I think Lew had planned to stay out a full hour on this eighth lesson, but after a look at my green complexion and the beads of sweat he said, "Take her back."

That took all my concentration. When we reached the dock I walked unsteadily over to the office steps and sat there, nauseated, for several minutes before I could get up and walk normally. Can I ever be tough enough to do this, I wondered. Somehow, I had to be.

*NC6194H log: May 11, 1947*

There is a phrase among airplane buffs and even a book entitled "eight hours to solo." I'd exceeded that amount of instruction time but hadn't flown alone. Did that mean I wasn't as good as the average pilot? Were my forty-two years too many? Was I too old to fly well? It was beginning to look that way.

A light breeze was blowing, and the late afternoon sun was bright on the water. With Lew sitting in his accustomed place in the front and me in the rear, looking over his shoulders, I was practicing landings. I was learning, all right, but was it too slowly? I was getting much better at judging just when the plane would run out of flying capability and could put it within a foot or less of the water at that moment.

It is much easier to land a plane when you use some power and set the throttle at a point where the aircraft flies just above stalling speed, slowly losing altitude. Eventually, the floats will slide onto the water with only a slight bounce or none at all. This requires some skill but it's nowhere near as difficult as landing a plane when your motor fails, and you are without power. That's why you learn to land "dead stick"—the hard way—first. It prepares you to make the best possible landing in case of a motor failure, and the sooner you master deadstick landings, the better.

Without power, I had to plan where to touch down long before I was near my proposed landing spot. My training routine was to fly downwind at an altitude of 600 feet, on a course parallel to the path I'd land on, cutting the power exactly opposite the spot where I wanted to land. I'd glide ahead and downward to 400 feet, where I'd make a left turn across the wind. Gliding down to 200 feet, I'd turn ninety degrees into the wind and see how close I could come to touching down on the spot I'd selected without having to add any power. I was coming close to my chosen points, and any bounces I made were small ones.

Lew signaled me to head in.

At the dock he hopped out but motioned me to stay in the plane, saying, "Let's see if you can do it alone."

I taxied away from the pier, turned into the light breeze, and lifted from the water. A flock of ducks flew out just ahead of me, used to the airplanes and in no hurry to get out of the way. I climbed to a reasonable altitude and did a couple of steep turns and two stalls. My stomach stayed in place. I came down and set a course to land on the far side of the lake, as far away as I could get from the office and the little group of pilots and their friends who I knew would be watching. Without Lew's weight in it, the airplane, flew differently. It was lighter.

My glide stretched out, and the Cub didn't want to stop flying. I was a little too far off the water, and when the stall finally came, I dropped three feet and bounced as far back into the air. It was the worst landing I'd made in more than a week. I could almost hear the laughter from across the lake. I took off immediately and started a wide circle.

I was ashamed but figured I had to make up for it on the next landing. This time, I would land a hundred yards off the pier. I knew the plane would soar longer because of its lighter load, and this time I was ready for it. I stayed just barely a foot above the water for my long glide, and when the floats touched down there was just the smallest of bounces. I moved the throttle forward and taxied in.

*NC6194H log: May 13, 1947*

Lying just north of Round Lake, Saratoga Lake is more or less round and measures about four miles across. Cottages are strung out along most of its shoreline. I had spent a lot of time fishing Saratoga. It was a little like home.

Lew had taken me through flying figure-eights around two conspicuous points on the ground and making S-turns over a straight road at a fairly low altitude. The goal of these maneuvers was to teach me not only to make smooth turns but also to recognize the drifting forces of the winds and correct for them. In this way, even in a good breeze I could make the plane fly a perfect pattern of curves and straight lines over the terrain, as perfectly as if the air were calm.

I'd done a stint at both these training exercises and had taken Lew back to Round Lake. Now Saratoga Lake lay beneath me. In spite of myself, I kept looking for a splash that would indicate a smallmouth bass feeding. My task, though, was to follow the edge of the lake at an altitude of 250 feet while maintaining a constant distance from the shoreline, no matter how sharply it bent or twisted. It was an impossible job because the contour changed more abruptly than I could turn.

The satisfaction of doing it quite well was like learning to write when I was a kid and making squiggly lines turn into letters and words. I even learned to handle distractions—like people who waved from cottage verandahs or squinted up at me from little flat-bottomed boats anchored beside patches of lily pads, their rods resting on the gunwales and tiny floats bobbing in the water nearby. I followed the shoreline around and around the lake for nearly two hours before changing to some other maneuvers.

That day I learned to control the plane well enough to lift one float off the water, then the other, on takeoff. Next I mastered landing the same way, first touching down on one float, then letting the other join it on the water. I was feeling more and more at home in the plane.

*NC6194H log: May 20, 1947*

I had flown the required forty hours. I had my ten hours of instruction and then some. I'd done my four hours of cross-country flying, and my logbook had been signed at four faraway places. I'd passed my written exams on meteorology, navigation, planes, and flying regulations. Lew decided it was safe to turn me loose with a flight examiner, who would decide if I really knew how to fly.

Taking a flight test for a private pilot's license when you've had only nineteen days to learn, when you know you were a little slow to solo, and when you still hate the thought of having to do a spin is cause for a lot of trepidation. But there it was. If I wasn't ready now, would I ever be? The examiner was years younger than I, competent and businesslike. He settled into the front seat where Lew had spent so many hours and gave me instructions:

"Climb to fifteen hundred."

"Do a three-sixty."

"Again."

"Now do a seven-twenty to the left."

"Let's find a straight stretch of road for S-turns."

"How about Pylon 8s?"

"Now, let's do *on* pylons."

The pylons I'd flown *around* at a height of 400 feet were big elm trees about a quarter of a mile apart. They looked too close together for the on-pylon maneuver, so I climbed up to 800 feet and found two other elms farther apart. The on-pylon maneuver means that you make several tight figure-eights around your pylons, as if you were pivoting around each elm tree on a string stretching straight from the tree to your lower wing tip, all the while maintaining altitude. In still air, this maneuver is quite difficult; with any wind it is an awesome problem. I didn't think I did it very well.

"OK, up to 2,000 for stalls," came the order.

They were a breeze. My stomach rode right along with me, and the airplane didn't lag back at the top of the climb. The examiner didn't ask me to spin. He just said, "Let's go back."

Did that mean I had failed?

I didn't know until he asked for my logbook and wrote "Approved" in it.

I had become a pilot and would soon be on my way to Newfoundland and my fishing camps.

# HOME AGAIN

◡

Flying in bright sunlight and a gentle wind, it was hard to remember the grim hour I'd spent crossing the open water of Cabot Strait, between Nova Scotia and Newfoundland. Below me, the Anguille Mountains sloped down to the sea. Then came the little village of Highlands, Robinsons, Fischells, and Flat Bay. I knew them all but was seeing them for the first time from the air. Across the bay I could see the white, bright buildings of Stephenville Airport. This would be my first touchdown in Newfoundland and a milestone.

My arrival was not as simple or as warm as I expected. In the first place I made a lousy landing. I approached the base and circled the field and the pond. There were no other aircraft aloft, and none were warming up or taxiing on the runways. I had no radio and looked for a green light from the tower. When none flashed, I circled twice more. Still no green light. No red one either, to warn me off. I headed for the pond beside the seaward runway. Whether it was a gust of wind that lifted me just before touchdown or plain misjudgment of my stalling speed, I hit the water and bounced back into the air, hit again, and bounced once more before settling into the light chop.

A few people were coming to the pier as I taxied in. Willing hands helped me tie up the plane. With my light pack in my hand I stepped ashore just as a car full of officials drove up. I thought I ought to go to flight operations. They took me to the Officers Club. And told me to wait.

I saw not one familiar face until Dave Sawyer came along. Dave was a warrant officer who had been there a long time. He was from Maine and was a fellow angler. I'd fished with him a couple of times during the war. He'd heard that a pilot named "Wolf" had just come in with a fishing rod in his plane. He didn't know I'd learned to fly. He was just curious. He was a welcome sight, and he helped me find out what was going on.

After the war, the U.S. government had given Harmon Field back to Great Britain, which renamed the base Stephenville Airport. No deals had been made yet for the commercial use of the facilities, and only military pilots could get permission to land. I'd barged in without a flight plan and without prior approval. On the Officers Club radio, the program I'd been listening to was interrupted with a "news flash from Gander." The announcer said that an American civil airplane had broken international rules and landed at Stephenville.

Eventually, however, it became apparent that I had no evil intent at the base and that a lone pilot in fishing clothes and a not very impressive Piper Cub would not seriously endanger the economy or peace of the world. Perhaps someone in Washington or Ottawa who'd been at the base during the war remembered me and gave me clearance. Two days later, base personnel gassed me up and let me go.

Following the railroad (the old pilots called them "iron compasses") and flying under white fluffy clouds, I headed for Corner Brook, where the big pulp and paper mill was sending clouds of sulfurous steam up toward me. I looked down and flew on, picturing Barry, a sturdy little kid of seven with a round face on which a smile like sunshine was always ready to break out. I also thought of Allan—ten, serious for his age, and eager to see the wild country and salmon rivers I'd told him so much about. Ella would be there, too, with her blue eyes smiling in welcome and her boys, Jonathan and Tony, in tow. We'd be together for a great summer.

The J3's motor was making its steady roar. The clouds were white, the sky was blue, and all was well.

A straight line from Corner Brook to Lomond takes you right over the hills on the north side of the bay and then over some fairly high mountains. Along the way, I crossed Old Man's Pond, a long lake set deep in the mountains. Flying at a thousand feet over the trees, I could see the dark, peat-stained water where it flowed through its narrow outlet and met the light blue water of the sea. The sun had grown hazy, and about three miles ahead things faded into an indistinct gray. The land began to rise under me and, it seemed, the clouds were coming down. I said to myself again, "There are old pilots and bold pilots but no old, bold pilots."

I tried to climb a little and found myself starting to enter the haze. I could still see the ground and make out the terrain ahead. It was barren country—just bare rock, blueberry bushes, and tuck-bush wherever there was enough soil for anything to grow. I saw a flutter of white wings as a flock of ptarmigan flushed below. A wisp of cloud passed me. I nosed down. Suddenly the haze was solid. I was in a cloud, with impenetrable gray all around me.

I felt the plane speed up, and I cut back a little on the throttle. It was a moment of terror. The seconds seemed like hours. There was no one to help me. Around me was the same air that had been so comfortable a few minutes before. But I couldn't see! How high was I above the ground? Where was I headed? Would I come out of the cloud headed right for the rocks, or would I hit the ground while still in the clouds? My eyes swept across the instrument panel. I had forgotten the ball-bank! That's the simple little instrument that tells you whether or not your airplane is in proper flying attitude. The little ball was way over to the left. Left stick! Left rudder! Slowly the ball came back to center. I slowed the motor. Was I right-side up? Keep the stick and rudder centered, I told myself. Slow down . . . but don't stall.

Suddenly, I could see the ground 100 feet below. Almost immediately, I was in the cloud again. Then out of it. The ground was lower—now 300 feet below me. I came out of the cloud in a gentle, gliding curve, my right wing high. Relief flooded over me. I had needed luck and I'd received it. I still had a chance to go on and become an old pilot. But the haze under the clouds was still hard to see through. Which way was downhill? Which way was the ceiling highest? I headed northeast. I thought I couldn't miss the road from Lomond to Deer Lake, one of the few roads in Newfoundland. It had been put in to connect a small, now-dying paper company with the railroad at Deer Lake.

I saw no lakes. There was no glint of water anywhere. Minutes ticked by. The terrain was changing. The trees were getting taller, and that meant a north slope, better soil. Yet the ceiling was coming down as fast as the land was lowering. Then I saw water ahead. It was Bonne Bay Little Pond, and there, on the far side of the road, was Jack Alexander's place.

Jack was surprised when I landed. He came out of his house swearing a little in wonder. He watched me hop out of the plane, submerging my ten-inch L. L. Bean boots in the process of turning the Cub around in order to lift the back of the floats up onto the gravel. Then he recognized me and poured out a dozen questions about the airplane and on where and when I'd learned to fly, ending up with, "Come in for a bite."

Jack was a bachelor, but his place was spick-and-span. Strong tea was steeping on the back of the woodstove. Bread made by his own hand came out of the breadbox. There was raspberry jam and, to finish off the meal, a dish of tart-sweet, preserved cloudberries, with cream from a neighbor's cow. There was warmth and friendship and time to relax from my scare in the skies. Jack couldn't know what I'd just gone through, and I wasn't going to tell him. If word got out that I'd almost flown blindly into the ground, no one would ride with me.

We talked of fish and fishing . . . and the fun of flying. Half an hour later, the sky cleared, and I flew on the few miles to Lomond, where Ella had bought a lodge.

She had named it Killdevil Lodge after the mountain across the bay, and this would be my pick-up point for fishing guests. I'd then fly them north for sixty miles to the camps at Portland Creek. I could handle a party of four in a single day. That was a whole lot better than having Norm Parsons take them down in his boat, a trip that might take one day and, then again, might require three. I'd have to take the sports one at a time, which would mean a lot of flying, but at that time of the year in Newfoundland, there was daylight from four in the morning till nearly eleven in the evening. There might be times when I'd be weathered in, but I expected them to be few. My only worry would be fog or high winds, and either one of those would stop Norman, too.

I circled high over the row of empty company houses, losing altitude, and buzzed Ella's lodge, coming out of a quiet glide into a roaring climb that shook the shingles. I climbed high enough to do a chandelle and then another while she and the boys climbed into the car and raced down to the beach. My floats had barely touched the shore when the children were climbing onto them.

As my legs stretched down for footing, the boys were hugging me. I gave Allan and Tony the ropes I carried under the front seat, and they scampered back ashore to secure the plane. Then Ella was in my arms, and we were a family again.

Before we headed to the lodge, there was one more detail to attend to. Allan came to me and said, "Have you got a half a dollar?" I reached into my pocket and gave him a fifty-cent piece. He walked over to the plane with Barry at his side. I followed to watch. Using the coin as a screwdriver, Allan opened the cover on the front left float compartment and looked down into it. Then he looked up at me and grinned. Barry looked in and made a grab with his hand. Then he grabbed again. Squirming in his hand as he brought it out was a little frog.

I had told the boys before we left New York that there were no frogs in Newfoundland. They'd asked why, and I had explained that being an island, Newfoundland did not have many of the animals and fish that were common on the mainland. Originally there were no rabbits, skunks, woodchucks, deer, or any of a long line of animals found in the rest of the Northeast. There were, however, arctic hares, caribou, lynx, otters, beaver, and bears. Rabbits and moose had been introduced and were flourishing. Foxes and mink, escapees from fur farms, were also doing well. The boys had asked if frogs could survive on the island, and I said I believed they would. The frogs would have plenty of black flies and mosquitoes to eat, and the winters in Newfoundland were no colder than they were at our home in upper New York State. They were just longer.

We'd started out with five small pilgrims that Allan and Barry loaded into a nest of grass and ferns in that float compartment. All but one made it. For years afterward, we'd hear them or their progeny making frog sounds in the swampy places that became their homes.

# PORTLAND CREEK

~

In Newfoundland, the flat north country has more water than the southern portion of the island, mainly because each winter's buildup of ice and snow keeps the lake hollows filled and the rivers running full. By contrast, the warmer, more mountainous lands to the south lose their snow, ice, and rain in an almost continuous runoff. This difference makes the north ideal floatplane country. Except for the mountain ridges and smooth slopes, lakes and ponds spread everywhere beneath a bush pilot's wings.

Allan and Barry had never been to Newfoundland before, but they had heard a lot about the camps at Portland Creek and were now going to see them. They sat together on a wide cushion in the front seat of the *Yellow Bird*, and they could hear me over the motor noise. As we lifted off from Lomond and headed out over Bonne Bay, I kept up a running monologue:

"That's the 'Eastern Arm' of the bay, and that's Killdevil Mountain on our right. It's 2,100 feet high. Maybe we can climb it someday—there's a trail.

"That's Norris Point, and that's the boat—the gray one—I caught the first tuna from. Only twelve fathoms of water in that narrow neck, but there's a hundred and twenty fathoms off Lomond at the bottom of the arm. Big whales and porpoises come in through here.

"There's Rocky Harbor. One winter day during the war, a DC3 made a forced landing on the bay there. It was frozen over, and the pilot thought it was an area of snow-covered land. But it was ballycater ice. The plane got all broken up, and the crew was killed.

Ballycater? That's what the Newfoundlanders call it when the sea ice is pushed together and is all rough—like a great white sheet of sandpaper.

"There's Sally's Cove. How'd you like to live there? Right on the sea? And catch codfish from your dory?

"That's Western Gorge. Isn't it magnificent? We'll fly right over it someday so you can see it close up. We'll take pictures."

Cow Head lay ahead of us, two great semicircles of shining white beach stretching out on each side of a rocky point that made a meager harbor for small boats. The short peninsula trailed off into a slowly submerging reef, and there, newly stranded, was a two-masted schooner. "I wonder," I said, "if they'll be able to get the boat off before a real big storm comes along to wreck it."

We circled low. There was a bunch of dories alongside and they were off-loading cargo. Maybe, I thought, if the ship was unloaded, it would float free at high tide. The men below waved us a greeting. Perhaps some of them had heard that I'd be coming down in a plane.

We came in over the telegraph wires at the mouth of Portland Creek, and I pointed out the spot where I'd had my tents the year before. We flew on over the river's mile of length and looked down at the new clearing, the tents, and the cookhouse that Eb had established at the "running out" of the pond. As soon as I knew I'd have a plane, I'd sent word that the campsite had to be moved. My landing point would have to be the smoother, safer fresh water of the pond, rather than the sea.

In February, Eb had sent me a short note in which he said he'd arranged for the new local schoolteacher to board at his house. Eb was learning to read and write, as I'd requested. His message was short but OK. I wrote back and confirmed that he'd be my foreman, and I sent him an advance on his pay and funds to cover the work that needed to be done. Now I would find out how well he'd managed. Things looked good from the air.

I taxied in to the shore, and the whole crew was there. Burly Eb was the first to greet us. Levi Humber, at seventy my oldest guide, was on hand. So were Herb and Arthur Perry, and Herb's wife, who would do the cooking on the big range that had been shipped from Corner Brook and brought up the river in a dory. Together, we walked the short path to the new campsite, and as we approached, we smelled a wonderful aroma. It came from a lobster chowder that Mrs. Perry was serving on the new screened porch that overlooked the Running Out Pool.

Now that the *Yellow Bird* had reached its base in the bush, the first thing we did was build a ramp for the plane. Eb had set up a portable sawmill at our site on the pond, so we had lumber for the ramp as well as for the cabins we were building. We designed a sloping platform such that if the plane came in at the right speed, it could slide up the ramp and be high and dry. At the same time, a man could push the Cub back down the sloping boards and get it into the water again when its mooring lines were freed. To complete the landing, a dozen fifty-five-gallon drums of auto gas had been off-loaded at the river mouth and brought to the lake by walking heavily loaded dories through the mile of rocky river.

Once things were in some semblance of order, I made an important side trip: I flew back to Stephenville to bring in Jack Young to work at the camp. He and I had spent many days on Newfoundland's salmon rivers and had camped in the interior, where the wild country stretched away endlessly and the caribou followed their age-old trails across the bogs and barrens. We had many campfires to remember, and a deep friendship had developed between us. Jack was the finest guide I knew. He knew the habits of the fish and game. He could make superb meals with a reflecting oven beside an open fire. He could turn the simplest foods into gourmet fare. He knew his island and loved it well. I had listened and learned to love it as he did. He was a man I admired.

I wanted Jack to help me in training the guides—none of whom, except Eb, could read or write—in the rigging of the fishing tackle and in handling all the complications of salmon guiding. I planned to build new camps on the isolated rivers within flying range and would be needing even more guides when the new sites were finished.

But there was another reason I brought in Jack. It was amazing how clever the men I'd hired were at building solidly with simple tools. But, as a showpiece at the Portland Creek camp, I wanted something I wasn't sure any of them could produce for me. I asked Jack to build a log cabin like one we'd hunted from years back in the Long Range Mountains. It would not be an ordinary structure but one that would be put together with nary a nail or spike, using no tools beyond an ax and hunting knife.

Sometimes I helped Jack with this cabin when I had a break in the long hours of flying. The logs that had been towed by dories from to the campsite were long and straight—spruce, fir, or tamarack that grew along the shores of Portland Pond. The floor was made level and solid with small, straight saplings fitted between the heavier logs. At the corners, each wall log was notched perfectly into the next one. The roof was birch bark, laid in great, overlapping sheets, then covered with sod from which the grass still grew. There was enough rain in Newfoundland to keep that wild hay green all summer, and the weight of the sod would hold the bark solidly in place and keep it waterproof.

We did fudge on the windows. Instead of leaving them open and covering them with birch bark at night or in storms, we installed panes of glass that slid across each other to let air through when needed. Finished off with rustic bunks and mattress cushions filled with soft, fragrant spruce boughs, this cabin quickly became the favorite of our guests.

Building it, however, came close to bringing me heartbreak. Jack and I were putting up the rafters for the roof, using logs that had been cut in June—when the sap is still running well. At that time, the bark can be peeled readily from the trees, making them smooth and clean but leaving them with a covering of sap that was as slippery as grease until the logs dried. We were handling a heavy one when Barry, who had been playing nearby, walked into the cabin.

Just then, the log began to slip out of my hands, and the boy was right below us as it started its fall. Jack tried to hold on to his end but failed. I yelled to my little son. Just barely in time, he moved aside but not quickly enough to prevent the log's striking him and knocking him over. I came down the framing like a monkey and took Barry in my arms, not knowing what to expect.

I looked at his face and saw that he was smiling. "You looked funny," he said, "like a spider coming down that wall." There was sticky sap on his jacket and in his hair, and there was a bruise on his shoulder. But that was all. It was one of those incidents where life or death is a matter of luck. Once over, they are soon forgotten, yet, in almost everyone's life, there has been a moment when tragedy was only a hairbreadth away.

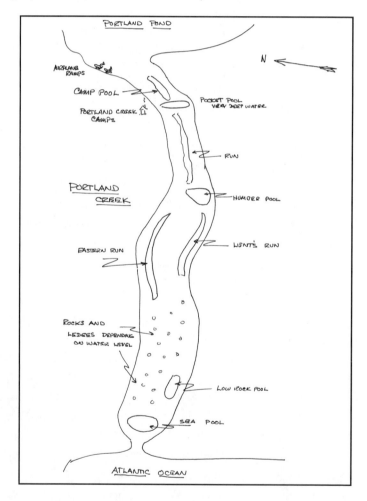

*Sketch of Portland Creek drawn by Barry Wulff*

# THE RIVER

❧

Throughout its mile-long course, Portland Creek flows over a wide, rocky, generally shallow bed that originates at Portland Pond. Roughly round and about six miles in diameter, this lake stretches from the Gulf of St. Lawrence all the way across the coastal plain to the long chain of mountains that parallels the coast for more than a hundred miles, from Rocky Harbor north. Through a short run of slow water at its eastern edge, Portland Pond joins Inner Portland Pond, which extends another six miles into the mountains. Whereas Portland Pond is relatively shallow, with a maximum depth of approximately thirty feet, Inner Portland has shores that slope swiftly upward for more than two thousand feet, and its depth is roughly equal to their height.

Although a small feeder stream flows into the inner pond at its farthest point inland, the main streams terminate in Portland Pond—Brian's Feeder from the north and the Southwest Feeder from the southwest. Both have runs of salmon and big, seagoing brook trout.

The river itself curves out of the lake, shifting from a southerly flow to one that is almost straight westerly to the Gulf of St. Lawrence. Portland Creek ranges in width from a little over a hundred yards to almost two hundred. Only at the Running Out Pool, at the top of the river, and at the Sea Pool, just above the salt water, is the bulk of the flow concentrated into a single, broad channel. The Running Out Pool, or Camp Pool, is a couple of hundred yards long, and just below it is the Pocket Pool, where a drop-off from the shallow Camp Pool stretches most of the way across the flow.

Immediately downstream of this point, the river grows shallow over its entire width, creating one of the few places where wading across is easy.

Below the Pocket Pool, the river finds a deep central channel called The Run, which extends for a quarter of a mile, long enough to accommodate three or four anglers. The Run itself is too deep to wade, but there is a shallow, fifty- to seventy-five-foot strip on either side, where an angler can always wade out to reach the salmon. When The Run shallows up at its tail, the water falls into a short but deep pool that stretches the full width of the river. This is the Humber Pool, one of the best spots for very large salmon.

Just below this point, the river splits. The southerly part of the flow goes down through Lent's Run before twisting back to rejoin the rest of the river. On the northerly side lies the Eastern Run, a conventional salmon pool a couple of hundred yards long. Deep against the northern shore, the bottom here slopes up gradually to a midstream gravel bar. Below Lent's Run and the Eastern Run, the two branches converge in a more or less uniform and wadable flow. Here, below big rocks or ledges, there are small, deep pockets in which large salmon often lie.

Then the main flow of the river drifts southward and forms the Low Rock Pool. From there, it moves into the Sea Pool, which is long and deep and which can rise and fall with the tides. Over the entire length of the river, from top to bottom, salmon are found lying in places that are not pools but that happen to please an individual fish. It was a dream river, my Portland Creek, where a dozen of my sports could each have a separate and adequate stretch of water to fish—all within less than a mile of their cabin.

I decided to set aside the Sea Pool and the run above it for the local people. I didn't want to take the river away from the Newfoundlanders altogether, and if I had the rest, I knew there'd be enough places to give the camp a good potential for profit. I explained it to the locals this way: Wherever a sport was fishing, he was accompanied by a guide who had a job. If a local fisherman took over that space on the river, there'd be a guide without a job because of it. That job would be the one the offending local fisherman or one of his friends could have had. In other words, if one of the locals fished in the river above the Sea Pool Run, I would not hire him at the camps; if he was already on the payroll, I would fire him. I felt that was fair and essential, both for the success of the camps and the economic benefit of the whole community.

Before starting operations, many a camp owner thinks he is going to do a lot of fishing. That's usually an illusion. There's too much work to do. But, over the years, he will get to fish a good deal, though always after all his customers have worked over the pools and given up. Or, he may take up the rod on the rare days when there are few guests and his fishing won't give them the feeling that any salmon he catches is one that they, themselves, might have taken the next day. Still, in time, the camp operator gets to know his rivers very well and learns to catch fish where others have failed. (Of course, I had yet another advantage: I had a plane to take me to wonderful areas that no one else had fished.)

There were times when I'd guide a particular friend just to be with him or to let his regular guide work on some critical camp chore. Then I'd take on the usual challenge of showing someone who didn't know as much about the river or salmon fishing as I did how to make exactly the right cast and the right retrieve to bring a salmon to the steel.

Guiding can be a frustrating business. When you indicate the spot where a salmon should be lying, your charge will cast out his dry fly and, because the cast wasn't perfect, he'll snap it right back in order to make a better one. All he does is to scar the water just over the fish's head on his pick-up and put the fish down. Then, no matter how many perfect casts he then makes over that spot, the salmon will not rise to his fly.

If, on the other hand, the sport simply lets that fly drift over the fish—even though the leader has landed in a mess—the salmon might well rise to take the offering or come up on a subsequent cast. Often, too, a beginner will pick up his fly during the retrieve just when it is about to reach the pregnant water. With a wet fly, certain speeds of retrieve seem to work best, but the typical sport will manage to be consistently faster or slower than that. In sum, there are endless ways your charge can fail to catch a fish that you could have taken easily. Mere words won't convey the skills he needs. But, because the unorthodox or crazy things some beginning fishermen do will sometimes catch salmon, you may learn a little more about how to stir the taking impulse in these moody fish.

I got to know Portland Creek intimately. I figured out just which rocks in various runs the salmon would lie beside or behind at each water level. I learned that the best way to fish the Eastern Run, which usually held some very large salmon, was to go through it first with a short line, standing well back on the gravel bank at the shallow side. Then, I would go through several more times, each time taking the fly a little farther out into the deeper water toward the far bank until finally I'd covered the entire pool. I found that each time I went down through that smooth, beautiful flow, the fish seemed to move a little farther away until, at the end, it seemed as if they were all strung out in a line over toward the far bank. If I gave them a rest then, before working through the stretch a final time, there was a good chance that one of those big, reluctant salmon would take the fly.

The Humber Pool, too, could be counted on to hold large salmon. It was there that I had a rise from a big fish late one season, when we had few guests and were closing up. Each evening, when the guests were giving up, I went down the path to pass a few casts over that fish's lie. Finally I hooked him. When he leaped, he looked as big as the forty-pounder that one of the locals once caught in the Sea Pool. He made that one great leap, and the fly came free from its hold.

The Caribous, a little pocket marked by three light-colored rocks that broke the surface in the middle of the great flat stretch between the Eastern Run and the Low Rock Pool, often held big fish. It was a tricky place to fish and, if you were guiding, you had to hold your charge well back from the deep pocket and have the angler make long casts over the shallow water that surrounded it.

The guides, many of whom had never had a rod in their hands before I set up the camps, got to know the river very well, too. Some of them could catch fish consistently in pools that I hadn't figured out as well as they had. Quiet, steady Tom Biggin often put his charges into big fish in Lent's Run. Yet, although I fished it fairly often, I never took a salmon of more than ten pounds from that pool.

And trout? When I first set up the camps, there were lots of them in the river, running up to four pounds, but as the seasons went by they became very scarce. Those sea-run brook trout seemed all too willing to take a fly and, with the concentrated fishing that went on in the salmon pools, I believe most of them were caught. They couldn't watch those beautiful salmon flies swimming over their heads day after day without making a pass at one.

The sports would usually keep them to have them cooked for breakfast, and it didn't take long before the catching of a good-sized sea trout was a rarity. The smaller ones, which hung out under the overhanging alders survived pretty well until the guides began to have their sports fish those shallower spots when they wanted a trout for breakfast. A dozen salmon fishermen on one short mile of water had a devastating effect on the trout population.

In spite of my trying to get most of the salmon released, fishing for them slowly began to become more difficult, too. Thus, I had all the more reason to set up camps on the other, nearby rivers whenever I could, and to work out some way to make my catch-and-release program more effective.

# THE COOKHOUSE POOL

∽

I had a lot to learn about winds. According to my advisors, they'd be my worst enemy. As I discovered one morning, the Cub was like a butterfly, practically helpless in a gale.

I had gassed up and was preparing to take off from Lomond when I looked across at old Killdevil Mountain and saw fog along the top. Just above it, an overcast stretched all the way across the sky. The air where I stood was calm, and the bay showed only a few areas of light rippling. The fog at the top of Killdevil was spilling over the cliffs and starting to flow down the mountainside, as if painted there by a great invisible brush. Funny, I thought, the wind must be bending down over the crest of the mountain and following down the slope a little way. It was like a white frothy frosting coming down the side of a long, green cake.

I forgot about the wind while I loaded the plane and climbed into the back seat. Once off the water I headed out the bay, climbing as I went. It was fourteen miles to the outer shore and Rocky Harbor, where the long, narrow, flat strip of land along the coast would start northward, forming an easy air pathway between the mountains and the sea. At Norris Point, I was at 1,100 feet and still climbing. Even so, the cloud cover was five hundred feet above me. I leveled off.

But my altimeter kept going up! I dropped my nose and headed down at lower power. Still the needle kept showing an altitude gain. Something was awfully wrong.

I looked down at the water and the shore below me. They were getting farther away, and the clouds above were descending. Then they swallowed me. I was in thick fog. The wind had sucked me right up into the clouds. I pushed the stick forward, and when the sound made by the Cub told me I'd picked up speed, I throttled back to idle. A pilot becomes very conscious of the noises emitted by his airplane as it flies. He can sense its speed from the sound. He knows, too, that the sound will be different if he "slips" at an angle to one side or the other. He reads it as a mother reads her baby's cry. It seemed a long time, but it was probably no more than a minute before I came down out of the cloud cover into the open air, where I could see again.

I guess I should have known. If the wind was spilling over the top of Killdevil and blowing sharply down the mountainside, then it had to sweep upward just as sharply against the peaks on the other side of the bay. I'd been caught in that updraft and carried to a level where clouds were forming instantaneously. It was a lesson I'd never forget. And I knew it wouldn't always be so easy to recognize the places where the wind was flowing into and out of a valley. There weren't always clouds in updrafts and downdrafts to make them visible.

I was learning the things every mountain flier must know. I would seek out the upwind side of the ridges and use the lift of the rising air to help keep the *Yellow Bird* aloft, thus saving energy and gas. And I knew now that I should not approach the peak of hill from the downwind side lest a down-driving gust push me into the ground.

I came to appreciate, too, that I could only climb at a rate of about three hundred feet per minute and that a minute would take me over almost a mile of ground. If I had a canoe or a load of lumber strapped to my floats, I could hardly climb at all, so I learned to circle several times to get altitude enough to start a trip. It didn't really matter that I was considered too old to learn to fly well. I would be careful and felt I had the judgment not to ask the airplane to do anything we weren't capable of doing. I'd had a couple of scares, and that was all to the good. I'd also had some good luck, and while it is said "It's better to be lucky than smart," I felt I needed to be both.

The rest of the trip was easy. When I reached Rocky Harbor, the sky opened up and the long strip of low land between the mountains and the sea was bathed in sunlight as I flew north. I was fortunate, I mused, that I hadn't had a passenger with me on this flight. The Cone party was back for another year, and I'd flown them in to the camps two days earlier. Suppose Caesar, the youngest Cone, who didn't really like to fly, had been with me. He might have decided that riding in the *Yellow Bird* was too dangerous and convince the other members of the party never to come back. I flew on.

It was like being in heaven, looking down at that unspoiled land below. There were marshes and ponds and patches of evergreens. The little freshets of water on the muskeg took on strange shapes that sometimes looked like animals or the profile of a man's head or the shape of a fish with its fins in all the wrong places. Puffy fair-weather clouds passed their moving shadows across the ground below me. I had to learn to judge how hard the wind was blowing, and those shadows could tell me both its velocity and its direction at cloud level. I could use the speed of my own shadow in still air—sixty-five miles an hour—as a basis for my guesses. How much would a wind like the one in which I was now flying push me off course if I were in strange country with no sun and no landmarks to follow? That was the sort of thing I had to discover.

There was a bunch of seals sitting on the rocks inside the inlet at St. Paul's. I dove at them, and they slipped off into the water. It was shallow, and I could still see them streaking along under the surface after the splashes. Because of human predation, the seals in Newfoundland were very wary. There was a bounty on harbor seals because they host a parasitic worm that infests codfish, and the rifles of the St. Paul residents had cut their numbers down to a very few.

I climbed up to five hundred feet again. At that height, I could still feel intimate with the land, but I could see distance better, and—most of the time—be within gliding range of a pond or a stretch of muskeg on which I could land the plane safely. Still, like Billy Bruce, I counted on my motor to run forever, even though the consensus was that all pilots have a motor failure once in every five thousand hours.

I swung out over the gulf to intersect Portland Creek at its mouth. I wanted to fly up the length of the river to see just where my sports were fishing. The Cone group were the only ones in camp, for the season had just started. With only four anglers on a river that could handle twelve, I knew there'd be some open pools. It was the first of July, and the salmon had just come in. All the fish in that early run would be big salmon of ten pounds or more. The grilse, smaller fish of about four pounds, wouldn't enter the river for another week or ten days. I hadn't caught a salmon yet that year and figured this might be a good time to do it.

I landed and secured the *Yellow Bird*. Finding that there were no pressing problems at camp, I went to the kitchen for a cup of hot tea and some fresh, homemade bread and honey. Then I walked to the new footbridge we'd put in across a tributary of the creek so that I could easily reach my tent, which was next door to the cookhouse. The stream formed a small, deep pool right below the bridge. Pausing to look down, I saw a small trout dash wildly for cover and had an idea for keeping the camp supplied with fresh fish:

I had ordered a kerosene-burning refrigerator, but it hadn't arrived yet. We had an ice supply that might last the full season, but then again, it might not. I realized that I could catch salmon and put them into this pool, where they'd stay alive until we needed them for food. Moreover, when guests arrived they could walk out on this little bridge, look down on the salmon, and be more eager to get out fishing—which is just how I felt at the moment.

Fortunately, although Marion Heiss and his guide, Levi, were fishing the Camp Pool, they were up at the head of it. There was no one at or near the Pocket Pool, so I put on my waders and went out there to fish. Luck was with me. I put on a #4 Jock Scott, and on the third cast, a salmon rose and missed the fly. Three casts later, he rose again and missed again. I changed to a Silver Blue. Bright, shiny flies are often best when the fish first come in. On the first cast, the salmon took the fly.

Like most of the early fish, he was a wild one. He made three jumps right in the Pocket and then, in an unusual move he went up over the ledge and into the lower part of the Camp Pool. Marion was playing a salmon that was tiring and had moved down to the tail of the pool. I feared that our lines would cross and was embarrassed that I, his host, might interfere with his fishing or cause him to lose a salmon. The fish crossed paths, and I had to pass my rod over Marion's. Then my salmon decided to work back downstream to the Pocket. In a minute or two Levi had Marion's fish secured with his tailer, and in a few minutes more, mine was ready for capture.

I brought him in close, then shifted my rod from my right hand to my left. I reached down and took a firm grip on the salmon's tail. Lifting him clear of the water and stones, I carried him the hundred yards to the little pool under the bridge beside the cookhouse. I left him there, and he lived healthily for a week before becoming the heart of a salmon chowder.

My policy of asking my anglers and guides to release their fish unless we needed them at the camp for food was still proving to be a hard sell. The guides would beg their sports to let them take the salmon home. Since it was hard for the fishermen to say no, a lot of salmon that should have been returned to the river went home to families that had grown tired of cod over the long winter. Fortunately, I eventually figured out a way to keep those fish in the river. Although anglers like to think that fly fishing can never hurt a river, every salmon that is killed cuts down that run of fish or, according to Darwin, lets the species deteriorate genetically because of lack of competition.

# FIRST SALMON

⁓

Faced with the inevitable decline of the fishing at Portland Creek, I knew that it was time to branch out to the other rivers nearby.

The River of Ponds was only eighteen miles away by air. It, too, flowed into a straight shore on the gulf. There was no harbor at its mouth and no settlement, only a few families who lived there to take advantage of the good cod and lobster fishing at their doorsteps. I'd explored it before and rated it as possibly the best salmon river in all of Newfoundland. The fish were large and plentiful. Only a few intrepid anglers had ever hiked their way for miles over a very difficult trail to reach its beautiful upper waters.

Moreover, those upper reaches encompassed a series of lakes where I could land my seaplane and set up camps. I decided to put the first one at Western Bluie in the middle of the area and, so, flew in some lumber, tents, and other equipment. I hired a couple of guides to set up the camp, and when it was finished, I flew in a couple of sports who were also good friends to try it out.

After Doc Glover and Bob Albee had been there a couple of days, I felt I'd better fly in to check up on things. I had brought Allan to the River of Ponds, too, on an extra trip the same day I took Doc and Bob up, when I was carrying only a few necessary supplies as a load and had room for him. I thought he might help in working on the new cabin or building a platform for another tent.

What was it Lew Lavery had said? "Never fly a minute but that you wonder where you'd land if your motor quits." It was eighteen miles from Portland Creek to Western Bluie, and I kept looking for safe landing spots along the route. Could I reach a pond from my present altitude? Was there a bog within range? If I went down in a bog, which I could probably do without damaging the Cub, I might be able to get a horse in there and drag the plane to a nearby pond if there weren't too many trees to cut. I could take off the wings to get it through a narrow trail and put them on again after I reached a pond.

If that wasn't possible, I'd have to use the wheels that Ella had brought with her as a safety measure. I could build a corduroy road of small spruces laid across the bog, wait for a good stiff breeze, take off with a little gas and no load, and land on the beach at Cow Head. I could have the floats carried out to the shore, even if I had to dismantle them, and could then have them brought to Cow Head by boat in order to make the Cub into a seaplane again. This would be difficult, perhaps, but certainly possible.

Ahead lay a ridge of high ground with no lakes. Dutifully, I climbed to 1,500 feet so that even at the point farthest from a lake or bog I could glide to it. When I crossed the middle of the high forested area, I could see Western Bluie.

Allan had become an avid fisherman as a very small boy, begging to go out with me and fishing on his own whenever he could. My elder son was precocious and daring, as I had been, wading to the greatest depth he could stand in, working on his baits and his tackle and his casting. He studied the woods and the animal tracks and their paths where we lived in New York State. Quite resourceful, Allan was mature beyond his years.

As I flew on toward seeing him again, I remembered a spring day a few months before, when I had to leave home for a lecture. I had waved good-bye to Allan from the front yard on the Battenkill, watching him at the head of the deep trout pool in front of the house. He was a tiny figure up to the tops of his boots, casting his fly into the swift run of water that dropped off just below him to a depth of more than a dozen feet. I turned, walked to the car, and started my drive to Boston.

Half a mile down the road I stopped, worried. I turned and drove back to the house. Without his seeing me, I looked out over the pool to see that Allan was still there and safe. He was, and I chided myself for doubting his judgment in wading. I had done those things, too, and done them safely. I walked back to the car and drove on to the lecture without a fear that he'd make a wading mistake. Life's full of hazards but if you can't believe in your own judgment, you miss out on a lot of living.

The guides and my friends were there with Allan at the camp that lay ahead. He was being looked out for and would be safe. I smiled to myself and hoped I'd be able to take him out with me on the river at the camp long enough for him to catch some trout and, possibly, a salmon.

I set a glide and came over the tents at about 200 feet. I could see the pool, but no one was fishing it. It was noon—lunchtime. Then I saw Allan, a tiny figure at the very head of the pool, where we usually caught only trout. He was up to the very tops of his hip boots.

I expected him to look up, but he didn't. Then I saw the flash of a leaping salmon, silver in a spray of foam against the dark water. Allan was playing a salmon. It was a moment to remember forever—the realization of a dream for him and for me. He was on his own, fighting that big, beautiful fish all by himself.

I swung out over the pond and landed, then taxied to the makeshift dock. I ran to where he was still playing the tiring salmon, with the guides and Doc and Bob coming along behind me. Allan brought the fish to the shallow water, and I lifted the salmon by the tail to carry him ashore for pictures. I hugged Allan then, perhaps for the last time as a little boy. He was growing up, this skinny little ten year old of mine.

The camp was OK. Doc and Bob were catching so many salmon they were ecstatic and were putting back all they couldn't eat at the camp. The guides, blond Fred Patey and black-haired Steve House, had everything under control except that a bear had been coming around the garbage pit. He hadn't broken into the camp, but they were worried. Would I bring in a bear trap?

I asked Allan if he wanted to fly back with me.

He asked, "Do I have to?"

I let him stay.

# Exploring for Salmon

࿇

Y ears earlier, the British Royal Navy had mapped the entire northern coastline of Newfoundland, and where they charted the bays, they went ashore to fish the rivers that held salmon. That meant every river of any size. But, the British sailors did not go far from their ships, into the wild and forbidding interior.

In fact, when I first came to Newfoundland in the early thirties, the current maps showed a great body of water, Lake Michel, centered far up on the northern peninsula. On earlier maps, it had appeared even larger. When I went down to the northwestern shore to explore the rivers there, I asked an old trapper about Lake Michel. He said he didn't know where it was. He guessed that long ago, some other trapper must have told the original mapmaker a tall story, as Newfoundlanders were prone to do to foreigners just for fun. Later, during the war, military planes overflew and mapped the area. They couldn't locate the lake, either.

As soon as I could find the time, I flew up to the northern peninsula. There wasn't even a moderately large pond near the vanished lake's location. Nothing but barrens and rock. On my way back to Portland Creek, however, I flew over Big Bluie Pond, at the headwaters of the River of Ponds. It was very real, and my first flight over it was dramatic.

I crossed the lake on that sunny afternoon at an altitude of about 500 feet and quickly found the inlet. I looked down at the mouth of the flow and the shallow water around it, keeping an eye out for salmon. Because of that season's dry weather, the water was only lightly peat stained, and from my altitude, I could see large rocks and logs on the bottom. I looked for individual salmon but spotted none. There were, however, a couple of long, dark rock ledges stretching out from the mouth of the river, and I made a mental note that they would probably be slippery if I waded out on them.

I circled around to look for any obstacles that might interfere with my landing or taxiing to the shore. As the plane's shadow crossed the ledges, my heart came up into my throat. The rock disintegrated into hundreds of fish that scattered in all directions. There were more Atlantic salmon than I had ever seen in one place. I circled again, landed, and taxied in to the shore. I was wearing waders, as I usually did on exploratory trips, and my six-foot fly rod was always within reach beside me in the plane.

There was no wind. The lake was mirror still. Breaking the surface here and there were little black triangles, which—as I waded closer—I could identify as the tips of salmon tails. They hardly moved, meaning that the fish were hanging just below the surface in a slightly head-down attitude. I moved out with the light flow of incoming water so as to send out a minimum of wading waves. The leader on the rod I'd taken from its hangers in the plane carried a dry fly, a White Wulff, my searching pattern. I cast it five feet in front of the nearest tail. The fly dropped gently. The tail disappeared, then a salmon's mouth opened and engulfed the fly. I set the hook, and the fish raced away amid the swirls and splashes of that great, spreading school.

He fought well, taking out backing on his first run in that big stretch of quiet water. He made several leaps and two other runs before he was tired. Then I brought him in to where I stood, knee deep, and picked him up by the tail. He weighed about twelve pounds. Working the hook free, I slid him back into the water. One after another I caught salmon from that school, never changing my fly. Sometimes I twitched it when I became impatient for a rise, but technique didn't seem to make much difference. Most of the time I just cast the White Wulff and let it sit. There were so many salmon there I don't believe any fly could have landed without being in sight of at least one fish. I caught a dozen salmon, releasing them all. Then, satisfied, I flew back to camp. Had I stayed on, I think I might have caught a hundred.

In the future, whenever I went back to Big Bluie it was alone or with special friends I could trust to keep this location secret. Each time, the number of fish seemed endless. Sometimes, on dead calm days, the drifting tails were there to see. Those salmon were making their seemingly endless wait for spawning time with their potential redds close at hand. Most of them, I believed, would spawn on the great gravel bars nearby, since the stream inlet was small and only a quarter of the fish congregated there would have filled it to overflowing.

This wonderful salmon spot was far inland, at the very head of the River of Ponds. If it remained a sanctuary, it would continue to provide a slew of salmon that would make for steady fishing as they passed through the lower pools where my camps would be. But if the inlet was damaged, the whole river would suffer.

Fortunately, it was a difficult place to reach. Summer travel over the boggy land was next to impossible. The inlet could be accessed by dog team over the snow in winter, but by that time most of the salmon would have spawned and would be either out in the lake or on their way back to the sea. A passerby wouldn't see them. But the country was opening up. Logging operations were reaching farther and farther back from the sea. Now bulldozers had replaced horses, and Bowater, the paper company, was making roads faster and cheaper than ever before. I just hoped they would be slow to reach the inlet.

The back country behind the shore on the northern peninsula and north into Labrador was still something of a mystery. There were bright and sparkling rivers known only to a few trappers, if at all. These held great runs of salmon just waiting for an angler's fly. It was my great good fortune to have the first light plane set up to explore the fishing, one that could land in rivers and other small waters and could gradually push northward—all the way to Davis Inlet, far north in Labrador.

Behind the mountains to the east of the main camp at Portland Creek lay a great valley with a large drainage that sloped from the high mountain crests on the western side of the peninsula, all the way to the low land at White Bay, on the Atlantic side. I wanted to see the river that drained that valley and, if it was what I hoped, I wanted to establish a camp there. I took Eb with me to help me choose the best site if we found good fishing.

We flew into the mountains over the lesser lakes behind Parson's Pond. Climbing to 1,000 feet above the crests, we could see White Bay and the open sea beyond it. Beneath us was typical Newfoundland high country. Here and there were a few scattered patches of scrub timber, usually in the cuts where a small brook ran or on the north side of the slopes where the retreating ice cap had made its best soil deposits. The rest was bare rock or muskeg-covered peat. This carpet of moss was dotted with freshets, where the water—held up by the sheets of rock below it—was too deep to be hidden by the vegetation. These threw sunlight back up at us as we flew over them.

Sometimes that muskeg would support the weight of a human being and sometimes not. Often a man could walk across once but on the return trip he'd plunge through to his knees or his hips and have to crawl or worm his way to a more solid area. In the summer, this country was impossible to walk through unless you knew your way. The caribou could do it, making paths that were permanent streaks on the ground below us, but these animals swim as easily as they walk and their paths were interspersed with water crossings. We saw several small herds of caribou—one spread out and feeding, the other walking single file over the peat on one of their chocolate-colored trails. Not one of these animals looked up as we flew above them. We climbed on, to 5,000 feet above sea level. From there we could see the entire pattern of the great drainage.

The dominant river in the area, called the Main River, had three separate branches. The most northerly one had no ponds in its flow. The central branch showed several ponds big enough to land in. And the southwest branch, which started in the high land just behind St. Paul's inlet, flowed through nine ponds that we could land in and take off from.

Rivers that have lakes or ponds in their flow are usually better for salmon fishing than those that do not. The ponds give the fish deepwater protection from birds or bears and provide large maneuvering areas in which the salmon can escape from seals or otters. In addition, the rivers with ponds usually hold larger salmon, perhaps for the same reason. Eb and I chose a pond about half a mile wide, landed, and taxied to the outlet. The shore was rocky, but the wind was light. I jumped off the floats when the water was knee deep and waded the plane to shore. We lifted one float up on a big flat rock and tied two lines to trees on the shore to hold the Cub steady.

My rod came out of its usual place, and with a box of flies in my pocket I was ready to fish. Eb went ashore to look for a suitable cabin site and to see whether there would be enough good trees close by to build a cabin or two. I could, if I had to, fly in lumber on the floats or even transport a portable sawmill, but if the logs were there all I'd need to bring in was sawn lumber for the floor, the roof, the bunks, and the tables.

The inlets and outlets of a pond or lake are good places for salmon to lie. When they get restless and want to move upstream or down, they can hold in the flow as it quickens or slows, experiencing the soothing feeling of moving water yet having the still depths of the pond close at hand in case they need to escape from danger. I moved to the running-out point, where the current began to quicken. Oily black and peat-stained, the water flowed over dark, moss-covered rocks. A salmon would be invisible here unless he flashed silver by turning his side to the sun or leaped for whatever reason salmon leap.

My first cast caught a trout of about twelve inches. I dispatched it quickly and tossed it onto the bank. The next cast took another trout of the same size. The third resulted in still another. In such untouched waters, there are often so many trout that it is difficult to catch a salmon. I caught one more fish and put it on the bank with the others to be the mainstay of our lunch when Eb returned. From then on, I put them back. I caught a dozen more trout before I'd exhausted that section of the pool. Then the fly swam through the water for five minutes without a touch. Were there no salmon here? Had I misjudged where they would be lying? Or were they simply not in the mood to take a fly? When Eb came back and started a fire, I waded ashore and cleaned the fish.

Over trout, bacon, bread, canned peaches, and tea we talked. There was a good site for a cabin and just about enough good logs to wall it in. Without a smooth beach, we'd have to build a ramp of lesser spruce poles, but there were plenty of those. The prevailing winds would come in off the lake, so the mosquitoes and black flies wouldn't cause too much trouble.

Black flies could be a real problem in Newfoundland, though not for Eb and me because we had developed a tolerance to them. A dozen years before, however, when I was out in the bush, I had been so bitten by black flies that I'd been feverish for a couple of days. After that, they didn't bother me. I could watch one land on my hand and chew a bit, then fly away. The little red spot that developed would turn black the next day, but there'd be no swelling, no itching. Twenty-four hours later, it would be gone.

But, some of the sports who came to the camps had no tolerance at all to black-fly bites. They'd turn into big, red blotches and swell up badly. So, we'd give our anglers headnets and show them how to tie their pants and sleeves tight against encroachment. We advised them to go out only when the wind was blowing. Wind complicates casting; bugs complicate living. Ironically, there is more marsh and boggy land—and less forest—in the high country than in the low land, so locations like the Main River were worse for bugs. We'd have to be careful whom we brought to a place like this.

We decided, though, that if Newfoundland's Natural Resources Department would open up a caribou season in early September before the salmon season closed (as they did in other parts of the island), we could offer a combination of salmon fishing and caribou hunting. Guests would have a good chance for caribou because the Main River area, deep in the middle of the peninsula, wasn't hunted at all by people from either coast. Judging by the blueberry barrens we'd flown over, there'd be a good chance for bear, too. It all hinged on there being salmon. There just had to be salmon!

Earlier, as we came in to land, I'd noticed a pretty good-looking pool about half a mile downstream. But the bog on both sides of the river there looked difficult to walk on. The pool itself wasn't long enough to land in and, anyway, I wouldn't have chanced a touchdown in water so black that it would hide rocks lying just inches deep. Besides, I wanted to fish that pool. The river was high from recent rains, and the water in the adjacent main channel looked deep enough for me to land the plane. Eb and I climbed back into the Cub, took off, and immediately started down.

Cub floats are about thirteen feet long and about eight feet apart. Each is eighteen inches wide at the widest point and sinks down into the water about eight inches. Rocks that don't project more than six inches above the surface will pass under the spreader bars between the floats without touching. This was the first time I had ever taxied on a salmon river. Fortunately, there was no wind, and following the channel was easy. I knew that if I proceeded slowly, there was no danger of damaging a float if we did touch a rock. We taxied all the way down to the pool without bumping a single one.

We tied up just above the fast water at the head of the pool and walked down. It was a beautiful spot. A current flowed between and around big, submerged rocks that twisted the flow on the surface but didn't break it. The water was five or six feet deep at the rocks, deeper below them. A salmon rolled to the surface halfway down the pool, and I waded into position to cast. He took the Jock Scott the first time it passed over him, but I lost him at his second leap. It was really just important that the salmon be there, not that I catch them. Continuing down the pool, I caught a trout at almost every cast. I was sure their splashings would have disturbed the salmon, but I turned back to fish down through the pool again, this time from the very top.

First I caught trout. Then when I reached the spot where the salmon had taken the fly, another one rose but missed. Two casts later, he took the fly. The Leica camera I wore around my neck was fitted with a fifty-millimeter lens, so the fish had to stay close if I was to get good pictures. That salmon jumped four times, right in front of me, and I photographed a couple of those leaps while I played him. When he was tired, I hand-tailed him, dispatched him, and slipped him into one of the plane's float compartments. We were a little low on fish at the camps, and I wanted to show the boys that we'd found salmon.

Eb came back from a walk in the bog, where he wanted to see if the cloudberries, which the Newfoundlanders called "bakeapples," were getting ripe. They weren't. He scanned the sky and said, "It's gonna blow."

I nodded. "Just one more fish."

Two casts later, I hooked another salmon. It was a four-pounder, a grilse and a very active fish. It ran farther and leaped more than the larger salmon, but it came to shore in less time. I unhooked him carefully and slid him back into his river. The wind was picking up. Another salmon jumped as we untied the plane.

The trip back upstream to the pond took longer, for the rising wind kept blowing us against the rocks on the northern shore. Eb dropped off into the water and either waded along next to the plane to keep us off the rocks or sat on the float and used the emergency paddle that was lashed to the floats.

A salmon leaped at the running-out as we reached it. Two more cleared the surface as we taxied out for takeoff. Why hadn't they leaped when we first arrived? Why hadn't the salmon in that pool responded to the fly?

We had no time left to fish for them. The storm was moving in. In spite of the growing breeze, our takeoff run was considerably longer than usual. The extra 1,800 feet of altitude in the Main River area made the air thinner there, and it provided less lift. I knew that I might not be able to get off that pond with a heavy load like lumber or a canoe, but I could surely bring heavy loads in. I cleared the trees with plenty of air beneath me.

The wind was strong and still rising, but it was blowing from the southwest, meaning that the landing back at Portland Creek would be toward the shore and easy. I settled in for the short flight, and my mind turned to the future.

We had a new campsite to think about and plan for.

# The Fun of Flying

❧

A pilot needs to keep up his flying skills. Being able to maintain full control of the airplane in unusual situations is essential to his safety.

So I regularly did chandelles, a beautiful maneuver where the pilot dives a little to pick up speed then climbs sharply until his plane is almost vertical. When the aircraft is about ready to stall—at just the right moment—the wings are leveled off, the nose comes down, and the plane heads back in the reverse direction with a good gain in altitude. The chandelle was a fighting maneuver used in World War I.

I also did plenty of lazy-eights. Here, the pilot makes S-curves back and forth over a straight stretch of river or shoreline, gaining altitude as he comes up to the top or bottom of each S and losing altitude as he comes back to cross the straight line at right angles with his wings level. He follows with the continuation of the endless S. The controls are constantly changing in this smooth maneuver, and it calls for good coordination all along the line.

Because my sons Allan and Barry together weighed less than a normal passenger, I could buckle both of them into the rear seat on a high cushion (so that they could see well) and take them with me when I went out to practice maneuvers. The one the boys liked best was the wing-over. In it you reverse direction in a minimum of lateral space. The wing-over could be a lifesaver if you were flying into a narrow canyon, thinking or hoping it was a pass through the mountains, only to have the canyon come to an abrupt end—as many do in Newfoundland. Faced with a solid rock wall ahead, you pull up into a vertical climb until your plane comes to the point where it is about to fall back. At exactly the right moment you put the rudder hard to one side or the other. The plane pivots on that wing and falls in a nose-down stall. As you gain flying speed, you lift the nose of the plane to come out of the stall. If you do things right, you'll be headed back on the course you came in on, at almost the same elevation.

In addition to including the boys in my practice sessions, I would take one of them along on my freight trips whenever there was space. Twice, Barry and I saw moose. The first one—a young bull with a small rack—was swimming across a lake, and we landed and taxied alongside him for a few minutes. I asked Barry if he wanted to slip over onto the moose's neck, hold on to his horns, and ride along for a while. He laughed, but as I moved closer he yelled, "No!"

The moose swam at a good speed, and I had to step the motor up from the 500 rpm of my normal idle to keep pace with him. When he reached the shore, he stood there and took a long look at us before he disappeared into the evergreens.

The second moose was a very big bull standing knee-deep in a small pond. When we first saw him he looked like a great stump, because his entire head was underwater getting lily roots. He'd bring these up with a lift of his head and stand there chewing. The air was perfectly still, and the pond in which he stood was like a mirror, without a ripple. I throttled back and circled. Barry asked, "How close can we go?"

"Pretty close, I think."

I cut back on the power and came around on a low, wide swing. If that old World War I German ace, Udet, could pick up a handkerchief with the tip of a wing, I decided that I could come pretty close to scratching that moose's nose as he stood there, like a statue, in a windless pond. I was no Udet, but I put one wingtip a foot or two in front of his nose. Then I had to apply power and look ahead. Over the sound of the motor I could hear Barry's high-pitched laugh behind me. The moose, he said, had reared up on his hind legs "with the most surprised look on his face."

When I looked back the big bull was standing motionless again. He hardly turned his head as we circled around once more. I waggled my wings as we passed in front of him, but he didn't move. We climbed higher and flew on.

We could never get close to the few bears we saw. There was something about the sound of my motor that scared them. It seemed to hurt their ears or frighten them in a special way. All those we spotted were already running for timber or deep alders in which to disappear. The one bear I saw with Barry was the closest. We had come around the edge of a mountain, and there he was, out in a bog, eating blueberries. He ran for the timber with amazing speed. There was a long, narrow freshet in his path, and he seemed to slide across the water in a great white splash and come out running on the other side. In seconds he had disappeared into the trees.

Coming back with Barry from one of my supply trips we witnessed something strange. As the camp at Portland Creek came into view, we could see the open sea beyond it and there, just offshore, was a big object that I'd just caught with the corner of my eye before turning to study the waves on the lake and figure out a path for my landing. Barry nudged me from behind and said, "That's a house out there!"

"A what?" I said, still looking down at the waves below me.

"A house—out in the gulf," he said.

Sure enough, what I had assumed to be a boat was a house afloat in the open sea. I swung out so we could have a look at it.

As we closed in we could see that the structure had a dozen or so empty oil drums lashed to the corners. It was floating fairly level, with the water halfway up to the open windows. A small trap skiff was towing it so slowly that we could hardly notice any movement. We waved and came close.

The man in the boat was Edgar House, one of the men who often worked for me as a guide. He waved back. I came by a few feet off the roof, and we could look in the windows and doorways. Barry claimed he could see a school of small fish swimming out the door. Later on, when Edgar came back to the camp to guide again, we questioned him about this strange incident.

He'd had a fight with his neighbor and had decided to move. He knew that because his house was built of wood it would float, but he reasoned that the empty oil drums would float it higher and, so, give it less drag through the water. His new spot was three miles down the shore. Sure, the trip had been slow going, but Edgar said that after we left him the wind helped speed him along. With logs and wedges, a pair of horses, and the help of friends, he'd set his house on its new site.

Barry asked, "Were there fish swimming inside? Little ones, like a school of capelin?"

"Yes, by God. There were," said Edgar. "When I got the house to shore and started blocking it up I found a couple of capelin that got in and didn't get out."

I also took Barry along on one of my exploratory trips back into the hills. Before we left, we talked of emergencies: If we went down, which of the survival rations should we eat first? I hadn't yet made the mature judgment that survival rations should be nourishing but should taste and smell like sawdust soaked in gasoline— something you wouldn't want to eat until you were damned hungry, and then only to keep from starving. Delicious things get eaten too soon. At that time I was carrying several cans of beans and peaches, along with raisins, dried apricots, sea biscuits, and such. Barry said he'd eat the peaches first and the sea biscuits at the very, very last.

Readily available, under my seat, I carried an anchor big enough to hold a twin amphibian. I also had a hatchet and a bucksaw blade, for which I could make a handle out of a bent spruce bough. And there were spare nuts and bolts, and tools I hoped I'd never have to use. I even had a can of tar to heat and use with rags to plug a hole in a float. With the nails I carried, I could build a ramp or a shelter. All this was extra weight that cut down my payload but might save our lives.

Another item we carried was not exactly for survival. That was a bottle of rum, preferably Lemon Hart or Hudson's Bay because they were 150 proof. It wasn't that I wanted to get intoxicated while I starved, but rather that I might want to open doors that might otherwise remain closed. I had learned this trick in the two summers I spent on a cabin cruiser exploring the Newfoundland coastline for the best salmon rivers and tuna spots. A drink of rum for the first citizen of any lonely outport would get you cooperation that money wouldn't buy. Even later on, when Allan learned to fly, he, too, would carry a bottle of rum in the front float compartment of his plane.

It was something special to watch your chosen Newfoundlander pour about four fingers of rum into a glass, look down at it fondly, then pour it down his throat at a single draught. His eyes rarely watered, and there was always a warm following smile as he put down the empty glass. When you did the same, even though you might water a bit at the eyes, a bond was established. You were friends.

On the exploratory trip I took with Barry, we were also carrying some paper bags filled with flour. Salmon poaching was a serious problem at that time. I had asked the government for wardens on all the rivers where I had set up camps (or planned to), and they had been promised. In fact, however, there was no Newfoundland Ranger of the colony's police force within ninety miles. Law enforcement was lax at a time when the price of salmon was getting up near forty cents a pound.

Knowing that poaching could put the camps out of business, the kids suggested that we bomb with rocks any poachers we saw from the plane. We talked about it, covering the use of bows and arrows, spears, and containers with smelly things in them. In the end, however, we settled on the flour-filled paper bags, which would, we figured, seem like explosives. Allan still longed for some cherry bombs.

We checked a spot back of Deer Pond where a good brook flowed into a smaller pond. I hoped it might hold really big trout, as Western Brook did—five pounds and over. No such luck. We caught a bunch of small ones and kept a few. I cleaned them while Barry got the fire going. We broiled them like hot dogs, holding them over the hot coals on forked sticks. We had salt and biscuits and a jar of jam. We made out all right.

We were flying across Western Brook on our way home when we saw poachers. Two men had a net beside a pool, and salmon flashed in the sun as they were dragged ashore. I lost altitude and circled around them, but there was no way to land, because the pool was too small. I opened the upper half of the door and latched it to the wing to keep it open. Barry shouted, "Can I?" and I nodded. I slipped in close, fifty feet over their heads and said, "Now!"

The first paper bag hit the water with little more than a splash. But the second hit a rock near the poachers, and the flour flared out like smoke. Barry dropped his remaining "bombs" into the alder thickets where the men had run to hide, and while they were not as spectacular as the one that had hit the rock, they gave off a little puff of white each time and kept the poachers moving. After a few minutes, we flew on, and Barry grinned all the way home.

One day we had some unexpected fun on the sea. I'd flown with the kids to Daniel's Harbour Pond, where we headed for Angus Bennett's store. Allan bought some candy and cloth for a kite. Barry settled on chewing gum. We'd run out of honey butter, and I needed some for my sports to spread on the fresh-baked bread due to come out of the oven late that afternoon, when they would be coming to the dining room for supper.

Afterward, we walked down to the cove to see what was going on. In the outports the docks and beaches where the boats are dragged out are the center of life—like the railroad station in a small town. A schooner lying a hundred yards off was picking up lumber brought out in smaller boats. A dory fisherman had landed a halibut that must have weighed close to four hundred pounds. He had caught it on a cod jigger and must have had quite a tussle getting it aboard.

There wasn't a breath of wind, but great, long rollers were crashing in on the short reef that gave the tiny cove its protection from the prevailing southwest winds. Barry pulled at my pants pocket and asked, "Could we land out there?"

I looked out to the sea and responded, "In those rollers?" Then, after I'd studied them a minute I said, "I think so, but are you sure you won't get seasick?" Both boys were sure.

I brought the bird in parallel to the massive waves, riding along one of the crests to keep my wings level and angling with the roller as it moved toward shore. The landing was smooth. I found that we could taxi along at pretty fair speed across the face of the wave or at an angle to it. It was like riding a roller coaster. I simply sped up to take off again. Several times, I lifted up on one float, changed over, and slid along the endless crest for awhile on the other. That was pure excitement. There were shouts and screams of joy from the back seat and wails of complaint when I finally lifted off to get the honey butter back to camp. After that, the boys would always wonder aloud if there were rollers off Daniel's Harbour, big waves that we could ride in the plane. But we never had those great, smooth swells come sweeping in again.

We had lots of fun flying over little motorboats—the small craft used for fishing in Newfoundland. Ranging in length from fifteen to thirty feet, they were open boats, and if it rained the occupants simply encased themselves in their oilskins and huddled down. Almost without exception, the motors were "one lungers," make-and-break engines with a single cylinder. For their size—and some of them were quite ponderous—they are the noisiest motors in the world. Each blast of the exhaust is like the firing of a cannon. The locals get used to it, but a stranger, riding with them, usually sits with his hands over his ears.

The fishermen use these boats to travel along the shore to and from their lobstering cabins during that season, from their homes to their cod-jigging grounds, and on visits to friends or shopping trips for supplies. The helmsman would sit hunched over at the tiller in the stern, staring forward toward a distant landmark or cloud, enduring the noise and waiting for the silence of his journey's end.

When we'd approach one of the Newfoundlanders from the stern I'd cut the motor and go into a long glide designed to bring the airplane perhaps ten feet over his head. He'd be sitting there enveloped in a cloud of noise when suddenly my shadow would cover him, and when I suddenly gunned the engine, the roar of my sixty-five-horse Continental and the air noise of my prop would drown out the sound of his own motor. The first time this happened to one of the fishermen, the fright was almost enough to make him jump right out of his boat. It was like a tiny rabbit being suddenly confronted by a great hawk. When reality returned, however, the fisherman would throw up his arms and wave. And laugh and laugh and laugh.

Most of these people were men we knew, friends who carried supplies for us, bringing fifty-five-gallon gas drums or fresh cod and halibut from their catches. When I had time, there was a "randy" (their word for a special ride) in the Cub, and on one or two such occasions, the fishermen got to see the same maneuver from *inside* the plane. Not once was there an objection. They took these buzzings as a good joke and the stories of their reactions were told all along the coast. After all, I was the one who could get them to the hospital in time, whereas if they went by boat they might well die on the way.

If I had one or both of my youngsters with me, I would often buzz the little lobstering shacks along the shore just for fun. They were always out in the open, so I could pick my approach and head into the wind for a quick lift from my dive. If I cut power and my approach was silent, the great, sudden roar of the engine as I pulled up would have a startling effect. I'd be looking ahead, making sure the climb out was safe. The kids, looking back, would see the door swing open and a surprised lobsterman rush out onto the gravely beach.

Normally, however, I always kept a respectable altitude when flying over the villages. I knew there might be sick people in the houses or those who didn't want to be disturbed. Even then there were some amusing incidents. Once, flying over Daniel's Harbour at about 250 feet, I looked down and saw a door open. A portly man came out, took two steps, heard the airplane, and looked up. For a moment he was transfixed. Then he put both hands up to cover his bald head and dove back into his house.

That man and I later became good friends. He sought me out, laughing, a day later when I was in Angus Bennett's store and said, "Next time come down closer. Come right in for a cup of tea."

# A Difficult Guest

~

Most of the Newfoundlanders rarely complained about my flying antics—or anything else, for that matter—but I wasn't always so lucky when it came to my sports. Getting them the fishing experience they wanted was often difficult, to say the least.

One of my clients—a Dr. Weston by name—said he wanted to fish the place he'd seen in my film lecture at Easton, Pennsylvania, the magnificent deep canyon where I'd caught such big brook trout. It was a film I'd made a few years earlier when we'd worked our way up the river in a small boat. Weston insisted on making this precise trip and wanted the same guide, too. Apparently he liked the look of old "Uncle Martin," whom I'd shown cooking a great trout in that old steel frying pan.

I could understand the doctor's desire to get in to Western Brook. Western Gorge was a rugged split in two-thousand-foot-high mountains, an extremely deep freshwater fjord that extended inland for about a dozen miles from the edge of the coastal plain. I had gone there originally because of its grandeur when looked at from the sea, but also because I thought there might be a stream feeding into it from a mountain valley, water that would offer good fishing in a spectacular setting.

Few people had ever been into the gorge. Except for the trappers and loggers, most of the settlers stuck to the coast. There was no timber on those high cliffs and mountaintops, but Martin Roberts from nearby Sally's Cove had been there trapping. He'd gone in on the ice during the winter and didn't remember much of a valley or a river at the inside end of the gorge. Still, he wasn't sure. He was a fisherman as well as a trapper, and I learned he was weather-wise and reliable. I hired him to take me in through the gorge.

I couldn't find a canoe, so I borrowed a narrow, twelve-foot, flat-bottomed cedar boat with twelve-inch boards for sides. It wasn't very seaworthy, so I had it carried—along with a three-horsepower outboard, a tent, and the necessary food—to the mouth of the river by a fisherman's trap skiff from Bonne Bay. Just at sunrise I brought the little boat safely through the surf at the river mouth, where Martin was waiting on the shore. We alternately rowed, waded, and used the outboard to get up to the big fjord that stretched inland through the gorge.

Using the outboard, we cruised inland. The water between the cliffs was so deep, Martin said, that even with two 900-foot lengths of cod line tied together he had not been able to reach the bottom. The fjord, he was sure, was as deep as the rock cliffs of its shores. It ended abruptly, surrounded by steep walls. No stream of any consequence flowed there, just a small brook that we judged to be spring fed. There was a barely discernible, treacherous path that led from the brook up into the hills where Martin had trapped for furs and killed caribou.

There was no level land anywhere in the area; we pitched the tent on a great sloping rock. While Martin worked on supper, I cast a fly where the small current flowed into the fjord. On my first cast—and for the next dozen casts—I caught a fish each time my fly hit the water. Each brook trout weighed about five pounds. I kept the first one for our meal and released the rest. It was a magnificent spot, but I knew that the cost of reaching the lake in a boat big enough to be safe in a storm would be prohibitive. And, although there were very large trout to be caught, I was sure that there were very few of them and that if I brought in fishermen in any numbers, the stocks would soon be wiped out.

Martin and I were up at dawn and on our way out in the little boat. With the outboard motor purring steadily we ran along the northern wall of the fjord, which was no more hospitable than the southern wall we'd followed on the way in. The rocks ran abruptly to the water on both sides, and there was nowhere to get ashore or pull the boat out. High clouds were rolling in from the sea, but Martin assured me that no storm would strike before that evening at the earliest. By noon we were back at the running-out of the fjord, and we fished from there down to the sea. The film I shot of the big trout in the river's pools was the footage that later so impressed Dr. Weston.

When he approached me at the lecture, I tried to discourage him. I told him I didn't have a camp set up on that river yet and said he'd have to sleep in a tent. I told him I could probably get Martin, all right, but explained that Martin was a friend, not a guide, and that he couldn't read or write. I said I didn't have a boat or canoe at the gorge either and probably couldn't get one there this season. I warned him that he'd have to walk down a trail to reach some of the best pools. The more I tried to discourage him, however, the more determined he was to fish Western Brook instead of Portland Creek. He arrived on July 19.

I'd brought Martin to a good campsite at the outlet of the big freshwater fjord the day before the doctor arrived. There was no time to have a boat dragged in from the village over three miles of bog, and I wasn't able to find a canoe to rent and fly in. Still, Martin had promised to clear out the trail down along the river from the big pond to the best pools, set up a separate tent for Dr. Weston, and make comfortable beds of spruce-bough tips.

I had brought in supplies for a week the day before our sport arrived. That included a lot of canned goods, ham and bacon, a couple of dozen eggs, and all the usual things. When I checked the campsite, I could see that Martin had done a very good job. The place was cleaned up nicely. There'd be some breeze from the big pond to blow the bugs away, and the pool at the outlet to the river was right in front of the tents.

I flew the good doctor in, introduced him to Martin, and checked over his tackle to make sure it was adequate. I stayed long enough to watch him wade out into the pool in front of the tent and hook a trout. He looked like a happy man.

Then the weather turned bad for two days, stranding me at Portland Creek. When the skies cleared, I flew over the camp at Western Gorge, planning to go directly to Lomond, pick up the fishermen who were waiting there for the flight to Portland Creek, and stop to see Dr. Weston on the way back to the main camp. But as soon as I spotted him on that overflight, I knew something was wrong. He was hopping up and down on the beach by the pond, waving a shirt or something. I landed and taxied in. After we exchanged greetings, he motioned me aside so Martin couldn't hear and said, "This man can't read or write."

I said, "You knew that. I'm sure I told you."

"He opens cans by the pictures and when there isn't any picture he just guesses. You can't imagine the meals I'm getting when I come back from fishing." He paused for breath then went on, "and he snores."

"How's the fishing?" I asked. I was looking at a fat five-pound brookie that was freshly cleaned and lying on some ferns by the campfire.

"Fishing is fine, but I have to get out of here. The bugs bite. My clothes are all damp even though he keeps a fire going in the little stove in his tent to dry them. I don't think he washes the pots and dishes clean. He uses a lot of sand but not a lot of soap. He's a little hard of hearing, too. I've just got to get out of here." The words poured out in a constant stream.

"Okay," I said, "pack up and I'll take you back to Lomond with me." I told Martin I'd be back to pick him up as soon as I could.

We reached Lomond in time for a late breakfast, and Ella took the doctor under her wing. She'd see that he got to the train. He had used up his deposit and a bit more. But he was unhappy, and I wasn't going to worry about getting any payment. I had to rush to fly the four sports to Portland Creek—one on each trip, an hour each way. I hoped the weather would hold and the day would last long enough. I took off with the first fisherman as soon as I could load him and his luggage into the plane.

Returning in two and a half hours, I found that the good doctor was still up at the lodge. The second fisherman in the party of four was waiting at the beach. I loaded him aboard with his duffel and took off. I flew him by the mouth of Western Gorge and gave him a peek at its dramatic depths. Then I took him low over the bogs and waggled my wings at a moose in one of the freshets. I got this sport set up in his cabin at Portland Creek and stopped by the cookhouse to pick up a quick sandwich of Mrs. Perry's good homemade bread, spread with bakeapple jam. I didn't take time for a cup of tea and ate the sandwich as I hurried back to the ramp and the plane.

When I taxied in to the beach at Lomond, Dr. Weston was there with the two remaining men from the incoming party. He was smiling again. I was surprised and asked, "Did you miss today's train?"

"These fellows have been telling me how great the salmon fishing is at your main camp," replied the doctor. "I've decided to go in there for the rest of my time. Can you get me in today?"

I told him I'd try.

It was after ten on that long northern day when I brought Dr. Weston in to the Portland Creek ramp. He'd eaten a couple of Ella's great meals while I was still functioning on one bakeapple sandwich, and that night he slept in a cot in a tent with a floor under it. Next day, he looked bright and chipper at breakfast when I left to ferry a couple of fishermen to the River of Ponds. After that I headed back to Lomond for supplies and decided to overnight with Ella and her boys. I needed a break, and I enjoyed it.

I probably shouldn't have stayed over. I tried to reach Portland Creek twice the next day and twice the day after that, but each time I got out to Rocky Harbor the shore was fogged in right down to the water. It wasn't until the third morning that I got through, and even then the ceiling was under fifty feet.

I thought I'd have to turn in at St. Paul's and then again at Parson's Pond, but I squeaked by. There was no wind, and the sea was smooth. I could have landed anywhere along the line and paddled to shore or taxied in to one of the little coves, where I could have pulled my plane ashore and waited for the fog to lift. I came over Portland Cove not far above the ground, and there on the beach— with a couple of Eb's youngsters beside him—was Dr. Weston, waving frantically. When I'd flown on to camp and was tying down the plane, my two boys came up to greet me. "What's wrong with Dr. Weston?" I asked them.

"He didn't like it here, I guess," said Allan. "He went down to the cove to stay at Eb's house."

There were three other fishermen at camp: two dentists from New Jersey and a butcher from Pennsylvania. The butcher was a good guy who fished hard and laughed a lot. The dentists were a jolly pair, catching a few fish but not working hard at it and generally having a good time with their guides. Apparently, they asked for an ax the second day they were at camp, telling Eb they wanted to cut down a tree—a dead one. Did he mind? He told them to go ahead as long as the tree was no longer alive. The one they picked was dead all right and good-sized, to boot. It seems that a woodpecker had come and banged furiously on the trunk first thing in the morning, when they wanted to sleep on. They were making sure he didn't get the chance to do it again. Dead wood is hard to chop with an ax, but the dentists finally got the tree down.

When I asked these three about Dr. Weston, they all shook their heads sadly. He wasn't happy, they said. He'd asked where the drinking water came from and when he found that the intake was deep in the Home Pool, right in front of the camp, he was horrified. They got Eb, and he explained that there wasn't a living soul in all the lakes and flows above the intake and that the water was as pure as God could make it. Unconvinced, the doctor countered that my kids had been swimming up in the lake. Eb told him that my kids were small and the pond was very, very large. He added that the boys were clean and took showers in the new shower house we'd rigged up with hot water coming from the heating unit in the big kitchen stove. Weston remained unconvinced.

Since their cabins were adjoining, the doctor shared an outhouse with the dentists. He had upset them because they'd seen him sneaking out there with a basin he'd filled with water and some lye from the kitchen to scrub down the seat after each time they used it. Finally it was all too much, and Eb offered the doctor the restful quiet of his own house in the cove.

Dr. Weston, who was due to fly out in the morning, was back up the trail by dinner time, and it was a meal to remember. As usual, the guides and the boys ate in a separate dining room. The dentists, the butcher, the doctor, a surveyor, and I were the only ones in the main dining room. The butcher had brought along some goodies with him from home, and each evening he'd provide something special for the dinner. This time he unveiled a short stick of salami, which he sliced and we chewed on as an hors d'oeuvre. Dr. Weston bit down on a pepper kernel, I guess, because his eyes watered and he made a face. But he got his slice down.

Mrs. Perry bustled in with a tray of glasses, water, and ice. I thought that in the spirit of the occasion Dr. Weston would have taken a drink even though it was water from the stream. But, just as he was about to lift the glass to his lips, one of the dentists whispered hoarsely to the other, "That must be the ice from the icehouse those salmon were lying on yesterday." The doctor never finished lifting his glass.

Not to be outdone by the butcher's generosity, Dave Snow (the surveyor) went to his cabin and came back with a can of Newfoundland seal meat. Opened, it was dark—almost black—rich looking, and oily. Seal meat is a delicacy when properly prepared, but it must have all the fat eliminated or else even most Newfoundlanders can't manage the strong taste. This smelled very good, and Snow passed it around. The butcher took some. Then I helped myself, and so did the dentists. Dr. Weston had just reached for a piece of the meat with his fork when one of the dentists leaned over his shoulder and said, "Gee, I think they left some of the fur on it."

The doctor withdrew his fork, rose, and went back to Eb's place. Later, Mrs. Perry took a plate of mashed potatoes, peas, carrots, and veal over to him, but Weston just left the food out on the porch. I went over and tried to make him understand that his dinner companions were just practical jokers and that he shouldn't take them seriously. But he wouldn't eat anything. He was adamant.

Next morning, the doctor took toast and canned fruit but no

oatmeal or eggs or bacon. He paid the balance for his time and sat in the plane, grim lipped, all the way to Lomond. Ella said he only smiled when she served him a second breakfast and when she got the driver to take him to the train at Deer Lake. When she bid Weston good-bye and said she hoped he'd come back, his parting words were, "Never."

# PINKY GOES WEST

꩜

Fuel was always a problem for us. At Lomond, where there were cars to be gassed up, it could come in by truck. Everywhere else along the shore, there were no vehicles and no roads—only boats. These generally used a special fisherman's gas called "acto." It would only run the Cub's sixty-five-horse engine if I mixed it half and half with fuel of a higher octane, namely automotive gasoline.

I reserved such fuel for emergencies, however, and normally used the gas the Newfoundlanders called naphtha, which was clean and unleaded, and had an octane rating of eighty. That was the recommended octane for the Cub's motor, so I had some drums of the stuff shipped to Daniel's Harbour, where it was used occasionally in washing machines and other small motors. The naptha was then brought by skiff to the river mouth and by dory up to the camp. It was a laborious process.

The best deal around was so-called blue gas. It was aviation fuel of ninety to ninety-seven octane. It had been loaded onto American or Canadian ships during the war for delivery to Russia. Many of these vessels had been torpedoed by U-boats near the Strait of Belle Isle, a hundred miles north of the camps. At that spot, only a twelve-mile channel separated the Labrador mainland from the island of Newfoundland. When the ships were torpedoed, dozens and dozens of the drums came ashore along the coast. The fuel was too hot for the one-cylinder engines most of the fishermen had in their boats, so a lot of it was simply discarded. When word got out that I'd buy it, a great many drums of blue gas were brought to

Daniel's Harbour. It was a little hot for the Cub, but mixing it with the cheap acto produced a fuel the plane could fly well on.

Fuel was a simple problem compared to engine and airplane maintenance. For minor motor tune-ups I could depend on Eb, but for anything serious I needed a qualified and registered airplane and engine mechanic. In addition, to fly legally I had to have inspections after every hundred hours of flying time. When my first one came due, I set off for Gander, a hundred and fifty miles to the east. It had become a major airport—a way point for transatlantic flights—and Pink Henderson had said I could get an inspection there. Pink was based at Gander, and I looked forward to seeing him again. He'd been friendly and had given me some good flying tips when I first met him at Harmon Field.

To appear on the map as a "lake" in Newfoundland takes a pretty big body of water. Gander Lake qualified. It's about thirty-five miles long and about five miles wide. The waves there can be dangerous even for planes much bigger than a Piper Cub. The seaplane base was on the lake not far from the runways. I think the powers-that-be hoped that one of the flying clippers might want to stop there sometime and they wanted to be ready for it. It would be several years before they wisely moved the base to the smaller, smoother Dead Man's Pond up on the higher ground. There, it was just as close to the airport buildings and was adequate for any seaplane, big or small.

I approached Gander carefully and low, because of my concern that there might be some other traffic—Connies or Sixes, big four-engine planes. The wind was strong and the waves were formidable. I circled the float to alert someone that I was about to land, and a man came out to look up at me. I knew that I was going to need his help because I had to come in downwind in order to put the side of the plane with my only door next to the dock. Maneuvering a float plane under such conditions can be like docking a sailboat with no auxiliary motor.

The mechanic who greeted me was an old hand. He took my wing as I slid up to the float, and I hopped out to tie up. He wasn't busy and immediately started to inspect the Cub. I watched and waited, and in a couple of hours he signed my logbook. I asked, then, about Pink.

The mechanic looked up slowly and said, "Didn't you know? Pink's gone west."

He told me the story. Pink had taxied his big Norseman out for a short flight. His wife was with him. The mechanic was on the float at the time and saw it happen. Pink lined up with the wind and started his takeoff run. The engine roared, and the plane started forward, increasing speed and lifting high on the step as it ran down the lake. The engine sounded fine, the mechanic said; he'd just given it an overhaul. The takeoff looked normal, but suddenly the plane skewed sideways and flipped over. It took a while to get a boat out there. When rescuers arrived, the Norseman was floating upside down on the floats. Pink and his wife were inside, both dead.

No one could figure out what happened. Only one possibility occurred to anyone: Pink and his wife had taken their little cocker spaniel with them; it seems that he often rode with them in the plane. Could the dog suddenly have grown anxious and slipped down by Pink's legs and the rudder pedals, somehow causing the veteran pilot to lose control? "We'll never know, I guess," was the mechanic's comment. Then he added, "The cocker lived."

The incident kept coming back to me on the two-and-a-half-hour flight home. Like so many airplane mishaps, this was a freak accident. Some little thing went wrong. Something unusual and surprising. Something separate from the normal worries of getting into fog and hitting a mountain. Or having to land on rocky terrain or in a place like Cabot Straight, where, if the waves were high no conventional aircraft or seaplane could hope to survive.

There would always be the little things to watch for.

# NIGHT LANDING

Ω

On my return flight to the camps, I landed at Corner Brook to buy liquor at the "Controllers," which had been set up there during the war, when the servicemen on R&R from Harmon Field had clamored for drinks. I had loaded a dozen bottles into the plane, along with some smaller, equally important things such as a prescription for one of the guides. The supplies I'd bought at Canada Packers would come down on the schooner that was leaving in a day or two, and they would be off-loaded at Daniel's Harbour. I had discussed credit with McKay at the bank. An old-timer from Calgary, he'd given me up to $10,000 credit just on my good name.

I walked down to the dock at the lake and looked at the sky.

The old-timers knew the weather. They had to. Their lives depended on it. They were fishermen, and if they failed to predict an oncoming storm, a stiff offshore wind could catch them and blow them out into the endless sea. Some of these Newfoundlanders could remember the times before they had motors, when they'd have to row for thirty miles in an open dory to get supplies—with no safe harbor in between. They clung to their weather sayings such as, "Look out for storms on the flood tides." "Let the weather settle until ten-thirty if you're worried about the day." "When you get a big, high pile-up of clouds to the southeast, look out for a hell of a storm." And, "Don't start out when there are two deckers of clouds, and the wind is working around against the clock."

As I climbed into the Cub, the clouds were, indeed, piling up to the southeast. A big, fat buildup was rising twenty thousand feet into the air and shining white in the afternoon sun. Regardless, I had to get back to camp, which was ninety miles northeast. A party was due to depart Portland Creek in the morning, and I had to be there to fly them out. Or to explain that the wind gusts were too strong, if, indeed they were. I was afraid they would be.

I taxied through the sulfur smell generated by the Bowater paper mill at the water's edge. Soon after takeoff, however, the air coming in through the cracks around the door panels was clean and fresh. I was rising over the hills to the north, and the sky ahead was clear. The ceiling and visibility were unlimited, except to the southeast.

North Arm appeared under my wing. That meant I could bend right and go to Lomond, where I could spend the night at Ella's and continue at the crack of dawn. Or could I? I turned to look back at the cloud bank. The sun was low. In another twenty minutes it would sink into the sea to the west, and it was a time of decision. I had yet to fly at night.

I knew that I could continue on and still change my mind, landing at St. Paul's, which was coming up below me as twilight set in. But St. Paul's was salt water, and I'd have the problems of tides and getting the plane ashore. I didn't want to anchor the Cub off the beach if the wind was going to blow. Still farther on was Parson's Pond, which was brackish water. There was little tidal flow, a better shoreline, and a friend's house I could pull right in to. By then, however, the sky would be really black. There'd be no moon or, at best, just a sliver later on.

I guess I knew all along that I was going to fly on into the night.

We had talked over such an eventuality, Eb and I. The Cub had no battery, no lights to see the instruments by, and no landing lights. Still, if I was going to be caught out after dark, he'd know what to do. The wind remained light—though building slowly—and that cloud bank was still a long way off.

Below me was country that I loved. A four-mile-wide stretch of relatively flat land lay between the mountains that paralleled the coast to my right. These peaks were bare, topped with weathered gray limestone above the tree line. From the smooth mountains the land dropped down through knolls and gulches to the level of the bogs and forests of the coastal strip. Across that strip, in a number of places, ran salmon rivers I had come to have a special feeling for—where the guests at my camps had been fishing.

The sun was still in the sky, but the Earth was growing dim. On this round planet of ours, three thousand feet of altitude prolongs the day by many minutes. I was flying in sunlight and it was hard to believe that down on the ground the sun was gone and the light was dim. There was no moon, but the stars had begun to show. Would I be able to see enough in the coming dark to know I was flying upright and level? I had heard the hangar talk: Even when flying over water in haze, it was possible to lose the horizon, become disoriented, and be unable to keep the plane upright. When you couldn't tell which way was up, you went into that deadly spiral that took you round and down with ever-increasing speed until you crashed.

I looked inland at the magnificent, sheer cliffs of Western Pond and let my eyes follow the winding reflection of light on the river as it came to the sea beneath me. Finally, my gaze fell on the fading glow in the clouds of the western sky. It was beautiful. How wonderful it was to be there, flying, looking down on places where I'd rowed, paddled, or walked through forests or over bogs to reach the salmon pools. But, in all its beauty, my world was growing dark. The lights at Parson's Pond glowed up at me. I remembered a fighter pilot telling me that in the blackouts it was amazing how easily one could see a very small light, even the flare of a match used to light a cigarette. It was heartening to see how clear the house lights were. Ahead was a fifteen-mile-long gulf of blackness that had to be crossed before I'd see the lights of Portland Cove's few houses and the camps. I held my course just over the dark land along the faintly glowing sea. I couldn't read the oil gauge, but the motor's sound was smooth.

I wouldn't have been able to consider a night landing at many places along the coast. There were boats at anchor or net floats and buoys at Cow Head, for example. Almost anywhere farther north there were logs that had broken loose from towing booms. But

Portland Pond had no logging. It would be free of floating debris and anchored boats. It was a place where I could land in the dark without those particular worries.

Portland Head is a six-hundred-foot high lump of rising land that breaks off to create a sheer drop into the sea. When I could make it out, I pulled the throttle back and felt the plane nose down and pick up speed. I was down to two thousand feet when I picked up the first glimmer of light from a house in the cove. Half a minute later I could see a light at the main camp at the outlet of the pond. Then I was roaring overhead.

I could sense the scurry within the cookhouse, where they had undoubtedly been sitting, enjoying the traditional dark-time snack after fishing. Now, Eb! I thought. Carry out the plan!

Sure enough, the winking flashlights soon came into view— two of them, bright six-volters. There was still a very faint glow on the waters of the gulf to the west, but the pond was almost as dark as the wide black band of mountains, which—in turn—almost blended into the sky. Suddenly I noted that the flashlights had stopped moving and were shining straight up from below. Now came the critical move: I had to put my plane into a continuous circle to find out which way the wind was blowing.

It was like being back at Round Lake and learning to fly. Centering on the flashlights, I swung left and established a radius for my turns. The seat of my pants told me that the little ball in the ball-bank was centered. First turn. With relief I felt the shudder of the airplane as I hit the turbulence in the air I'd made with the propeller at the start of my swing. I had to keep on circling in the very same path.

The pressure on the seat of my pants felt "right." Motor steady, controls unchanged—720 degrees, 1080 degrees. Smooth circles. I was still in the turbulence. I passed directly over the lights on the seaward side of the circle. The center of my circling had moved toward the lake. This told me that the wind was blowing in from the sea, meaning that I should make my landing to the west, toward the land at the camps. I flew inland over the pond, and the flashlights began to move once again.

I flew into the blackness for a distance I judged would bring me almost to the eastern side of the pond, then I turned back to the camps. I was about to make my first night landing. How nice it would have been to have an instructor with me to talk me through it! My eyes were completely accustomed to the dark, and if I had turned on a flashlight to read the instruments on the dash, I would have been blind the moment I turned it off. So, there was no way to be sure my throttle was set at 1,500 rpm, which in my practice gave me the best landing glide. I set it as best I could by remembering the proper sound. I'd have to keep my nose slightly up to keep the floats from digging into the water and flipping the Cub over on its back when I touched down. I would also need to keep the wings level by the faint glow of the stars as I felt my way down. It occurred to me then that I should have waited for a moonlit night. But that would only have postponed the inevitable.

I could see the two lights at the camp and turned slightly right to bring them into line as they should be. I could feel the mild sinking sensation as the plane glided along, slightly nose up, reaching down for the water. The lights were coming closer.

Too close! I put on full power and lifted up, heading for the stars. I flew half a minute farther before I turned back over the lights and headed out above the lake again.

With the camp lights in line once more, I throttled back, guessing again at 1,500 rpm. Were my wings level? Seconds ticked by. I saw that the lights were in line but still far away. My glide was steady. But was my nose high enough?

Then there was a splash and a little bump. The welcome sound of water swished under the floats beneath me. I was down. I was home. I taxied in toward my camp and my kids.

# MERCY

❧

The lad came trotting down the path in front of the tents. I picked up my cup of tea and walked to the door of the cookhouse to greet him. He was out of breath, having come over the path from Daniel's Harbour, running most of the way. He blurted out, "Nurse Bennett says she has a woman who should get to the hospital right away."

I put on my sweater and told Eb where I was going, then I hurried down to the ramp, gassed up, and took off.

Nurse Bennett was an English woman who had married Angus Bennett when he was overseas in World War I. Angus, of course, was now the merchant who ran the store and almost everything else in Daniel's Harbour. Nurse Bennett ministered to the ills of all the people for more than fifty miles along the coast. There was a cottage hospital at Bonne Bay, sixty miles to the southwest, and there was the Grenfell Mission Hospital at St. Andrews, almost three hundred miles away around the shore, on the eastern side of our northern peninsula. Between them, at scattered settlements, were Nurse Bennett and four others like her. The health of the people of the outports on that shore lay largely in their hands. These nurses did what they could. In emergencies they acted as doctors and even did amputations when necessary. They sent patients to the hospitals if there was time.

The pond at Daniel's Harbour was small and round, only eleven hundred feet in diameter. Fortunately, although there were trees on its northern side, the western side was open bog, and there were no obstructions there. As I approached in the Cub the wind,

Lee Wulff competed successfully as a member of the Canadian team in the bluefin tuna match of 1937 at Wedgeport, Nova Scotia.

The boats used in trolling for bluefin tuna at Wedgeport were commercial fishing vessels rigged with rudimentary fighting chairs and rod holders.

Lee, left, cranks over the propeller of his first J3 Piper Cub, the *Yellowbird,* at Round Lake, New York, in May 1947 as flight instructor Lew Lavery looks on.

The motor vessel *Red Wing,* operated by Norm Parsons, heads out to sea from the mouth of Portland Creek after dropping off and picking up anglers.

Jack Young begins construction on a cabin at Lee's main camp on Portland Creek.

Young, a superb craftsman, shaped and fitted each log and timber by hand.

Ella Manuel played a critical role in Lee's operation, greeting and housing anglers at Lomond before they were flown to the camps.

At Killdevil Lodge, Ella provided her guests with wonderful food, warm hospitality, and a breathtaking view from the front lawn.

For many of Lee's "sports," a ride on the train called the Newfie Bullet was part of their journey to and from the camps. Here, Ella waits with a group at Deer Lake.

Lee takes a nice salmon at the River of Ponds, just steps from where he touched down in his plane.

Here's the first cookhouse at the Portland Creek camp. Lee, center, is flanked by locally hired guides, including Manuel Caines, far right.

Arthur Perry, left, and his brother Herb, directly behind the sport in the checkered shirt, helped Lee make the camps a success.

The falls on the Humber River were dramatic and provided a formidable barrier to migrating salmon like those leaping here.

Lee prepares to land a salmon with the tailer he invented.

Allan Wulff, left, and his brother, Barry, hold a 25-pound Atlantic salmon at the Portland Creek camp. Lee and the boys slept in the cabin visible in the background.

An avid photographer who understood the value of publicizing and promoting his operation, Lee always had his trusted Leica camera around his neck when he fished.

Lee compares notes with sports and guides at the Sea Pool on
Portland Creek. From left to right are guide Levi Humber, sport
Alex Rogan, guide Arthur Perry, Lee, and sport H. G. Tapply.

Allan Wulff, already a good pilot at age sixteen, poses with *Rudolf*,
Lee's red-nosed J3 Cub.

Although Atlantic salmon were the glory fish at the camps, Lee put his anglers into lots of trophy-sized brook trout like the one he's holding here.

Camera in hand, Lee takes a break atop the incomparable Western Gorge. Unpredictable winds made the flying here very dangerous.

Lee and one of the guides prepare a shore lunch at the head-waters of Western Brook Pond, deep within the fjord at Western Gorge.

The gorge cuts deep into the Long Range Mountains, which form the backbone of Newfoundland's northern peninsula.

Lee's first Cub, the *Yellowbird*, met a tragic end when a hurricane tore through Bonne Bay.

In the 1940s, Lee didn't have access to high-modulus graphite blanks, as evidenced by the deep bow in his flyrod.

Wearing the chest waders in which he frequently flew, Lee boards the *Yellowbird* at Bonne Bay in 1947.

Lee frequently used a Link canoe, which could be taken apart and stowed in two canvas bags that were lashed to the floats of the Cub. (See photo at top of page.)

Allan Wulff and Lee share a rare moment of relaxation, using one of *Rudolf*'s floats as a seat.

Allan Wulff regrades the sand where the float planes were beached at the Portland Creek camp.

Barry Wulff prepares to net a nice trout in Western Brook Pond.

Newfoundland offered many challenges to novice pilots like Lee, not the least of which was a lack of smooth, level shores on which to beach a float plane.

Lee and his beloved *Yellowbird* take off from Lomond with Killdevil Mountain in the background.

as usual, was blowing in from the west. I circled the village once and saw that the residents had heard me and were on their way to the pond. They were at the boggy shore when I landed. Willing hands swung the plane around and lifted its tail up onto the grass. I had taken the front seat and didn't get out; I just kept the motor running and supervised their getting the small woman—all bundled up in warm clothing—into the rear seat. I helped her buckle her seat belt.

Nurse Bennett's look told me there was no time to talk, so I didn't ask questions. She shouted, over the motor noise, "I've wired Bonne Bay. They know she's coming. Good flying." I just checked to see that the patient was comfortable and taxied out.

Good judgment helps in taking off from a small pond like that one at Daniel's Harbour. You have to be sure in your mind that you have a long enough run. You can't stop if you're more than halfway along in the process. There's a tendency to try to get off the water as soon as possible. You have to fight it. If you try to lift off too soon, you put your wings at too great an angle of attack, which slows you down if you're not already up to flying speed. The fact is you're committed, anyway. Once you're up on the step beyond mid-run, there's no way you can stop short of the far shore. The best course is simply to stay on the water as long as you can, gaining as much speed as possible. Then, just as your floats are about to touch the grass on the far shore, you rise up over it. The first time I took off from the pond, I tried to lift too soon, just got off, and dragged across the marsh, barely flying. From then on I always used the entire "runway." This time, we came off the water flying strongly and climbed toward the south.

The air was smooth, and my passenger said she was comfortable. I had a lot to think about: One of the anglers at the camp had wanted to change guides. All the Newfoundlanders were competent, knew where the salmon were, and could net or tail them well. I knew it was just chance or poor fishing that was keeping the unhappy sport from catching fish. So I had talked him into one more day with the same guide. The kind of change that he wanted me to make is usually disastrous. If the guide that replaces the rejected one is a friend of the first man, he'll use all the tricks in the book to keep the angler from taking any salmon. He'll have him cast over barren water, pick the poorest pools, and choose the least likely flies for him to use. That way it vindicates the first guide and implies that the fault lay with the angler. I sure hoped the dissatisfied sport would get a fish today.

A while back, the guides had complained a bit about my clients being too finicky. They said these fishermen wanted the dory held at a very difficult angle. They didn't want to stop and eat at the customary time, when the guides were hungry. The clients, they said, asked for ridiculous things at strange times. In response, I'd gathered the guides together and asked that they be particularly patient for the good of the camps. I explained that their time with any one difficult fisherman was limited to a few days or a week and that for so short a period they should just shrug it off. I wasn't sure how much I'd impressed them.

Two days after the meeting, a group came in from New York. One man had started complaining about things while still in the airplane. He was well liquored and quarrelsome. Eb had assigned him to Edgar House, the same structure that had been floated across the sea to Daniels Harbour by its owner. Edgar himself, a big moose of a man who weighed 220 pounds, picked up the man's bags and carried them to the cabin. The fisherman followed and entered just as Edgar dropped the bags on the floor and turned to ask if there was anything else he could do. The New Yorker, whom we found out later was a middleweight boxer in college, said something like, "Don't drop my bags on the floor like that you big goon. I've a notion to knock your ears back."

In his report of the incident, Edgar said he just smiled politely at the man and went back to the bunkhouse.

I asked, "Didn't you say *anything*?"

"Well," answered Edgar with a smile, "I kinda looked down at him and said, 'For you, sir, that would be a two-handed job.' Then I walked out." In fact, however, Edgar served as the guide for this sport, and the two seemed to get along fine. The man caught some decent fish.

My attention suddenly returned to the flight. I looked out at the ground below and saw that we were passing over Parson's Pond. Subconsciously I'd been aware of occasional pressure on my back when my passenger's knees would push against my seat. The next time this happened, I turned and asked, "Are you all right?" She nodded but her face was set, her teeth gritted. I refocused on flying the plane. A few minutes later, however, the pressure on my seat back was there again. And then again. Suddenly the light dawned on me. I timed the interval between the last push and the next one—six minutes.

I'd read about babies being born in taxicabs during snow-storms, with the drivers acting as midwives. But in a J3 Cub? Western Brook was just behind us. Deer Pond was coming up. Only steep shores and uninhabited land between us and Bonne Bay, which was fifteen miles away. I pushed the throttle full forward. For the first time, the Cub flew all out at more than seventy miles an hour. The tachometer was vibrating at the red line.

We landed with just a little bounce and came in swiftly to the beach. Two nurses were waiting there, and they helped my white-faced passenger out of the seat and along the float to the shore. Supporting her, they walked the hundred yards to the hospital and disappeared inside.

Later, when I saw Nurse Bennett again, she said, "I thought there was more time. If you had known there wasn't, you would never have taken her. It was good you did. I got a wire. Everything's fine. Mother and baby are both doing well."

# FILMING

❦

Western Brook was so clear that when viewed from the air, it didn't seem to contain any water. In the river's flow to the sea, there were three ponds not far below the big initial one. Each was small and shallow. As we came over the longest of the three I looked down at a great rock, only half of which was above the surface. This monolith was the size of an army truck, and behind it a great furrow ran for two hundred yards in the gray clay bed of the pond. That furrow was mute testimony to the great force of the ice and wind that had slid the big erratic along the bed of the lake the spring before.

I didn't want to risk landing in one of the small ponds because I wasn't sure of their depth, so I decided to set the plane down in the big pond. I had brought Allan with me to work on another movie for Piper Aircraft. I had simply been too busy to spend time on the film earlier in the season and had let a lot of good opportunities go by. Now it was late in the season, but I had to come up with some exciting footage. I knew that Western Brook was my best bet. Outside of the hard-to-please Dr. Weston, I'd put no fishermen in there, and although the poachers would have done some damage, it was still the right choice. Many of the fish at my regular camps had been caught, and those that remained had seen too many flies.

Since it was mid-August, few salmon would still be in the pools at Western Brook. Most of the fish would be up in the safe, deep waters of the big pond, waiting for spawning time a month and a half away. Periodically, a few might drift back into the flow at the outlet to feel the comfort of moving water or for some other reason known only to salmon.

We came in and landed where I knew the water was deep only because I'd waded there; due to the water's clarity, it didn't seem to be more than inches deep from the air. The floats slid easily up onto the pebbly beach.

I enjoyed film work and for many years had been making movies to accompany my lectures to outdoor clubs. I'd learned how to use untrained people like guides and fishing companions to help out with the shooting. I could get them to hold a camera vertical and keep it steady. I could give them the lens choice, the distance, and the iris settings. I could have them shoot each scene of importance two or three times so that I was sure at least one version would come out well. This practice raised the cost of each film but paid off in quality.

The movie for Piper Aircraft was a new challenge. This was to be my first film with a sound commentary. I knew I would have to think a little differently in the planning of my shots. Normally, if an otherwise beautiful campfire scene with a tent in the background ran for ten seconds without any action, the audience would get bored. But, things would be different if I dubbed the sound of an ax over that scene and then cut to the guide dumping sticks down beside the fire and adding one to the blaze. In this manner, I would be able to hold that first beautiful but static scene longer just because of the life the off-scene chopping sound would add.

The theme of the film was the Cub, me, and maybe Allan, too, if I could work him smoothly into the story. Previously, I had filmed my learning to fly at Round Lake and had shot some footage on the way up to Newfoundland, as well, to show something of the trip. A sequence showing the capitol building at Augusta, Maine, with the sun gleaming off its golden dome had seemed especially beautiful. There'd also been some good shots of Nova Scotia. I had asked Allan to film me taxiing in to the ramp at Portland Creek and to document some takeoffs and landings at particularly beautiful places, some of them with early snow beside the water. My son had become a good cameraman. He had learned enough so that I could depend on him to get the shots I wanted and to tell me if he didn't think they'd come out well because of camera shake or some other reason. I was counting on him to help make the film for Piper.

We fished first at the outlet of the big pond, where we had the best chance for a salmon. The streambed sparkled in the sunlight over a layer of water-worn red, yellow, and green jasper pebbles. A fish coming to the shore in that day's bright sun would move over a beautiful background. I set the 16mm 70DL camera with its three lenses on a tripod on a rise at the edge of the pool; I knew Allan could work well from that vantage point if I hooked a salmon.

The first thing I did was to wade quietly out into the pool to see if I could spot any fish in the clear water. In fact, I located four big ones and a single grilse. I didn't think I'd disturbed the salmon much, but I let some time pass so they would feel rested and secure. It was a great advantage to have found out exactly where they were lying, because Allan would be able to line up the camera to cover both me and the fish.

The initial drift of my dry fly went over the first salmon without a response. On the third pass, however, one of the fish rose and took it. This was a big one, perhaps the biggest of the four. Allan started the camera as he saw the rise. The fish came into the air with a great leap and ran down through the pool. I coaxed him back partway, bringing him up from the shallow water at the tail of the pool to the deeper flow of its center. I moved downstream to stand abreast of him, for I don't like to have a fish below me in the current. I want the flow of the water to make the salmon work, not add additional force to the strain he is putting on my tackle. The fish jumped, settled down again for a moment, then jumped again. Allan got the second jump from start to finish. I could hear the camera running and turned to see if Allan had used the right lens to get both the fish and me in the picture, since we were close together. He had. Then the salmon raced downstream, out of the pool.

I followed, giving all my attention to keeping my footing and holding the line above the rocks that poked up from the streambed. We had raced a hundred yards before the fish paused and I was able to look for Allan. Sure enough, he was following me with my two light cameras. I watched him leave one ashore and wade out within good camera range while the big salmon rested. I got downstream of the fish again to put pressure on him from below and make him work against both my pull and the flow of the current. He put up with this for only a minute or two, then came racing down by me. I had to make another downstream sprint to stay close to him. The fish stopped again in some fast, shallow water. Allan came running down the bank with a camera. More by luck than design, he filmed two good jumps with me in the picture. Then I sang out, "He's going to jump again!" and Allan got another shot of the fish, up close.

The salmon was tiring. In a minute or two I motioned to Allan to come close as I brought him in. There was an anxious moment when the fish swung away into a bad angle and I had to call "Cut" and wait for Allan to rewind the camera. But our luck held and so did the weather. It was in sunshine that I was able to lift the thirty-pounder's tail and half carry, half drag him to shore. He was a fish to be proud of—for any river or any film. We had captured the high moment we needed. Now we could hope for some big trout.

We gathered our gear and paddled downstream to the first of the small ponds in the flow. While getting the cameras out of the canoe, I saw a big trout roll in the pool beside us. I put on a high-floating, white dry fly and began to cast. Allan was all set with the telephoto lens. When a trout rose and missed the fly, I told Allan to concentrate on that spot and cover the drift of the fly over it. On the second cast the fish took, and we had a good shot of the rise—not to mention footage of the brookie's struggle against the rod. This trout weighed just a little over two pounds and was fresh from the ocean—beautifully silver. I put him back knowing that there were much bigger fish in these waters. Allan filmed the release, too, which would add to the story.

I caught four more trout, all in the same size class. Like the first one I'd hooked, these fish were silvery and had just come in from the ocean on their spawning run. Their sea coats would change swiftly in the fresh water, and within a few weeks they'd revert to their usual, brilliant brook-trout coloration. Small schools heading inland from the ocean often stick together for a while, and we had struck one of those groups. After a few more fish, the rises ceased. In all, I'd hooked and released eight. In just a few minutes of filming, we had captured rises and catches that would impress the viewers back home, where trout of this size were few and far between.

Allan looked at me questioningly, "Shall we go?"

I shook my head and kept on casting. I knew that the first trout I'd seen was much bigger than the ones I had caught, and I wanted him for the film. Finally I gave up and went ashore to mark the boxes of exposed film. Then I sat with Allan, and we shared a bag of raisins. The sun stayed bright, making for good camera weather. I decided that if the trout I'd seen didn't rise after the rest I was giving him, we would move on to another pool.

The big fish rose to the third cast, giving us just the kind of action we needed. At six pounds, here was the trophy for the film. He was the kind of brook trout our audiences would gasp over, the kind that were rarely caught anywhere in the United States anymore—a trout to dream about. Unlike the others, this was not a fish just in from the sea. He had been in the river for some time. His coloration was brilliant in greens and yellows, reds and blues. The film would show him in all his glory.

Now it would be Allan's turn to fish.

We canoed another half-mile downstream, to the next pond. This time I took the cameras and Allan used the fly rod. There were trout here, too. All those he caught had been in the stream awhile and were brilliantly colored. The first two or three were small ones of less than two pounds. Then Allan found the right spot and hooked a five-pounder. It was a joy to watch him play that big fish and to film it. He had to wade out into fast water, and his boots were slippery on the rocks. He kept his balance well, although once he went down to one knee and shipped some water.

When he finally brought the tired fish close to shore, I moved in for a tight shot of his small hand stretching to its limit to reach around the trout, just behind its head, to strip it, lift it up, and carry it ashore. The sequence was a good one, and the film would show Allan, a boy, with a big trout that any grown-up angler would be proud to catch. More important, I would have that footage for all time to help me remember him as a precocious ten-year-old fisherman, budding cameraman, and potential bush pilot.

We were shot with luck that day. In a single outing I had done what I'd set out to do—show that a Piper Cub would take one to the otherwise unreachable places where the fishing was best. I was paying my debt to Piper Aircraft.

# SEASON'S END

## SEPTEMBER 8, 1947

⌀

The sun was high and shining down through a slight haze. Three thousand feet below me was the Codroy Valley and the Little Codroy River, where I had first fished in Newfoundland many years before. Ahead was Cabot Strait. The season was over. I glanced at the gauges, noting that my oil pressure was fine. The Cub and I had made it through the summer, and I was on my way home to Shushan, in upstate New York.

Behind me lay a good, successful season. The guides had earned more money than they'd made in any summer for fifteen years. They'd accepted my training and worked well. Virtually without exception, my sports had been very happy with these guides and, almost always, with the fishing. Before I left we had a celebration. There were a dozen bottles left in the store of liquor I kept on hand for guests, and I decided it was time to use them.

First I explained to the staff what a cocktail bar in New York or Chicago would be like. I said it would be friendly, crowded, and noisy, and that usually there'd be a piano or some other sort of music. Our dining room at Portland Creek was comfortable for twelve, but there would be twenty-three of us. We whipped together some small tables to replace the big one we usually ate from and covered these with oilcloths. So, the room was crowded with tables and people, all jammed in together with bottles and glasses and hors d'oeuvres. A lad from Daniel's Harbour with a violin came over to fiddle for us.

Fred Guinchard, the warden, gagged on his first martini. He tried the olive and spat it out. After two drinks of rum, he tried a martini again and downed it, sans olive. The two bottles of Lemon Hart—a hundred-and-fifty-proof rum—were the first to go. The bottles of bourbon were the last. But emptied they all were. It was a party to remember. At the end of it, Arthur Perry, the drinkingest of all my guides and the best maker of dogberry wine on the coast, sat down on the bench beside me and said, "Where's Mr. Wulff? Where's Mr. Wulff? I have to tell him about a big salmon we lost in the Eastern Run. My sport says he's coming back next year to catch him. He promised!"

I told him Mr. Wulff had gone to bed and that he'd better go to bed, too. He staggered out to the guides' tent. In a few minutes he came back, muttered something about "No bunks," sprawled out on the floor, and was asleep in seconds. He was the last. I threw a tablecloth over him for warmth and went to my tent and to bed.

All that lay behind me now. All I could see ahead was water. Nova Scotia might not be as easy to hit on this crossing as Newfoundland had been when I was going the other way. I'd be approaching it like the point of a blunt arrow. My course was 240 degrees magnetic, and I watched the compass needle closely. There was a lot of ocean out there. Still, I was flying in smooth air and it was a good time to reflect.

All the kids had enjoyed their summer. Ella had stayed with hers at the lodge in Lomond, making a couple of visits to the camps at Portland Creek. My boys, Allan and Barry, had been there with me most of the time. With Eb's help, they had built a little rowboat they named the *Titanic*. They had stayed overnight with the sons of some of my guides and made lasting friendships there. They were healthy, happy kids.

All the film we'd shot had gone in for processing and should be waiting for me when I got home. Barring some undiagnosed fault in a camera or some disaster in the processing, our footage would be good. Editing would be my next job. What a great break it was to have had good weather in the last two weeks of the season—and particularly on that day at Western Brook.

My eyes flicked to the compass and the oil gauge regularly. The sun was warm through the Plexiglas of the windshield. It would be easy to get drowsy, and I remembered hearing of pilots who fell asleep under the steady drone of the motor and the comfort of smooth air. One had flown into a mountain. There were few distractions to keep me awake, nothing out there to see. The waves below showed whitecaps, but the air above was smooth.

I kept looking at my watch; the seconds went by all too slowly. Where was Nova Scotia? Had I been fooled by the wind down there? There was wind at three thousand feet, too, but I couldn't feel it. I only knew that it was on my nose and couldn't push me off course. But was it actually much stronger up here? Should I fly lower? But then I wouldn't be able to see as far. I could have gone higher, but the winds were sure to be stronger up there, and the Cub would only fly at sixty-five miles an hour.

Ten minutes more, and there was still no sign of land. The sun was beating down, and I was feeling warm. I opened the window a little. It was suddenly hard to hold the compass right on 240 degrees. The oil pressure was steady, but was that a strange sound in the motor's rhythm? I noted that the auxiliary tank was empty, as was the five-gallon can. I worked the wobble pump to make sure. The main tank was almost full, meaning that I had almost twelve gallons left—three hours, for certain. I looked ahead at the sky. It was empty.

Another ten minutes passed. I wondered how much longer should I fly if I didn't see land. If I turned back and took a course of 60 degrees, I couldn't miss Newfoundland. Was I getting wind drift? Suppose the wind was actually blowing from a different direction at three thousand feet than it was on the water's surface? Back home, pilots could check with a forecaster before taking off and find out what the winds aloft would be in both speed and direction. No such help had been available in Newfoundland.

There was a ship below me, a freighter heading backward on my course. Did it come from Nova Scotia or far out to sea? Five minutes later, when I looked back, the ship had vanished into haze. Wasn't it time to turn back and wait for another bright day? That might take a week. I continued to look ahead. Nothing.

Way to the right, I thought I saw a line of clouds out over the Gulf of St. Lawrence but couldn't be sure. It was time to start worrying about gas and the point of no return. Was I headed for Nova Scotia or Africa? What about that low line of clouds. I decided to turn to 310 degrees and fly for ten minutes. If I didn't see land over there, my course to Newfoundland would be about 55 degrees. I looked at the map again.

Very quickly, the low clouds become more definite, turning into a line of low hills, indistinct in the soft haze. It could be no other land than Nova Scotia. I flew on by sight instead of compass—on a course of almost 300 degrees. That must be Sydney way off to the right. Lord, I had come pretty far down the coast! I *had* been headed for Africa!

I knew there was gas at Sydney, and the sun was still high. I circled several times before landing, but there was no sign of Billy Bishop at the dock. At sunset I tied up alongside a fishing boat at a pier in New Glasgow. The skipper looked at the sky and promised me there'd be no wind that night to damage my plane. I slept with the crew in their cabin and ate breakfast with them. I gave each of them a ride in the Cub before heading south to Wedgeport. There'd be old friends there and gas to take me on my way. If the weatherman smiled, just one more day would take me home.

Later I was to find that the compass in the plane was off by almost forty degrees. I never thought to check it against another one, outside the plane, before I took off. Some change in the metal near the compass on the instrument panel must have affected it. It had been scary out there, well beyond the sight of land. But as long as my motor ran and I didn't go beyond my point of no return—or some sudden, unpredictable, and very hard offshore winds didn't come up to slow me down—I could always have made it back to Newfoundland.

Maybe.

# START OF ANOTHER SEASON

## JUNE 13, 1948

ᐧᐧᐧ

I was over Nova Scotia again at three thousand feet, flying north through bright skies over a sunlit land. Ahead of me, however, a solid, white blanket of fog lay over the sea. Still, I knew it was a thin one because I could see the top of St. Paul's Island, twenty miles off the coast and right on my path. There, a few green tree-tops poked above the layer of fog that covered everything else.

I had gassed up at Sydney, and my tanks were full. I was a lot more knowledgeable than I'd been the year before and had become more cautious. And there'd been a lot more flying in the States during the winter to add to my experience. I had flown to North Carolina to hunt quail and to Florida to be among the first few to catch a bonefish on a fly. I'd been lucky and I knew it. From time to time I still repeated to myself: Old pilots . . . bold pilots . . . no old, bold pilots. If I remained careful, I'd have a lot more years of flying.

The fog below me was beautiful, but I knew that it could be deadly. Fortunately, there had been no wind at Sydney, and I was pretty sure that beneath the fog, the sea was calm. But if I had an engine failure and had to pass through that blinding blanket, at what altitude above the water would I emerge? Caution told me to turn back; the sunlight, light winds, and smooth air beckoned me onward. What would Billy Bishop have done? I decided to fly toward Newfoundland for half an hour.

I was sure that I had a good summer ahead of me. Camp bookings were good, and Eb had replaced all the tents at the main camp with cabins. The film I'd made for Piper Aircraft—*Wings for an Angler*—was a great success. Using it and my other movies, I had generated twenty-seven bookings for April alone. Ella and the kids would be along in another week when their school year was over. I looked down at the fog. There was no water showing below and no land to be seen ahead. I made my periodic eye swings across the instrument panel. Sure, the motor seemed to be galloping a little, but I was beginning to recognize that it always did that over water.

Almost halfway across, there was still no sight of land. But I knew that if I could reach the big island and find a few fog-free square miles, I could almost count on some water to land on. There was a pond at the head of the Little Codroy River, just a dozen miles from the nearest point at Cape Ray. There was also a protected cove at the river's mouth. I kept flying on my course of 60 degrees, magnetic.

Way up ahead, poking through the fog, a dark spot developed. I watched it grow, ever so slowly, and become the top of a mountain. I guessed that it was Table Mountain, which was near Cape Ray and right on my course line. This time I had checked my compass carefully before I took off and knew that its reading was true. I thought of the Little Codroy again and recaptured a mental picture of the forty-two-pound salmon that Peter Daniels had caught at the Widow's Pool. I was coming home to my favorite fishing.

The area of clear air at Table Mountain proved to be small, and I couldn't see the coast. The cove was socked in and so was the pond, farther inland. I turned north, worried. Where was my open spot, and where was my pond to land on? I could make out the dark tops of the Anguille Mountains. The fog had become much thicker, and I guessed that the layer now measured five hundred feet instead of the fifty at St. Paul's Island. Then, as I reached the mountains, I looked ahead and—just as on my first trip across the strait—I saw sunshine on St. George's Bay. Stephenville was on the horizon. My second, less worrisome, crossing was over.

This time my landing at the old Harmon Field was smooth as

silk. There was no political turmoil, either. That base, like Gander, had been opened to civilian planes in the last year. A mechanic came out of the shed to gas me up. I asked about Dave and Dellie Sawyer, and found they'd gone back to the States. The sky was blue and inviting. Gassed up, I flew on. When I got to Portland Creek I knew Mrs. Perry would put a fresh, steaming lobster on my plate every day till I tired of them.

# EARLY FISH

❧

The salmon came into the River of Ponds as much as ten days before they arrived at Portland Creek. It was, I believe, a matter of water temperature—the earlier rivers were the ones that warm up sooner. But the date when the salmon showed up was always a matter of guesswork. I'd taken a couple of fishermen in to the Western Bluie camp at a time when I was pretty sure there would be fish in the river. Two days later, I went in to check on conditions.

When I landed at the camp there was no one in sight. I guessed that one sport and his guide had taken the canoe and gone downstream, while the other angler, with his guide, went upstream toward Eastern Bluie, over the trail we'd cut. They'd have heard the plane, of course, and would be coming back soon. It was close to lunchtime, anyway. I looked things over. The camp was clean; everything was in order. I got my rod out of the plane to fish.

The pool in front of the camp was inviting. The salmon were due in, but I hadn't seen one jump or roll in the ten minutes I'd been looking around. I waded out to the deep water and began to cast. If the water is cold, salmon may lie in a river for days and never leap to show themselves. If sports do only a little fishing in those early days and don't see a fish or get a rise, they will likely feel that there just aren't any salmon yet and become discouraged. Then they'll decide to sit in their cabins and play cards until someone sees a fish jump or catches one so they can be sure there are salmon on hand. At such times, the guides needed to prepare extra-good meals and tell long, amusing stories. Of course, there were plenty

133

of trout to be caught, but for a sport who has come a long way to catch salmon, brookies are a pretty poor substitute.

I made two casts to a lie where I knew a salmon should be holding. Then three. On the fourth cast, there was a swirl behind my fly. Some anglers like to rest a fish if he comes to a fly and refuses it at the last minute. I was impatient, however, and hoped that the fish was, too. He was. I cast right back to the same lie, and the fly stopped in mid-swing. The rod bent, and the salmon went into the air with a beautiful leap, falling back with a great splash. The world was as right as a world could be.

I dropped the front of the leather camera case I wore around my neck, clearing the lens of the Leica. That case was part of my costume. I put it on in the morning just as I put on my shirt and pants and shoes. As an outdoor writer I knew how important good pictures were to the editors who bought the stories. Good leaps were the best photos of all. I'd started a new trend by taking photos of the fish I caught as I played them. I would hold the tackle tightly in one hand—ready to give slack if needed—while I operated the Leica with the other. I could wind a new frame into place with just a quick movement of my thumb. In this instance, I captured two good jumps.

There was a hail from the bank. Guide Fred Patey stood behind me and watched as I brought the fish in. The salmon weighed twelve pounds and was solid, shining silver save for the dark blue of his back. Bright and strong, he was fresh from the sea, with two tiny parasites called sea lice clinging to his side.

"They'll be glad to see that," Fred said. "We haven't had a rise."

"Where's your sport?" I asked.

"He'll be along in a minute," Fred answered. "He just wanted to make a few more casts while I got the fire started for lunch. Steve and his man went down to Barrisses Pool in the canoe. Thought the salmon might be up that far but not here yet."

Fred's "minute" grew to be a pretty long one. The guide assured me that everything was going along all right and that the two sports weren't grumbling too much—so far—for the lack of salmon. They had caught some trout and joked about it's being a hell of a long way to come to catch trout, and small ones at that. The River of Ponds didn't have a lot of super-sized trout like those in Portland Creek or Western Brook.

"I have to get back to Portland Creek," I said finally. "Hold the fort. I'll pop by again tomorrow or the next day and bring in some lobsters. You can get their mouths set for a feast." I rose to walk to the plane.

Fred's angler came down the path before I could taxi out. He was wearing a grin a mile wide. Over his back, its tail tied to a stick, was a nice salmon. "Hi! Lee," his voice purred. "They've finally come in. I saw another one jump while I was playing this fish. I'm going back there after lunch."

All was well in my new world, too.

The Western Bluie camp was empty a few days later, when the two fishermen went out. I had a full day before the next group was due to arrive and decided to fly in with Allan to see if we could have the pleasure of catching some salmon and get some pictures to build up my files, too. No writer of salmon articles and stories can have too many photos of leaping fish.

The clear sky was bathed in the sun's brilliance, and the ponds were just as blue beneath it. I was surrounded by my favorite colors: the blue of bright water in sunshine and the velvet green of the softwood forest. It was so beautiful that sometimes I felt a little stab of pain when I looked at these scenes hard enough to build them into my memory against the cold, gray, rainy days that were sure to come. There was a light, warm breeze blowing in from the gulf, and I knew that it might mean fog on the morrow, when I had to pick up the next two fishermen at Lomond.

I treasured the times when I could fish with Allan. He seemed to love fishing as much as I did, and I wanted him to know and understand the salmon, which I felt were the most exciting of fish. They were different. To catch them you had to reach their minds instead of their stomachs. You had to stir a memory or create a challenge. No salmon on its spawning run ever has to take a fly.

We tied up at the camp beach and got out our tackle. We each had a camera, and when one of us hooked a fish, the other would take pictures of the jumps until the salmon was released. We had a double chance whenever I was playing a fish because we'd have two cameras going on the jumps. Sometimes the light was better from one angle than the other. I hooked the first fish, and Allan put his rod ashore to wade out near me with his camera.

That fish leaped with a wonderful abandon. He was still super-charged with all the energy he'd brought in from the sea and had lost none of his brilliance or strength. We got some good jumps. Then, the faintest shadow crossed the pool. I looked up to see the sun catch a tiny wisp of cloud that was moving eastward toward the mountains.

I broke off the fish intentionally and yelled to Allan to get ashore and help me unload the Cub. We'd taken the lumber ashore but still had some supplies in the plane. We rushed. One bag broke open as I lifted it up, and beans spilled all over the place, some of them getting down under the floorboards, where they would re-main for the life of the Cub. They say a pilot should never take off in a hurry lest he forget some important part of his procedure or checklist, something that could hurt him later. As soon as I could manage it, however, we were airborne. We found ourselves on the inner edge of a great, low blanket of fog that was quickly sweeping in from the sea and spreading over the lowlands. This was not the place or time to get fogged in. Once I left Western Bluie I just *had* to make it back to the main camp or be stuck somewhere, perhaps for days.

Eighteen miles to go. Could I get back to Portland Creek before the pond was completely fogged in? There was still a chance. I'd thought of turning back to Bluie as soon as I lifted off but had de-cided to try to make it to camp. Once beyond the ridge of trees I curved toward the mountains. The last fog-free place would be right where they started to rise above the level land. I could see the next pond down the line and headed toward it . . . then flew on to the next one. Each could give me a safe haven. I'd have to land on the last water I could see. The fog was moving in on top of the trees under us, pushing the plane closer to the base of the hills. I caught the glint of bigger water. It was Portland Pond and the channel into the inner lake. I breathed a sigh of relief. We slid onto the water with a few hundred yards of clear air to spare.

Allan looked out at the solid fog around us and said, "What do we do now?"

Camp was about six miles away across the pond. I taxied slowly south so that if I hit a rock there'd be a minimum of damage to the floats. I didn't know the far shore of the lake very well, and it was hard to see through the Plexiglas. I opened the upper part of the door and latched it to the wing, finding that I could see better with my head out the window. The wind was increasing, and the waves were building up. We inched along. It was going to take a long time to taxi home following the shore.

Allan called out, "I smell smoke." Then I smelled it, too. Wood smoke! It had to be from the camps. I let the plane swing into the wind like a weathercock. Looking out through the door I could see the white lines of drifting foam on the waves, the lines that tell you the true direction of the wind better than any other indicator. I powered enough to lift the plane onto the step and level off. Once we were away from the shore, I knew there was nothing but open water between us and the camps. Now and then the smell of smoke confirmed our direction.

I judged that we should come in to shore at a southward angle that would let us turn aside before we hit the beach. (Once the power is cut, boats and planes slow down quickly.) For a full four and a half minutes our eyes bored into the fog. I decided that I'd better slow down.

Suddenly, there it was—the blackness of the trees. I pushed left rudder and cut the throttle. We were in a quickening flow—the river! I moved on slowly, avoiding the rocks that were dimly visible in the gathering dark. I knew every one of them from wading while fishing. We came in to shore at the tail of the pool, right in front of the cookhouse. It was the first time I'd ever brought the plane down there. Eb was standing on the bank. The others— guides, sports, and Mrs. Perry—were coming out the door, backlit by the lamps that were already burning bright.

Barry was there, too, with his ready smile. "I heard you first," he said. Barry had the best ears in camp; he always heard the plane before anyone else. "How did you get down in the fog?" he asked. "They said you wouldn't get back tonight, and we were worried."

We walked back with them into the warmth of the cookhouse. The fog had developed at the camp about 1:00 P.M., shortly after we left. It was thick and built up quickly, making the day darker and darker. There was a report that a plane had crashed somewhere, but there were no details. They had worried, of course, but it wouldn't be the only time I was thought to be missing. Everyone's anxiety quickly waned in the safety of the camp. There was steaming tea, black as the top of the stove. There was a warm loaf of bread, freshly out of the oven. There was happiness . . . and work to do in the morning.

The plane crash had been Tommy Mantinon in his Norseman. Six people died when he hit the trees just short of his landing. I'd caught big trout with Tommy at Star Bog in the middle of the island when he could fly and I couldn't. He was a laughing guy. Everyone liked him.

I wondered if my time, too, would come in the fog.

# AL AND OKEY

～

Two of my good friends, both pilots, flew down to fish with
me in early August. Al Nogard was a Federal Aviation Ad-
ministration inspector stationed at Albany, New York. Okey
Butcher, a buddy from my hometown of Shushan, New York, had
also learned to fly from Lew Lavery at Round Lake. For them, it was
simple logic: If I could make it to Newfoundland, so could they.

Al was a superb pilot with all the possible ratings. They flew
down in Okey's Aeronca Chief—a very light float plane like mine,
but with its two seats side by side instead of one behind the other. It
had the same sixty-five-horse Continental engine that powered the
Cub. Okey and Al followed my route "down," as we always said in
Newfoundland, gassing up where I always refueled and crossing the
strait from Dingwall to St. George's Bay on a beautifully clear day at
seven thousand feet.

Neither man had ever fished for Atlantic salmon, but they had
heard my stories and seen my films. With Okey's great understanding of wild things I knew he'd be a good salmon fisherman.
So would Al, who was just plain smart. I set Okey up with Arthur
Perry, who knew the most about the river. I turned Al over to Levi
Humber, who—in spite of his many years—was still able to throw
a seventy-pound pack on his back and march off with a spring in
his step. After the first day of fishing, when Okey caught a salmon
and Al had one on, I asked the two guides about my friends. They
reported that both were pretty good at casting and asked the right
questions.

That evening Okey pulled a bag of fly-tying materials out of his gear and came into the dining room to tie a few flies. He didn't know the old standard Atlantic salmon patterns so revered by veteran anglers, but he did know trout flies and bass bugs. We watched with interest as he took up a large 2/0 hook and proceeded to wrap bucktail around it in a haphazard fashion, leaving wisps of hair projecting away from the shank in all directions. He muttered something like, "Salmon're bigger than bass. Big fish, big flies." Then he held out his creation for Al to inspect.

Perhaps because they don't really want to eat the flies they do take, salmon are very difficult to understand. Most anglers in Newfoundland believe that the best flies are small, roughly the size of the stream nymphs and airborne insects they feed on in their parr stage. A fly like the one Okey had tied was startling to the other salmon anglers in camp. One of them said, "No salmon will ever rise to a thing like that."

Okey's response was, "Want to bet?" To which the angler replied, "If you can catch a salmon on that thing I'll eat the fly."

I figured Okey made a real mistake when he said, "Ten bucks to you if I don't."

In the early season, when the salmon have first come in from the sea, they are more likely to take large flies than in August, when the water is low and the fish have seen a lot of anglers' flies. They become dour in the lower, staler water and seem to rise better to the eights, tens, and twelves—very small flies for so large a fish. This was August, and it looked as if Okey would have a problem on his hands.

The following morning he tried his new fuzzy floater for a while without success. At Arthur's urging he put it away and finally caught a small salmon on a #8 Gray Wulff.

In the evening he tried the big fly again—for a longer time—and had no luck. Just before dark he changed to a #8 Night Hawk, which Arthur called a "Noydok," and raised a grilse but failed to hook him. Al had already caught his second salmon and was feeling good about his fishing.

The next morning Al caught another grilse, but Okey—still spending most of his time with his Fuzzy Wuzzy—was blanked.

That evening, at Arthur's pleading, Okey went back to small Night Hawks, Silver Grays, Black Doses, and other customary salmon flies. Again, however, he failed to get a rise. Al had moved one fish but was unable to hook him. The rest of the anglers at the camps were having slow fishing, too.

The following morning Okey was scheduled for the Humber Pool, where some of the biggest salmon tended to hold in low water. He'd reverted to standard salmon patterns and had started out with a little double-hook Jock Scott. On the first cast, he raised a salmon that came with a rush and missed. Quickly, Okey switched to his ugly creation and cast it out. Almost as soon as the fly touched the water the fish took it. Feeling the pressure of Okey's powerful strike, the salmon made a great, cartwheeling leap that ended when he fell, head first, onto one of the big rocks protruding from the pool at the edge of the deep water. He started to sink, stunned and quivering, but quick as a cat Arthur slashed out and scooped him up with the net. It was all over in seconds. The fish weighed twenty-two pounds. Arthur skinned it out for Okey to take home for mounting.

The man who said he'd eat the fly weaseled out; he paid Okey ten bucks instead. He was, I felt, a poor sport. He could have filed the hook into fine steel dust and chopped the bucktail up into little bran-sized chips and eaten it, mixed with cornflakes and covered with sugar and cream. I'm sure I've had worse things pass through my stomach.

Shortly thereafter I flew some provisions into the Western Bluie camp and brought out the two anglers who had been fishing there, leaving the place empty for a couple of days. Since Okey and Al had their own plane, I suggested that they fly in and try the fishing.

I went one step farther. Knowing that I could trust them to keep my secret, I told them about the great shoal of salmon at the top of Big Bluie, the uppermost pond in the watershed. Okey and Al jumped at the idea and agreed not to bring out any fish—no matter how many they caught. They also promised to tell the guides that they'd only taken one or two salmon, which they'd put back. My instructions were that they could have one day—and one day only—at Big Bluie because if they went back a second time, guides Fred Patey and Steve House, who were no dummies, would smell a rat.

On their return, Okey and Al reported that they caught close to a hundred salmon at the inlet to Big Bluie and released all but one injured fish that they brought back to make their story of ordinary fishing believable. They also had good action right at the cabin and at the pools just above and below it. One stray, bright fish—coming in late—had been so wild at the strike (Okey used heavy leaders and struck hard) that he'd greyhounded across the pool like a marlin and had ended up high and dry in the bushes on the far side of the pool. Okey and Al had to take the canoe across the river to find and release the salmon.

They were the only ones I ever sent or took in to the Big Bluie Inlet, and they went home happy, having had the kind of salmon trip no one would ever have again. A few years later the paper company put a logging road from Hawke's Bay right to the shore of Big Bluie Pond so that they could log the hills around it and tow the timber to a truck-loading site. That made these waters accessible and the salmon easy to haul out. In a few years they were gone. I'd counted on them for brood stock and after they disappeared, the run of salmon in the River of Ponds dropped dramatically.

It made me wonder how long our declining fishing would still be good enough to satisfy my sports.

# REQUIEM

◡

A nother season was complete, and it had been a good one. I knew that I would break even and that the prospects for coming years were good. I would continue to pick up most of my anglers at my lectures, where I'd have a chance to look them over a bit and try to discourage any I thought might later cause problems at the camps. Though effective, such strategies weren't foolproof.

The past season had brought me a problem fisherman, a doctor. He was an acquaintance, and he'd insisted on being at Portland Creek at the very best time for fishing. I told him I thought the third week in July would be the safest bet. As it turns out, I guessed wrong: this wasn't a good time that year. My sport was unhappy and didn't want to pay his bill. I had to tell him then what I should have told him in the first place: that of the six weeks of fishing I had available, two would be very good, two would be fair, and one or possibly two—when the water was too high or too low—might be bad or terrible.

I told the doctor that if I knew in advance which week would be best, I would just open the camps for that time and charge six times as much. I said that anyone could look at the catch records for our rivers and make a decision. Everyone, I explained, had to take his chances. In the end I asked him, "If you were treating a pregnant woman and told her exactly when she'd give birth, and if you missed the date by a day or two, would you not charge her for your services?" Since he still wasn't persuaded, I simply said that if he didn't pay his full rate he could find his own way home. He paid.

Some of the problems that occurred were so absurd that they had to be considered amusing, and many of these involved my efforts to maintain schedules.

When you drive the twenty-five miles from Lomond to Deer Lake, there's a place where you top a hill and can see the town of Deer Lake about nine miles away. On this particular day, I approached that spot at a modest speed because I had plenty of time to meet the party of four coming in on the train. To my surprise, from the crest of the hill I could see the smoke of a train already standing in the station. I put on some speed, thinking that either my watch was wrong or that for some unaccountable reason the train must have come in early.

When I got there, things were quiet around the station. I walked the length of the platform and saw none of my incoming party. They wouldn't have had time to get a taxi, and even if they had I would have passed them on my way in. I went to the station office and inquired.

"No. There was no one on the train for you."

Puzzled, I debated a course of action. There was no telegram saying they had missed connections anywhere along the way. The people at the office would have mentioned a message, since all telegrams went through the railroad stations, and the station agent was the telegraph operator. Should I wait and have the station agent tell me if a wire had come through for me? Had my anglers missed the station and gone on? No. The train had stopped for all of ten minutes, and there was a big sign proclaiming "Deer Lake" in plain view on the platform. I went back to the office again and asked, "Are you sure there wasn't anyone on the train for me and that there is no message?"

The station agent looked up from his accounts and said, "Nope." Then he added, "But that was yesterday's train. Today's train is an hour and a half late." True to his prediction it came puffing into the station ninety minutes later. My sports were on it.

That five-hundred-mile-long, narrow-gauge line ran a rather ragged schedule. In the winter, when the snowdrifts were deep, the trains could be stuck on the Topsail Hills for as much as a week until the plows cleared the tracks. In the summertime it was rare to have a serious delay unless there was a derailment or a bridge washout. If the trains were ahead of time, the story went, they might stop at a particularly good spot for fifteen minutes to pick blueberries. During the war the GIs dubbed the train the "Newfie Bullet," and the name stuck.

I had written in my brochure for the camps, "Nothing moves too swiftly in Britain's Oldest Colony. Don't write! Wire!" I remembered a time when I was tuna fishing at Lomond and waiting for a telegram with instructions from the Tourist Board at St. John's. The wire was an important one and was made up of 103 words. It took less than two hours to come through from St. John's to Woody Point, at the outer part of Bonne Bay. But it was another three days before the wire reached Lomond, seven miles away—even though there was a wireless connection between the two points. When questioned, the operator at Woody Point said, "Obviously it was too long for a telegram, so I put it in an envelope and mailed it."

The airwaves weren't always reliable, either. In our second summer at the camps, the word on the radio for several days indicated that a hurricane was moving north. The storm was far away at first, and we paid little attention except to listen to the reports of damage and wonder what it would be like to experience a hurricane. It had been a long, long time since Newfoundland had seen or felt one. Besides, our weather was great. The second season was at its end, and all was well. The camps were closed, and we were all at Lomond readying ourselves for the trip back to Shushan.

I took all four boys out in a dory to the seventeen-fathom ledge near the Little Southeast Arm of Bonne Bay to jig some cod. At dinnertime the fish were on the table, our favorite fare among all the northern species. Salmon, of course, has a much more exciting taste, but as a steady diet we all voted for the more delicately flavored cod.

The 6:00 P.M. news said the hurricane was off northern Nova Scotia and could be coming our way. I made plans to pull the Cub up onto the beach and tie it down securely. After dinner we got together the stakes and ropes we would need, along with the sledges for driving the stakes. We were all ready to go to work when a radio flash told us that the hurricane was three hundred miles south of Burgeo, on Newfoundland's south coast, and moving eastward. It would pose no threat to the island.

I heaved a sigh of relief. We put away the ropes and stakes and sat by the fireplace reminiscing about the special things that had happened that summer. At 10:30 we went upstairs to sleep.

At 2:30 A.M. all hell broke loose. Wind roared in with a deafening noise. Shutters slammed closed and then tore loose. Doors banged and banged. There was the crash of glass breaking. We lit lamps, but the wind blew them out. We found flashlights, jumped into the car, and had a hairy ride down to the cove where the Cub was moored. She was bent and twisted and upside down, with only her floats on the surface. The wind was deafening—roaring in with great gusts, tearing off roofs, and overturning small houses. It hit the triple screw S.S. *Preventer*, a big converted destroyer used to tow log booms, and caused the ship to bang against the pier with great screeches of bending metal as the hull tore at the pilings. We went back to the lodge and sat there, listening.

It was a long, wearing night. The boys slept a little, but neither Ella nor I closed an eye. We wanted coffee, but we let the fire go out in the stove rather than risk the chance of its setting something ablaze, for the blasts of wind had blown off the top of the chimney.

In the morning we viewed the wreckage. Trees were down everywhere. On the mountainsides whole forests were flattened. The big white birch in front of the lodge was as bare of leaves as it ever was in winter. The white clapboards of the building were green, painted with tiny bits of the leaves the wind had torn from the tree. All the small boats from the cove were either cast up on shore or missing and somewhere out on the bay. The battery-powered radio announced that a Sabena Airline DC6 had crashed while trying to land at Gander.

My own plane was a wreck. I salvaged the floats but left the rest for Eb, who I thought could resurrect the motor and perhaps make an airboat that would slide on snow, bogs, and water. Summer was gone and so was my beloved *Yellow Bird*. Sadly, we all rode back to Shushan in the car.

# FORCED LANDING

~

With the Cub gone I needed another plane. Clearly, a four-place aircraft would save a lot of flying; I could do in one trip what had taken me three trips in the J3. As yet Piper didn't make a four-place plane, so I chose an Aeronca, a brand that had just come on the market. It had four seats, a big cabin, and big, wide wings with an overall span of thirty-eight feet. Its motor was a 145-horsepower Continental. The makers advertised exceptional performance. If the front seat on the passenger's side were removed, there was room for a stretcher, something that might come in handy.

After taking delivery of the Aeronca, I flew down to Newfoundland in it for the 1949 season, getting the feel of the airplane. Since it wasn't a tandem—with single seats, one behind the other—I couldn't see as well on the left side, where a passenger would be sitting. Then, too, instead of a stick to control the ailerons there was a wheel in front of each seat for the pilot or trainee to use. This design was a step forward, and I'd gone into debt to keep pace.

The weather was good over the Cabot Strait, and I crossed in sunlight at 7,500 feet. Soon afterward, I landed at Portland Creek to be greeted by an admiring crowd that gathered around the beautiful, new, maroon-and-cream airplane. Each guide looked forward to riding in it. The seats were softer and the appointments more elegant than in the utilitarian and drafty Cub.

I'd found that my takeoff run was a little longer, even with the Aeronca's big, broad wings. I had to have a little more speed to

147

leave the water—over forty miles an hour—and that meant I couldn't get into quite as small a pond as the old Cub had handled. But I now had a battery and lights for flying at night, and an electric starter to save me getting out and pulling the prop through every time I wanted to get the motor going. I found, however, that if I throttled back I could barely keep flying at thirty-three miles an hour, which the J3 had done with ease.

Each airplane flies differently. Each has its own special characteristics, its strengths, and its weaknesses. Some planes are relatively stable in stalls and spins, while others are wild. It takes time to learn all of a particular design's special traits. The Aeronca Sedan had a quirk that its manufacturer's hadn't intended, and it came as a real surprise to me.

My good friend Neil Marvin and his wife, Connie, were fishing at Portland Creek. Things had slackened off momentarily, and I had a free afternoon. "Neil," I asked, "would you and Connie like to fly over to the River of Ponds with me for an afternoon of fishing? I have to take over some supplies." Neil jumped at the chance, but Connie, who didn't really like airplanes and flying, declined.

I made my customary check of the oil level and examined the gascolator for water in the fuel. I had a preflight look around the controls and floats while one of the guides pumped in gas from a drum beside the ramp. When the tanks were full we took off. Isaac Bigin, one of the guides, came along to check on things at the outpost camp.

It was a fine, sunny afternoon with light winds. All the ponds beneath us were flashing in the sun. It was a "milk run," a flight I had made so often that I knew every little pond, bog, and freshet we passed over. I looked for moose and saw none, but pointed out some landmarks to Neil along the way. I circled some pools on one of the feeder streams to see if we could spot any salmon.

Halfway along in the flight I began to climb because we were coming to a wide belt of timber where there would be no ponds beneath us. This procedure had become a habit: If someone I was flying into camp should ask me, "Where do we land if the motor quits?" I could point at a distant lake and say, "Way over there." Any pilot who lasts long in the bush has to have plenty of ingrained caution—no matter how daring he seems. When I advise any angling friend who's going off into the bush in a plane, I recommend, "Look for a pilot with some gray in his hair."

As soon as I could see Western Bluie Pond I nosed downward. We took a long swing over the new cabin at the Forks and flew low over the Spring Tilt, where the water boils up out of the ground to make a seasonal stream that flows over what later becomes a dry riverbed. The salmon run right up to that first, big welling-up of water. The bottom wasn't gravely there, just rocky, and I wondered where those salmon would go to spawn.

When we landed, Neil rigged up his tackle and rushed out into the pool. Isaac and I went over to look at the newly finished cookhouse and cabin. The era of tents was passing; no one wanted to stay in them any more. If I told a perspective client about some excellent fishing but said he'd have to stay overnight in a tent to enjoy it, that angler would opt to stay in a cabin somewhere else instead. I was going to have to raise my rates to thirty dollars a day—or more—to make up for having to fly the portable sawmill and a two-man crew into every site where I wanted a camp.

As soon as our inspection was over, I joined Neil at the pool while Isaac took the canoe and went down to look at the Forks and the new trail that had been cut along the Spring Tilt. Neil had already caught a ten-pounder, and soon after I showed up he hooked a nineteen-pounder. I took pictures as he played the fish. It was a wild male and must have jumped fifteen times. Neil thought about having it mounted for a minute or two, then gave up the idea and turned the big fish loose to swim lazily back to his lie in the deep water. I caught a twelve-pounder and released it. It was 7:00 P.M. when we stopped fishing. We were going to be a little late for supper.

We flew out easily, and I climbed up over that broad belt of timber.

Then the motor stopped.

When you're flying along and everything is under control, sudden silence hits you like a hammer. You think, This can't be happening. Then you start to look for the trouble. A quick glance at the gas gauges revealed the problem. They read "Empty"! I'd been regularly checking the left gauge alongside my head, and a minute or so earlier it had read almost "Full." I swung the plane in a flat gliding circle and picked out the nearest pond. It was a long way off. The Sedan was a little heavier in its wing loading than the Cub, and I could only count on from eight to nine feet of horizontal glide for every foot I sank down toward the ground. I settled the plane into its best glide angle.

I tried to start the motor. The propeller was windmilling, so the Continental should have fired if there was any gas getting to it. It didn't. The only sound was the soft hush of the air going by and the purring of the prop's slow rotation. None of us said a word. The pond I'd picked out was over a mile long. There'd be lots of room to land there . . . if I could make it. The water looked to be at the very end of our gliding range. Why hadn't I flown a little higher to establish an extra cushion? Maybe I'd been thinking, subconsciously, of the old Cub with its flatter glide. There was thinking time as we settled slowly toward the trees.

The pond was coming closer. It was fringed with a rim of trees, and there was a big bog right next to it. If we can't make the pond, I thought, at least we can slide into the bog without hurting anyone—if it's level and free of any rocks. If it wasn't, there might be some damage to the plane and, perhaps, to us.

The bog was nearer now and coming into better view. I could see that we weren't going to make the pond. It had to be the bog. I could make out some rocky places in what, at a distance, had looked like smooth muskeg. Now I could see the red of blueberry bushes and knew that they grew on hard, rocky ground. I could also make out rocks that were mostly hidden by the low bushes but were certainly large enough to tear a float off and send us cartwheeling.

Then, without thinking consciously, I remembered some hangar talk: "There's always a little gasoline in your primer line," someone had said. I pushed the primer and then pushed again. The motor roared, and the windmilling prop swung up to speed.

Two seconds . . . five seconds . . . ten. Then that welcome sound died away—but not before the lift carried us just over the treetops. We touched down on the water between some rocks but struck none. When the plane stopped, we just sat for a few moments without making a sound. Then I got out on a float and took up the emergency paddle to push us to shore.

We held a council. Isaac explained that we were about ten miles from the coast and that there was no trail anywhere near our location. He said that even in the dark he could work his way across the bogs, barrens, forest, and tuckbush to the telegraph line and coastal path somewhere near Bellburns. He would then follow it to Daniel's Harbour. The question was: Should Neil stay with me or go with Isaac? Neil thought of his young bride and knew she'd be pretty upset when he was reported missing. He decided that the sooner he got back to Connie, the easier it would be for her. Neil headed out across the bog with Isaac.

I looked the plane over. What had happened to drain out the fuel? Where had it all gone? And why? We'd had no smell of leaking gasoline. Yet the tanks were bone dry. I opened the cup that catches water and dirt just above the carburetor. Nothing flowed out of the gas line. The tanks were completely empty.

I started a fire and put some water on to boil in an empty can I carried in the floats. I happened to look up at the plane and noticed that the left wing's gas cap was missing. That still didn't explain why we'd run out of fuel. It couldn't all have splashed out of both wing tanks in less than five minutes of flying.

I had a sleeping bag in the plane, and I took out the front seat on the passenger's side to make space. I'd be comfortable enough. I had emergency rations in the floats but wouldn't touch them for a day or two at least. I'd wait till I needed them badly, when they'd do me the most good. I was sure I could catch trout in the pond and add to that a rabbit or two I could snare. I thought of Isaac and Neil hiking in the bush and didn't envy them. I settled down to sleep.

It was late afternoon on the next day when help arrived in the form of a jerry can full of gas on the back of a lobster fisherman and trapper from Bellburns. (He later turned out to be one of my best guides.) Isaac and Neil had had a rough trip out. They'd come to a big bog and had decided to cross it. It was almost dark and they felt they could see better out in the open than if they had to travel through the trees. Besides, they reasoned, it would be a lot shorter. When I got back to camp, however, Neil told me the crossing was more like crawling than walking. And the bugs were bad. It was long after dark when they struck the coastal path and, moving along it, came to the houses.

I strained the gas into the tank through the felted funnel I carried to keep my fuel free of water. I plugged the open tank tightly with a rag, pushed the primer shaft a few times, then touched the starter. The motor soon caught and—with the trapper aboard—I took off with a minimum of warm-up. All the way over I worried that the same thing might happen all over again. We didn't have much gas; it barely showed on the gauges. But, everything went smoothly, and in fifteen minutes we were back at the camps.

Eb and I finally diagnosed the problem. The little folder about the plane explained that the Aeronca Sedan had a tank in each wing. They drained down a common line to the carburetor. There were no valves in the line, so the gas could flow freely from one tank to the other. The gauges were vertical plastic loops that showed the actual level of the fuel inside the tank. Then came the joker: Inside the aluminum tanks were collapsible neoprene bladders that swelled up when gas was poured in, expanding until they filled all the space in the aluminum tanks. But these liners collapsed again as the gas went out of them. When the cap wasn't put on one wing tank, the pressure of the collapsing bladder had forced all the gas out of both tanks through the single open neck. Meanwhile, the constant pressure of the collapsing inner liners was flooding the gauges and continuing to tell me that they were still just about full. It was a simple explanation and an unfortunate adventure. But it could have been disastrous.

Hangar talk says you'll have an engine failure once in about five thousand hours. This was to be my only one in what turned out to be more flying time than that.

# Troubles

❧

When I first fished at Portland Creek and had Arthur Perry as my guide, I learned that the only other angler in the area was Cornelius Wentzell. "Nell," they told me, fished with a long spruce pole that had guides made of telegraph wire, and he used waxed carpenter's cord for line. He had heavy Japanese gut for leaders and a few flies that navy officers had given him.

The other locals, who were not then either guides or fishermen, had no tackle. If they wanted a salmon they got one with a spear or net. But eventually, when they saw the sportsmen fishing and enjoying it, salmon angling became the "in" thing, and they all wanted to do it. I implored our sports not to give the guides fishing tackle as it would only mean that they, or their relatives, would soon compete with the paying customers for fishing spots on the river. But the guides were charming and friendly, and it was not long before everyone in Daniel's Harbour or the cove had an outfit to fish with whenever he wanted to. And fish they did.

Sometimes the locals would try to find a vacant spot, but often they'd arrive early out of spite and hog a pool all day. They would even barge into a stretch of water where one of my sports was fishing with his guide and cast next to his line—if not right across it. One time three ex-guides decided to take over the pool right in front of the camp at Portland Creek. They came early and stayed all day, every day, bringing sandwiches for lunch. The fact that they were taking jobs away from their fellow villagers didn't seem to bother them at all. But their presence forced me to fly my clients to outlying camps, where guides from the nearby settlements got the paychecks and bonuses.

There was nothing I could do, legally, to stop the ex-guides. Barry and Allan, however, cooked up a scheme to bother them a little.

From time to time, these fishermen would get tired of standing in the current and would rest on barely submerged rocks where they could sit—comfortable and dry—in their waders. After dark one evening, Barry and Allan took some short, flat-headed roofing nails and sharpened them to needle points. With caulking putty they fastened the nails to the tops of those barely submerged "sitting rocks." The following morning there were a couple of yelps of surprise and pain, and two pairs of leaking waders. That didn't stop the nuisance, but it did delight the kids. Within a few days, the ex-guides had to leave anyway to get on with their haying while the wild grass was still in good shape.

One day I noticed a tent pitched on the right-of-way across the river. I'd bought the land on both sides of the river, but a right-of-way for logging and personal passage extended thirty-five feet from the water's edge.

I went over to investigate and found three burly men sitting around a campfire. One was an ex-guide who had been fired for fishing in one of the pools I'd dedicated to the camps. The others were friends of his from Parson's Pond. "This is a right-of-way," I explained. "It must be open for travel at all times, and you cannot block it with any tent or permanent structure. You cannot camp here or on my land along the river."

"We know it is a right-of-way and that it is for public use," said the ex-guide. "So you don't own it, and we plan to use it."

I was ready with a response, "You know, of course, that I, or anyone else, has the right to walk over any part of this right-of-way at any time. And now I'm going to exercise that right." I pulled up the tent's stakes, let it fall to the ground, and walked over it. The tent was up again that night, so I crossed over to it, taking Eb with me. Again, I pulled up the stakes, dropped the tent, and walked over it. Recrossing the river, we stood and watched while the three men gathered their tent and gear, and set off down the trail toward the cove.

I put the incident out of my mind, but a few days later, I was visited by a tall Newfoundland ranger, resplendent in his uniform. He happened to be passing through, he said, when he found that I'd broken the law by taking down and damaging a tent, and he was going to give me a summons to court in Corner Brook.

I invited him into the cookhouse for a cup of tea and some lobster chowder. I explained, "That right-of-way—like those on all the rivers and ponds of Newfoundland—is for travel. If you give me a summons I will get into my airplane and fly to Roches Line, where Commissioner of Justice Winters has his summer home on a pond and stream. I will put up a tent and throw beer bottles and garbage around. If I know the chief justice he'll be very upset, but I'll show him your summons and tell him you said it would be all right."

He put his little book back in his pocket and sat looking at his half-finished pie for a spell. Then he said, "I guess you're right. I'll tell the boys they can't camp there."

I understood how the natives felt. They lived near the river and wanted to fish. Unfortunately, when the public fishes without restraint, the salmon disappear—as they already had in so many Newfoundland rivers. There, no one fished at all anymore. Because of our efforts to protect our salmon, the camp at Portland Creek was successful, and the people of Daniel's Harbour and Portland Cove enjoyed a greater summer income than they'd had for many years.

Newfoundland was going through a transition from being a colony of Great Britain to being a province of Canada, something that would have far-reaching effects. Joey Smallwood had become premier, and he gathered a new group of men around him to run the province. I invited Smallwood to the camps to fish, and he arrived with one of his sons and a member of his cabinet. They all caught fish and seemed to be having a great time. On the last evening of his three-day stay I was able to go out with Smallwood, taking the place of his regular guide. I'd known him for many years, ever since he was the radio commentator for the Gerald S.

Doyle news and was known as the "Barrel Man," the name given the lookout on old sailing ships.

The premier caught two salmon that evening, and in between fish I gave him a rundown on the precarious situation in Newfoundland, on how well the camps were working in spite of the obstacles I'd run into, and on the need to save the good rivers like Portland Creek and build back the ones that had been devastated by poor management and lax protection. He asked how the local people felt, and I told him of their conviction that everyone should be able to fish—anywhere and at any time. I added that I could understand their wishes but said that only with strict controls could they reap the rewards that the residents of the cove and Daniel's Harbour were enjoying now. They had to choose between making a living or exploiting a diminishing salmon fishery that would eventually disappear. I told Smallwood of the studies that showed that wherever everyone fished—without strict restraint—the salmon soon disappeared.

After the second fish, which was an active high-leaper, the premier filled me in on his dreams of big tourist hotels, of his certainty that somewhere in Newfoundland and Labrador there had to be valuable mineral deposits that would mean rich mines and mining income for the province. His dreams, I realized, were not of fishing camps and tourist-fishermen. I had made my pitch, which I'm sure was quite logical, but had failed to impress him. He saw controversy in any conservation measures and—smart politician that he was—wanted to avoid it. When he went back to St. John's he turned over the management of the salmon fishery to the federal government in Ottawa.

I did get one thing out of Smallwood's visit: a warden for Portland Creek.

His name was Fred Guinchard, and he lived not far from the river. I let him set up a tent by the right-of-way, midway in the river's length. He was always welcome at the guide's table or in one of the bunkhouses. Fred had relatives all over the place, but he took his job seriously and tried to stop poaching before it got started. He often stretched fine black sewing thread across the path between two pools at ankle level to tell him if someone had passed that way. He also roamed the river at night. For a time I don't believe there was any poaching at Portland Creek, and no one was apprehended. Then an eighteen year old named Sam, a cousin of Fred's wife, was caught with seventeen salmon he had snagged at the first pool of the feeder stream nearest the camp. The original eight-fish daily limit had already been reduced to four, so he had far too many.

Fred reported the case to the head warden at the Department of Natural Resources by wire, and we waited. And waited. After a couple of weeks I began sending telegrams. I wired the Tourist Board. I wired the Department of Justice. Nothing happened. There had never been a court case anywhere in the area before, and no one had ever been arrested. It began to look as if nobody ever would be.

I solved that problem by getting into my airplane and making the long, slow, three-hundred-mile trip to St. John's and working my way through the bureaucracy to Les Curtis, the attorney general. At the end of the second day I was promised that if I would fly a judge in from Stephenville Crossing he'd hear the case. That meant a total of almost a thousand miles of flying.

Judge Power set up court on the cookhouse porch, overlooking the Camp Pool. Evidence was given and a verdict handed down—a $100 fine, which the defendant and his father agreed to pay. The judge went home, and I felt justice had been done. But that was not the end of the matter. I loved the trees around the camp and made sure nothing damaged them during our operation each season. When I returned to Portland Creek the next spring, revenge was evident. Every tree within fifty feet of a camp building had been girdled with an ax and was dead or dying.

In June of that year, Sam was caught again—eleven months after the previous year's incident—this time with eleven snagged salmon. I didn't have to fly to St. John's. A few telegrams brought word that if I'd fly a judge over from St. Anthony—three hundred and fifty miles away—he'd hold court.

Like the first case, it was held on the cookhouse porch and, as before, Sam was found guilty. Suddenly, however, things were different. Sentence was suspended, and no fine was mentioned or levied. The judge went home. A superior court judge from New York, who happened to be in camp at the time, was amazed that there was no penalty for a second offense, and so was I.

Almost a year later, when I arrived at the camps in May, I met the Ottawa official who appointed the wardens. He said, "I know you're not going to like this, Lee, but I've appointed Sam as warden." That season, Sam got married and was on his honeymoon. He spent little time on the river, and the poachers in his area had it easy.

Right then I felt like giving up the whole business. And I should have. The salmon belonged to Newfoundland and the province was going to do what it damn well pleased with them. I was up against a stacked deck. But I had parties on the way in, and the place was good for my kids. I kept hoping that someone in the provincial government—someone powerful enough to do something about the situation—would see the truth and decide to help out. Time passed and I hung on.

# THE EARLY BIRD

⁓

The premonition that this particular sport would be trouble-some was strong long before I picked him up at Lomond. Cliff Darden was a friend—no, an acquaintance. I'd been trout fishing with him once, as part of a group. He had fished hard then, rising early and getting out on the stream before the rest of us were starting our breakfasts. He fished late, too, after we'd all come in for supper. This was to be his first salmon trip, and I wasn't sure how well he'd fit in at the camps.

The great difference between trout and salmon fishing is that there are few salmon pools, and they have to be shared sensibly and fairly. Salmon will only choose to rest in lies that they consider both safe and comfortable. There may be such pools only once every mile or so in a river's length. Trout, on the other hand, feel safe in shallower water and—having the need to feed, too—will spread themselves through the full length of a stream. There is room for many more fishermen on a trout stream than there is space for an-glers on a similar salmon river.

We were sticking to our established policy of assigning each an-gler a particular pool or stretch of river for his mornings, rotating fishermen and locations throughout the week. The few afternoon hours were the least productive time of the day, so we let the river rest then to improve the evening fishing. If, however, one of our sports wished to catch trout during the afternoon, he could go to one of the feeder streams. Dinner was at 5:30 P.M., and from then till darkness, which might come as late as 11 P.M. in the early season, each guest was free to fish wherever he chose, as long as no other angler was working that piece of water.

If, by chance, an angler got up and fished before breakfast, he did so without a guide, and the rule was that he had to stay in the pool that was assigned to him. Moreover, after breakfast he had to return to that pool for the rest of the morning.

Cliff Darden didn't like limitations. He was out in the morning before breakfast on his first day and on his second. He fished without a guide . . . and he fudged. One of the guides, who had gone home the previous evening and was returning for breakfast, saw him fishing a pool that wasn't his for that day. Cliff knew the camp rules and had broken them. But I didn't want to send him home, give up the revenue, lose him as a friend, and have him bad-mouthing the camps among his cohorts. I wondered if there wasn't some way I could solve the problem. I struck the idea of getting up early and taking him off in the plane to a place with plenty of salmon. When I asked Cliff if he'd like to try some really untouched fishing, he jumped at the chance.

I set the time for early the following morning. Mrs. Perry, bless her, was up baking bread in the kitchen at 5:30. She gave us oatmeal and bacon and eggs. We were off long before breakfast time.

We flew over the crests of the Long Range Mountains to the eastward drainage and a stretch of the Main River. It was the middle of a fifty-mile-wide expanse of wilderness without a living soul in it. I impressed Cliff with how far from civilization we'd be and how few people ever see the real wilderness. It had the look of a beautiful day. The wind was light, and the low sun was slanting down on the alders at the bank as I taxied the Aeronca to shore beside the outlet of one of the ponds in the river's flow. As we coasted in to the beach I dropped off the float and waded ashore toward the brush with a rope in my hand to secure the plane.

As I reached the bushes they parted, and a bearded face with a wild look on it peered out at me. Then a man stepped forward. That surprised the hell out of me and certainly shot my story of the lonely bush.

The bearded stranger turned out to be one of a group of five young men who had decided to make a wilderness trip and had chosen to cross the wild, northern peninsula from St. Paul's Inlet on the gulf side to the waters of White Bay on the Labrador Sea side. The map showed only a short distance from the head of St. Paul's drainage to the head of the southern Main River branch on the White Bay side. They had started out with two canoes and hundreds of pounds of tents and supplies. They hadn't hired guides, and I guess were either so cocky or so withdrawn that none of the St. Paul residents told them their plan was crazy.

They soon found that the short distance from the point at which St. Paul's was a navigable stream and the top of the mountain was just about straight up. They left their canoes and cached a lot of their supplies, deciding to take what they could carry and build log rafts on the White Bay side of the mountain when they reached it. Arriving at the top they could look back at the hard climb and look ahead to easy going over almost solid rock across the mountain peaks. They pushed on.

The whole thing was a mistake from the beginning. As soon as they got off the very high ground they began to run into small ponds and marshes around which they had to make long detours. They fought their way across bogs and through tuckbush where it took almost an hour to travel a mile. By the time we met they had abandoned most of their gear and were down to one light tent, some cooking gear, and a few supplies. They had counted on a trip of just a few days and at the end of a week they were almost out of food. They'd been hiking down the small brook that flowed into the pond we were on. The bearded fellow had forged ahead to reach the water and try to catch some trout. The others were back breaking camp and would be coming along. Could I bring them some food? Did I have any fly dope? The bugs were killing them. Would I fly them out?

I promised I'd fly in a load of food later in the day. I was too busy with the fishing parties due at camp to fly them out. The pond we were on was too small for a Norseman to get in and out of, but I told them that if they'd go down to the next pond downstream I'd send one of the bigger planes to pick them up. Cliff and I caught some trout and a salmon for them, and I gave the young man some fly repellent, some trout flies, and the spare fly line that I carried.

We then flew on and fished the lower pond's outlet. We had an hour of good fishing, releasing five salmon. Cliff wanted to save his, but I told him they'd make us overweight, and so we couldn't carry them. On our way back we saw smoke coming up from the spot where we'd met the bearded stranger. All five men were there. I waggled my wings and kept on flying back to camp and a second breakfast.

When I returned later in the day with the emergency food, they were established in their one remaining tent on the shore of the larger pond. All were bedraggled, red eyed, and bug bitten. I told them the Norseman would be in the following day, weather permitting. They gave me some messages to send by wire and started preparing a meal.

On the next afternoon, the Norseman apparently flew over the camp at Portland Creek on its way out with the hapless explorers and waggled its wings. I wasn't there. I was making the second flight of the day to Lomond.

# DISASTER

❧

Keith Kennet and Bud Norris, old customers and good friends, were happily ensconced in the Jack Young cabin. The weather and water conditions were excellent, and they were catching a lot of fish. Then, when their week came to an end their luck changed. The morning they were due to leave camp turned out blustery, with a twenty-five-mile-an-hour wind from the east and higher gusts. I couldn't fly them out, and Keith was unhappy. He was a man who operated on a tight schedule and had planned to attend the Bohemian Grove meeting in California. It was of great importance to him, he said, insisting that the wind wasn't too bad. He said that I should fly him out, but I decided to wait for better weather.

Keith was like few other fishermen who came to the camps. Apparently he fished and did everything else on a set schedule. When his week was over he lost all interest in salmon. A more typical angler would have made the best of it and enjoyed the fishing as long as he was stranded by the weather and couldn't do anything about it. Bud Norris kept right on fishing and enjoyed it. Keith sulked in the cabin, playing solitaire or reading a book.

The next day's weather was just as bad. I kept hoping the wind would slacken, but it held all morning. Keith was very unhappy and threw things around in the cabin to show it. Nonetheless, I did not give in. I was not yet completely at home in the Aeronca. We'd had fairly mild weather up to that point in the season, and I hadn't had a chance to check out the plane in rough water.

Finally, the winds began to let go. When they'd slowed down to a level that I felt the old Cub could have handled, I decided to re-lent and go. I taxied downwind in the gusty breeze without any problem, but when I cut power and tried to turn into the wind, the Aeronca only got halfway around. Then a gust got under the up-wind wing and lifted it. The downwind floats sank deep in the water, and the plane refused to swing around into the wind. When an especially hard gust hit the uplifted wing, the Aeronca flipped over onto its back.

The air trapped in the wings and fuselage let us settle slowly, and we were able to get out through the door in plenty of time and sit on the floats. Some of the guides had been watching from the ramp, and they rushed out quickly in one of our outboard-powered skiffs. They threw us a line, which I made fast to a float, and then came alongside to take us aboard. Heading into the wind, they kept the plane from drifting back into the rocks of the shallows downwind until Eb came out in another boat with a heavy anchor that he put upwind to secure the Sedan's position. Then we all went ashore.

I had a heavy heart. I was without a plane in midseason.

Most aircraft are designed to weathercock—that is, turn into the wind automatically. If a land-based plane was put on floats and if it consequently lost good rudder control and didn't weathercock, it was required to have an additional lower stabilizer fin on the tail assembly to correct the fault. The Aeronca had no such fin. I'd made a mistake in buying a newly designed airplane that hadn't been thoroughly tested in at least a year of flying. I should have picked up a used Stinson or some other model that had a proven record as a seaplane, even though it might not have been manufac-tured any more. Or I could have purchased one of the new Seabees, although they had their problems, too.

I sent a guide to Daniel's Harbour to wire Norm Parsons in Norris Point, asking him to come down and get our two stranded anglers. But I knew his boat couldn't take the kind of weather we were having, either. It was not until late the following evening that Norm reached the mouth of the river. We ferried Keith, Bud, and their belongings out to the *Red Wing* in a dory. Norm was loathe to go because he'd just made it over the bar in a rough sea and was sitting in a fairly secure anchorage, but Keith was persistent. After half an hour of discussion they set out on a night run for Lomond. I never learned whether or not Keith got to the meeting in Bohemian Grove for even a single day. I had other worries. My fishermen would now have to come and go by boat until I could get another plane.

I wired my friend Al Nogard to see what he could suggest. He worked wonders, arranging for me to buy a J3 Cub on wheels and to have his friend Gene Guether fly it down. The floats from the wrecked *Yellow Bird* were still at Lomond, and we would put the replacement plane on them as soon as it arrived. As well as being a skilled pilot, Gene was a top mechanic. He would repair the Aeronca if it was fixable and fly it back to the States for full repairs and the required inspections. We turned our attention to salvaging the upturned plane.

Diving underneath I could see no structural damage. The floats were still full of air. By this time the wind had died out, and the waves had subsided. Now, however, I had to get the plane into deep water (so I could turn it right side up), and that was a long way off. We dared not let the Aeronca touch an underwater rock, which would bend the frame and tear the skin beyond repair. We took a page from a Horatio Hornblower story and "kedged" it to deep water. We hooked a long rope to a heavy anchor, then tied the other end of the line to the plane and rowed the anchor as far ahead as we could. When it had a good grip on the bottom, we pulled the Aeronca up to the anchor. We did this again and again until we had reached deep water.

It took a little thinking to get the plane right side up without doing any damage. For one thing, the frail, fabric-covered wings were full of water and heavy. They needed to drain slowly as we brought them up into the air. For another, the floats were full of air and would resist being submerged. To overcome that I drove nail holes into the two front compartments so that the noses of the floats would sink more readily. Pulling the plane downward with a rope on her tail, we brought the wings up out of the water gradually, then plugged up the nail holes in the floats and bailed those compartments dry. Finally, we towed her to the ramp.

The next step was to dismantle the engine. Eb took over that job, and I went back to managing the operation at Portland Creek. There was no way to reach the outlying camps, so those trips had to be canceled. Norm Parsons brought the fishermen in and took them out again in his boat. Fortunately we had a couple of weeks of good weather, and there were no holdups.

Gene made the flight down in the Cub without difficulty, crossing the Cabot Strait in bright sunlight at over eight thousand feet. I'd made arrangements for him to land on the paper-company farm alongside Deer Lake. He had to make two low passes to buzz the cows away before he had a clear stretch to land on.

I'd brought the floats up from Lomond and with them three, twenty-five-foot-long spruce poles. With these we made a great tripod and rigged it with a block and tackle to lift the plane high enough to remove its wheels and put on the floats. We then filled the tank with gas, slid the Cub along the ground for the short distance to the water, and took off for Portland Creek.

When we came taxiing up to the ramp the boys stared at the new plane. The previous owner had painted the metal cowling at the front of the fuselage a bright red, leaving the rest of the plane Mr. Piper's favorite color—bright yellow. The previous Christmas season had seen great popularity for Gene Autry's singing of *Rudolph the Red-nosed Reindeer*, and our second J3 was immediately nicknamed *Rudolph*.

Eb had done a great job of cleaning up the Aeronca's engine. Gene had brought spare magnetos and a few other things he thought might be needed. Within three days he and Eb had the engine running, and the plane had been checked over thoroughly. When Gene said it was ready to fly, I took it up for a couple of hours, doing gentle maneuvers at first—always within gliding range of the big pond—and then trying a few more strenuous things. I had no problems. The next day, Gene took off for the States in the Aeronca for its post-accident inspections. Rudolph became our one and only airplane for the rest of the season.

# WESTERN GORGE

⁓

T he camps were getting a reputation. The top periodical of that time, *Life* magazine, decided to run a story on Atlantic salmon fishing and sent a team down to make the fishing at the camps the heart of the piece. John Hamilton was the writer and Howard Sochurek, an award winner, was the photographer. I flew them in, one at a time in *Rudolph*. Whenever I wanted them to cover an outlying camp I made two trips to make sure they got the best possible photographs. I took them to the River of Ponds and to a new camp I was building a hundred miles farther north, on Castors River. Located deep in the wilderness, this water and its salmon fishing were untouched. Finally, I took Howard to Western Brook. John had decided to stay at Portland Creek and talk to the staff and the anglers.

I planned to build a camp at Western Brook eventually, but up to that time—except for the disaster with Dr. Weston—I'd used it only for day trips. The running out of that great, crystal-clear pond was something I saved for VIPs. You could look across at the tall, vertical cliffs that rose from the water's edge and opened a gorge that penetrated a dozen miles into the mountains. There were occasionally very big salmon lying in the Running Out Pool, fish that came out of the lake to feel the soothing effect of the flowing water. It was there that I'd taken Ed Gilligan, outdoor editor of the *New York Herald Tribune*. Under my guidance he caught a salmon of almost thirty pounds, an event that led to some excellent columns about the fishing on his trip.

I've never, ever been able to decide which kind of water I like best for my salmon fishing: Is it rivers whose waters are stained dark as tea by the peat of the long-dead forests that underlie the bogs in which they rise? Or is it the gin-clear flows like the Fox Island River and Western Brook? There is a mystery to fishing the dark water, where one can only picture in his mind the salmon that is lying somewhere under the surface. The top-water swirls and ripples can suggest to a knowledgeable angler just where the fish should be lying, but he can never be sure there is even a single salmon in the whole pool unless he sees one jump. Even then he doesn't know exactly where the fish lies or how his fly is approaching it. This may be the greatest reward in salmon angling: presenting a fly to a spot where instinct or judgment tells you a big salmon should be lying, and finding that he's there and will rise to your fly.

In crystal waters an angler can often see the fish he's casting to. If the guide climbs a tree he can see salmon even in very deep water. He can tell his sport where to cast, whether the fly is tracking right, and whether or not there is even a small movement by any fish in response to his presentations. An angler who approaches such water cautiously can often spot the salmon before he casts anywhere in the pool, and working slowly into position, he can watch the reactions of the fish he is casting to. Any slight movement of a salmon as a fly passes over him is usually an indication of interest and the probability that the fish can be caught.

On that day at Western Brook with Howard Sochurek, I waded in slowly at the bottom of the pool and worked out to a depth where I could see the best holding water. I spotted a very large salmon and waited for some ten minutes before I cast my fly. I drifted a big White Wulff over him. For the first half-dozen casts he made no move, but on the seventh he rose up under the fly, nuzzling it with his nose but failing to open his mouth and suck it in. Had I struck and snatched that fly right off his nose he'd have spooked and certainly refused any fly I offered after that. It is a sign of maturity in a dry-fly fisherman that he watches his fly closely, doesn't make a spastic yank, and lets the fly float on—like a natural insect—after such a false rise.

That salmon showed no interest in the fly on the next cast.

Some anglers believe in resting a fish when he has come up and missed their fly. I prefer to hope that the salmon is as impatient as I am and can't wait for the fly to come drifting over him again. I cast back three times without result. Then I rested the fish.

I tried again with a Gray Bivisible #8, then a #6 Royal—both to no avail. Going small and trying a dozen casts with a #14 spider did not move the fish either. Before leaving a salmon that has risen once, I always make my last cast with the fly that first elicited attention from him. So out came the #4 White Wulff again, and I drifted it over his lie. He rose and took it.

I struck. As he felt the steel the fish jumped, cartwheeling. I believe his tail must have struck the taut leader and pulled the fly free. At any rate, he fell back to the water with a great splash and swam off.

I looked over at Howard. "Did you get that jump?"

He shook his head. "Only the splash when he landed."

There was, of course, no way I could tell him in advance when a salmon would rise or make a sudden leap. It takes a lot of film or luck or special instincts to capture a rise or get really good jumps.

I went on to fish farther up into the pool. Four salmon came to my dry flies, and all were landed. I played them carefully, maneuvering them into position between Howard and me. Quite often I can make fish jump on demand in a particular spot by varying pressure and positioning in playing him. On at least a dozen jumps Howard felt that he had clicked his shutter at just the right moment and captured the salmon in the air, with me in the background. He covered the casting, playing, hand-tailing, and releasing of each fish. He even thought he might have gotten one of the rises. When he was satisfied I said, "Let's go home."

Howard had other ideas. While he'd been photographing he'd been looking at the gorge with its dramatic gray cliffs, which rival those of Yosemite. He said, "Let's fly into that gorge. I'd like to get some pictures of it." I thought hard. I found myself wishing that Old Martin or some other old timer were there to advise me. The sky was cloudless but had a strange, opaque sort of mauve color. There was not a breath of wind. I was reluctant. Howard was eager, insistent.

I'd seen Western Gorge from top to bottom and from the inside out. I'd had my qualms even when Martin and I had gone in and come out on days that he was sure would be windless. Without his understanding of the weather I was loath to fly into the gorge. Often, when I had the boys with me and was checking the ridges for updrafts or downdrafts, I'd fly over the mountains about fifteen feet off the ground. As we passed over the sheer edge of the gorge, the land underneath would suddenly drop away to a depth of more than two thousand feet. It was a startling sensation and always drew a gasp from the kids or anyone else. I had flown partway into the gorge with Ella one day when little puffy clouds were forming all around us, but I stayed at a thousand feet or better and was ready to duck out at the slightest feeling of unstable air.

At Howard's insistence I agreed to fly in a ways at mid-level. We entered the gorge at a thousand feet, gray rock walls towering above us on either side. There were changes in the formations where different pigments had settled to create the rock millions of years ago. Some of those sedimentary layers, which were originally horizontal, were now stretching almost vertically from the water far down below us right up to the rim. It was a very special sight. Below us was the windless pond and its reflections; overhead loomed that strange and beautiful mauve sky. I opened the upper half of the door, and Howard took pictures.

Then he complained, "I can't get good shots from here. The walls are too high, and the water is too far down. You've got to get me down to water level. I want to land."

That's when I should have held back. But, I thought, the salmon usually tell me when lousy weather is coming by refusing to take my flies. They didn't. Besides, there isn't any wind now, and there hasn't been any all day. I flew down through smooth air and landed *Rudolph* at the one place we could get ashore—the inland end of the pond. Howard climbed a short way up the slope and began to shoot more film.

The slightest breath of air brushed my cheek. Then a flurry of little waves drifted across the surface, just offshore. I called to Howard, "Come on, let's go!"

It was as if he hadn't heard. I shouted more loudly, then got out onto the float and waved frantically. Still no response. I moved forward on the float and swung the prop. The motor caught and roared into a steady rhythm. I swung the plane around and poked the nose of the floats in to the sloping rock. Only then did Howard come—slowly—and climb aboard. I let the Cub drift back till I could make a forward turn, roaring into a takeoff.

Howard was heavy—well over two hundred pounds—and he had a lot of cameras and gear with him. With no wind but little whirls here and there on the water, I had to work up to over forty miles an hour before I could get the floats to break free of the glassy surface. Then there was wind all around us, whistling down from the rim of the gorge.

We lifted, then we dropped, caught solid air again, and continued our slow climb. A patch of smooth air got us up to five hundred feet. Then we were pushed back toward the water—even though the throttle was full forward and the nose of the plane was set upward for a climb. We lifted again, momentarily . . . and dropped. One of Howard's cameras drifted, gravity free, over my shoulder and banged against the instrument panel. I grabbed it with my right hand and pushed it back over my shoulder. "Hang onto that thing!" I yelled. "Suppose it got down on the floor and jammed a rudder pedal!"

Looking below us I could see black patches on the water where the wind was blasting hard against it. We were being pushed rapidly down toward the waves. Try to keep level, I thought. Keep the nose down. Stall out and you're dead.

There is a well-known aviation writer who maintains that there is no cushion of air at the surface when the wind blows hard against it. He uses as proof the observation that a bug striking your car's windshield hits hard and squashes. There's no cushion, see? Thank God this "expert" is wrong. His theory might work for heavy bugs like beetles—as well as for helicopters or fast, small-winged planes—but how many butterflies wham into your windshield? None at all. A J3 Cub is more like a butterfly than a beetle. We were pushed down almost to the water and shuddered there for seconds before we crossed into rising air and were hurtled upward several hundred feet. Glancing up I could see a pair of gulls soaring in the updraft at the gorge's rim.

"Please," I whispered, "let me get up over that edge."

Where the black squalls hit the pond they picked up sheets of water and lifted them a hundred feet or more into the air. They were like lacy clouds, rising then falling back to the pond. While we were inside one of them I saw the flash of a rainbow for a brief moment before we felt a rattle like hail on the airplane and passed on into clear air on the other side.

Twice more we were pushed down almost to the water. Each time, there was a cushion. At last I found an area where the air was rising: Just as it came pouring down over the edge of the cliffs on one side, it had to lift somewhere else to get out of the gorge. The gulls had indicated where the updraft would be because they would never have been found in downward-flowing air. We were like the proverbial pea in the policeman's whistle until we flew into that wonderful updraft and climbed with it, up over the rim. The coastal plain was out there below us. We were safe at last.

The gas gauge on a Piper Cub is a cork that floats in the tank ahead of the front seat. A heavy wire, bent sharply at its top, protrudes upward through a hole in the filler cap. When the tank is full the wire stands about nine inches above that cap. As the gas is used up the wire drops down. When the tank is empty the wire indicator sinks right to the gas cap and rests there motionless. As Howard and I leveled off, the bent-over tip of the wire was hitting the gas cap, bumping up a little bit and settling down again under the influence of the small amount of gas that was sloshing back and forth at the bottom of the tank.

We had come out over the top of the gorge at better than two thousand feet. I put the plane in a slight climb to gain altitude with a minimum sacrifice of distance. The higher we flew the greater the number of ponds and marshes I could reach in my glide if we ran out of gas before we got home. When I was within range of Portland Pond I relaxed. Western Gorge had given me its most impressive memory.

# THE LONG WAY 'ROUND

W hen the time came to fly home from the camps in *Rudolph* I didn't feel that the engine had the power it should. There was nothing I could put my finger on, but it seemed to be running rough, reminding me of the worrying sound of the *Yellow Bird* when we flew out over the water. Eb couldn't find anything wrong and neither could the mechanic who serviced the paper company's newly acquired Grumman Goose amphibian. Everything checked out, and I put it down to my imagination.

Neville Whitehurst, the canny English wartime pilot who flew the Goose said, "Lee, don't go back across the strait. You know and I know that the motor is all right, but just suppose it quits halfway across. You'd feel damn silly on the way down. Be smart, lad. Take the long way 'round."

The long way meant three hundred more miles of flying, but the water crossing at the Strait of Belle Isle was only a dozen miles instead of the hundred I would have to face at the Cabot Strait. I had long since given up the idea that I might survive a forced landing in the cold, rough waves out there. I decided on the long route home.

Once I crossed the Strait of Belle Isle and turned south, I was flying over unfamiliar territory. My first landing was at Harrington Harbour in Quebec, where I worked my way through a lot of fishing boats and nosed into the pier without banging my wings on anything. Gassed up, I continued westward to the Hudson's Bay store and its few surrounding houses. Jim Massey, the "factor" (proprietor) at the store, sold me gas and invited me to stay overnight at his house. I spent a pleasant time with him and his family, and in the morning they waved me on my way. I always found a warm welcome and a home wherever fate set me down in the wild country. One of Jim's sons, Ian, later became a fine bush pilot, and I saw him frequently in my later years of flying in Labrador.

My map indicated that the next likely fueling stop was Natashquan. In fact, I spotted the big gasoline-storage tanks long before I made out the buildings of the town. The main pier was clearly too high to go in against with my long wings, and I could see no other place where I could safely get to shore. Then I remembered passing a little cluster of houses beside a small pond a few minutes earlier. I turned back.

The pond was adequate for landing but not by much. Half a dozen houses were strung along the road, where a bridge crossed a small brook that ran across a narrow strip dividing the pond from the salt water. I made the landing and taxied to the shore beside the bridge. The houses emptied, and a crowd gathered around me. I brought my French into play—barely remembered from my year of art study in Paris more than twenty years earlier—and convinced one of the men to take my ten-dollar bill and go off to fetch a couple of five-gallon cans of gas. I settled down to wait.

Despite my being rusty with the language I managed a conversation about the plane and about fishing along the shore. No. They didn't see any horse mackerel, which they called albacore, in their waters. Yes, there were a lot of salmon in the Natashquan River. It was too late now because the season was closed, but if I'd come back in June they would arrange it so I could catch some fish. They said a man named Knapp owned the lodge and the river. Then the gas arrived, and I strained it into the tank.

Once, when I was learning to fly, Lew Lavery stopped my take-off before I got started, insisting that I swing around and take in about twenty yards of water I had behind me. "Always use all the runway you can get," he said. "You never know when you'll need it."

In Natashquan I taxied all the way to the far shore of the

pond—downwind—over the course I'd be using for my takeoff. The water was brown, and I couldn't see much of the bottom. There were occasional patches of grass growing in fairly shallow water, but I passed over it easily. The wind had lessened, and there was just a light breeze coming in from the sea.

At the edge of the pond I turned, pushed the throttle forward, and began my takeoff run. I was just getting on the step when my floats touched something soft— like a mud bank—and the plane lagged for just a second. However, it then went back up onto the step and picked up speed. Again, though, there was a moment of slight slowing. The bridge and the people on it were coming up fast, but *Rudolph* just didn't want to leave the water.

The bridge was too low and too narrow to fly under, and I was too close to abort. The people standing on the span were beginning to panic and run. I'd just about decided to fly into the hole under the bridge, which would fold the wings back on each side to absorb the shock and probably let me stay alive. Then, with my last hauling back of the stick, *Rudolph* jumped into the air. I just made it over the bridge but couldn't clear the telephone wires. I passed underneath them, stalling because I'd asked the Cub to do more than was possible. We slid downward through the air over the far side of the road, hit the water of the open gulf hard, and bounced high. Nosing down at the bounce with full throttle, I kept *Rudolph* in the air and flew on to the west. I'm sure that there are people still living in Natashquan who remember the crazy American in his red-nosed, yellow plane—the greenhorn who didn't realize he was taking off from a brackish-water pond on a falling tide. I'm sure it must have been as scary for some of them as it was for me.

The rest of my trip was uneventful except that I was weathered in at Sept-Isles (Seven Islands) for five full days of solid fog. This route truly proved to be the long way home. The journey took eight days instead of my usual two.

*Rudolph*, like the *Yellow Bird*, came to a sad end. I'd landed the plane on the grass at Shushan and planned to put it on wheels. Then I intended to reinstall the floats in the spring and take off on a wheeled "dolly" positioned under the floats. Two months later, however, while the plane was parked at Okey Butcher's airstrip, it was caught in a sudden, ninety-mile-an-hour gale that came roaring into Shushan in the middle of the night. There was sixty pounds of weight under each wing and under the tail to secure the Cub, but Rudolf flew nonetheless, ending up halfway across the field in a tangled mess. The wind also tore the roof off Okey's hangar and flipped his own plane out onto the field, leaving it flat on its back and badly broken.

Newfoundland is not the only place where strong winds blow.

# THE PACER

⌐⌐

*R*udolph was gone. Repaired and relicensed, the Aeronca
Sedan had been sold. Ella and I had decided to go our separate ways, but she'd continue to run her lodge at Lomond
and welcome my fishermen. Word came through from the north
that Eb had died of a heart attack at a Christmas Party in Daniel's
Harbour. I had taken the boys on a hunting trip to Mexico during
their Christmas vacations, using Piper Aircraft's new four-place
plane, the Pacer. In exchange for that footage, I received a Pacer on
floats.

This plane was lighter than the Aeronca, and it was not as
roomy. On the plus side, the Pacer's 150-horsepower Lycoming engine would give me a cruising speed of 115 miles an hour. When
the weather threatened and the time a trip would take could be the
deciding factor, that would be an advantage. However, there were
disadvantages, too. The shorter, narrower wings had less lift, and I
would require greater speed to leave the water on takeoff. That
meant a longer run before becoming airborne. I wouldn't be able
to get into the smaller ponds that were easy enough for the J3 Cub
or the Aeronca.

The Pacer was delivered just in time for the 1952 season, and
there was much to learn about its quirks and performance. How
fast would I have to go when taking off from glassy water, and how
much of a load could I carry,? How far could the plane glide in case
of an engine failure? This was a new design, and pilot reports on its
flying characteristics had not yet come in.

The trip to Portland Creek was uneventful. I flew the roundabout northern route through clear skies and light winds, and made the trip in two days.

Another pilot, Frank Frazee, joined me at the camps. He flew down in his 165-horsepower Stinson "Station Wagon," which was also a four-place plane, though considerably roomier than the Pacer and almost as fast. The number of reservations was increasing. Clapboard buildings and log cabins had replaced all the tents. We had a larger icehouse and kerosene-burning refrigeration. I'd set up a shower house with plenty of hot water, two stalls, and a changing room. A fifty-yard-long breakwater gave us a safer mooring place for the planes and boats.

I'd also bought a Ford tractor with Bombardier tracks. Though it was designed for snow travel, I was sure it would cross bogs, as well. It would let us pull out the stumps of the trees we were cutting to create a three-thousand-foot runway that would let DC3s—carrying more than twenty anglers each—fly directly to Portland Creek from airports in the States. There was great cheering when six men got the tractor ashore from a cod fisherman's trap skiff. There was wonderment and more cheering when I drove it across a stretch of marsh where a man couldn't walk without sinking to ankle depth and wondering with every step how soon he would plunge down to his hips. The outer world was coming to this lonely north shore, and it would never be the same.

Whenever I had spare time I practiced with the Pacer. With its shorter wings and higher speed, my flying had to be more precise. One of the maneuvers I performed whenever the water was smooth enough was to flip the plane up onto a single float—one wing high, the other low. It took nice balance to run across the water in a straight line while heeled over. Even more was required to make a perfect circle and then, by flipping over from one float to the other, to make a second circle in the opposite direction, completing a figure eight. In the slower airplanes my speed had been under forty miles an hour for that maneuver. In the Pacer the circles were larger, and my speed was fifty-five miles an hour.

The one-float maneuvers reminded me of the most beautiful flying I ever saw a bird do. I was anchored in Bonne Bay while fishing for tuna in 1939 and came on deck to find an early-morning fog that blotted out everything that was more than a hundred feet away. The air was still and the water oily smooth, with slow, easy swells moving in from the outer bay. A slim-winged, gray bird about the size of a small gull appeared out of the mist, one wing high and the other barely touching the water. In that attitude it circled the boat, making a fine, continuous pencil-like wake on the water with its lower wingtip. That bird flew up and over and down the swells as they moved slowly shoreward, always with one wingtip barely touching the surface. There was no visible motion of its wings and no updraft to support its body, yet the bird easily made that perfectly balanced circuit of the boat and disappeared into the mist.

When the skipper came up from below I told him what I had seen. After my description he thought a bit and said, "That must have been a hawk." I determined later that the bird must have been a sooty shearwater, a species of the open seas that rarely comes to land. It had been an amazing sight.

The one-float ride and high-wing attitude wasn't just a practice maneuver. The need for it arose one afternoon when I'd flown three fishermen to George's Lake to catch the train, which always stopped beside the lake to take on water for its steam boilers and would take passengers aboard there (or at any such stopping place). When the train puffed on I taxied out to take off. The wind was blowing hard, but it didn't seem any worse than when I'd come to land. I reached my sixty-mile-an-hour flying speed and took off, banging a little harder than usual on the last wave. Then I was airborne, and everything seemed normal—until I looked down and saw with dismay that the front strut attaching one float to the fuselage was broken and separated. The rear strut was still intact, but the nose of the float had dropped about a foot. I had a problem.

There was no way I could land in rough water without that float's digging in and flipping the plane over onto its back. I might die as Pink Henderson had. I needed to find smooth water, but where?

I decided on Deer Lake, which had beaches along its southern edge. The wind was southerly, so that shore would be in the lee, but I'd have to make a crosswind approach. Gusts were coming in over the trees and bouncing off the surface of the water about a hundred feet out. I approached at a low angle to the beach, fighting the turbulence and touching down on the good, offshore float. I held the other one up as long as I could. By that time I had slowed down and was fairly close to shore. As the wings leveled, the loose float dug in. The plane shuddered, twisted toward shore and . . . we slid safely onto the sandy beach.

After getting out my tools and taking off the broken strut pieces, I measured the distance between the bolt holes on the good float and cut a piece of fishing line the exact length of the strut. On a short stick I marked the width of the block it had to be bolted to. Then I walked to the road, bummed a ride to town, found a plumbing shop, and had a piece of inch-and-a-half galvanized pipe cut and bent to the right width, and drilled for the bolts. In less than two hours I was back at the plane. With the help of the taxi driver I put the makeshift strut in place and bolted it tight.

I reached Portland Creek just ahead of darkness, happy to be home and glad that I'd be there in the morning to keep a promise to two of my anglers—a man and his wife—who insisted on going to church the next morning. They were Catholics, and I told them there wasn't a Catholic church anywhere along our shore. I said that I could manage the next best thing: a Church of England at Hawke's Bay, thirty-five miles to the north. The service was a pretty good one.

# Happiness and Sadness

〜

Because of the outlying camps we could still offer excellent fishing, and most of our sports were happy. The happiest of all was Bob Jacobs, a New York architect. He first arrived in 1949 with the three Cone brothers, who had been fishing with us ever since I started the camps. They were seasoned salmon anglers, while Bob was a novice. They showed up a little early that first year, and I flew them in to Western Bluie on the River of Ponds. It turned out that the run in that river was later than usual.

When I checked on things the second day no one had caught a salmon, but Bob was beaming. He'd landed more and bigger trout than ever before and was in seventh heaven. The others would only fish for trout if they needed them to eat, and with Bob in camp, there were plenty for the frying pans. The Cones played cards, keeping their tackle ready and at hand. Meanwhile their guides spread out along the river for a good part of each day to spot leaping fish that would indicate that salmon were in the river and where.

When the fish did come in, Bob was so excited that he glowed even when telling of the smallest one he'd caught. He was hooked. From that time on he returned to the camps every year. He loved the guides and used their words and way of talking, but with his own exaggerations. He would ask for an "haxe" to cut a bit of brush along a trail. He would say, "That salmon come to m'fly right savage." or "He's a new fish, bright as alvor." or "I tricked 'e with a Noydok."

Bob always found time to help around the camp where he was

staying, and the guides loved him for it. If they told him of a particular pool that was too far to walk to, he'd go there if he could talk the teller into taking him.

Bob used to amaze the Newfoundlanders with his almost daily swims, for he went in no matter how cold the water or the weather. He was a tall man, with big bones and big feet. He'd played water polo at Amherst and always kept himself in fine shape. Few Newfoundlanders could swim. They were always on the water in boats, but they were like cats and almost never fell in. They figured if they did, they'd drown for sure. Bob offered to teach them to swim, but he had no takers. It was he who suggested that I hold school sessions at the camp to teach the guides to read and write, taking part of the afternoon chore time to do it. I thought it was a great idea.

Maybe it was a case of old dogs and new tricks, but that didn't work, either. One of my best guides, Maurice (Mush) Caines, was the ringleader of the opposition. I had said that if any one of them learned to read and write, all the thoughts and wisdom of the world would be available to him and that he could communicate with others who were far away without involving a third party. Mush simply replied that knowing how to read and write wouldn't help a man cut a tree down one bit faster or shoot straighter at a caribou. I just couldn't convince him, and he was able to persuade most of the other guides. The school idea died there.

Bob liked deep water. He always seemed to be in up to the top of his waders and was sometimes over the top, something that never seemed to bother him no matter how cold the water. He fished all of the rivers and would often sleep in just a pup tent on the overnights. My favorite memory of him is from Castor's River, the outpost farthest north of the main camp at Portland Creek.

I had gone down to Labrador to check out the St. Mary's River and to leave a gas cache there. On the way back I didn't stop for fuel at Flowers Cove because I had just enough to get back to the main camp and didn't want to waste any time. I crossed over Castor's River just above the lower camp, not far from the salt water. When I looked down at the river, there was Bob out in the middle of it. We'd had a flood of rain, so the river was high and swift. Bob was up to the top of his waders again. I waggled my wings in salute. He took off his hat and waved it vigorously.

At that moment a rock must have rolled under his feet, for he lost his balance and simply disappeared in the deep, brown, white-capped flow. Seconds later he came to the surface—like a seal—about twenty feet downstream, got his footing, and laboriously waded the sixty feet to the shore. I circled to be sure he was OK, but I didn't have the time or gas to land and joke with him. I knew he'd be laughing.

Ironically, Castor's River was the setting for this, one of my happiest moments, but also for one of my saddest. Close by the lower camp there was a crystal stream with several great, deep holes in its flow. They were loaded with trout—big ones. Those fish were part of a run that came in from the sea, and they were as large or larger than the trout of Western Brook. Many were over six pounds.

It was a fragile thing, that trout run, so I put a one-fish-per-trip limit on it. My guests were the only ones who fished this stretch of water, and the local people in the settlement a few miles down the shore seemed to realize that those trout were bringing some prosperity to the community. All went well for the first year, and the second year was as good as the first. Then disaster struck. One of my Castor's River guides, a man from the settlement, was caught stealing from a suitcase belonging to one of the guests. He took some money and a pocketknife. The angler wasn't worried about the money but he did want the knife back as it was something he'd had a long time and treasured. I succeeded in recovering the knife but not the money, which I replaced from my own wallet. I fired the guide.

He needed the work badly and wanted to be back on the job. He offered to let me take the money out of his wages. I hated to have the rest of the guides think that if they stole and got caught—but replaced the loot—they would not be punished. That story would go all down the coast and might lead to some additional thievery. So I refused.

Then he said, "If you don't hire me back I'll ruin the trout pools."

That sort of blackmail, too, can be catching. Give in to one blackmailer and you'll have a lot more individuals who will try to bend you to their will. The guide stayed fired.

For the next two weeks I was helpless while he did what he had threatened. At that time the Newfoundland limit on brook trout was thirty-six per day. Each morning he and one of his grown sons would walk by the camp on the short trail up to the pools. Each evening they'd come by again carrying heavy sacks loaded with those big, beautiful brookies. Low water had concentrated the fish in two deep spring holes. If they could not be caught on bait—and if no one was watching—they could be "snatched" with a weighted treble hook and pulled from the pools, or even speared. I found a spear hidden in the bushes not far from one of the pools.

Right from the start I talked to the local warden and wired the Department of Natural Resources. Unfortunately, the warden was a cousin of the ex-guide. He said that the law was the law. So did the Department of Natural Resources. How I wished they'd paid attention to my old Tourist Board reports requesting a daily bag of five pounds in addition to their limit on numbers.

In two weeks there wasn't a trout weighing as much as a pound left in the stream, and the next year there were no big trout there to delight my guests. Nor were there any the following season, nor the one after that.

# Final Flight

⌒

It was warm in the kitchen, and the heat was welcome after my stint of lying on the gravel next to the ramp as I patched a small hole in one of my floats. The weather was damp, and the fog was so thick that early afternoon seemed like evening. There'd be no flying. I sat on a bench against the wall with a cup of hot tea steaming on the oilcloth-covered table in front of me. By the stove Mrs. Perry was mixing a pudding. The fishermen and their guides were in their cabins. Allan and Barry were visiting friends in Daniel's Harbour. It was a good time to sit still and relax.

The radio on the kitchen shelf was pouring out the usual music for that day—lively jigs and reels. Momentarily I was caught up with thoughts of work that could be considered pressing. I was also wondering how things were going at Lomond. A party of four should have been arriving that afternoon. I couldn't be there to meet them, but I hoped they'd understand. Ella would send them out to jig for cod or troll for mackerel in the cove. Or they could take the car and fish for trout in Bonne Bay Little Pond. She'd take care of things.

The news at 1:00 P.M. said that a pilot was overdue on a flight from Goose Bay to Flower's Cove, which was 120 miles north of us. The plane was a Norseman, owned by Wheeler Airlines. Most of the Norsemen had radios and instruments, but that wouldn't help unless there were stations on the ground within range to orient them. The only bases that could assist the missing pilot were Goose, Gander, or Stephenville, and all of them were more than 150 miles from Flower's Cove—well beyond range. I got up and moved to the stove to pick up the pot that always simmered there, refilling my cup with steaming tea. I stirred in a teaspoon of sugar and walked back to the bench.

Then we heard it. A heavy motor. Overhead.

I ran outside to listen. The plane was coming from the east, and it had to be in the overcast. With that much darkness the cloud cover must have been all of six thousand feet thick. The sound came closer. Then it was directly overhead. The plane was low—no more than a thousand feet high. I had no radio with which to contact the pilot. My frequency only worked for VHF stations in the States. I had a helpless feeling as I heard the motor drone on westward, out over the gulf.

I pictured the pilot blinded by the overcast, knowing that his altitude would let him fly into a mountain but wanting and hoping to be low enough to get under the fog. He'd be boring holes in the thick clouds with red-rimmed eyes as he flew on, his throttle on a low setting to save gas and keep the plane aloft as long as he could. He'd watch the gas-gauge needles settling closer and closer to zero. He'd be looking for any sight of land or water, hoping that it would not be the gray rock of a mountainside, dead ahead. Where had the winds drifted him off his course? He could complain bitterly in his mind that he hadn't ditched two hours earlier, when he could have been reasonably certain about coming down over the gulf or the Atlantic.

We heard the sound of the motor fade away. Mrs. Perry asked, "Wasn't that a Norseman?" I nodded. We turned back into the warmth of the kitchen. "Your tea will be cold," she said. "I'll pour you another cup." We sat for a long time in silence.

The 6:00 P.M. news said the Norseman was still missing. I checked the reports for days afterward. The plane had disappeared without a trace.

# THE NEW PILOT

Through the years, Allan had ridden with me in my airplanes whenever he had the chance. I let him take the controls from time to time, and as he became older and more proficient, I allowed him to try some of the simpler maneuvers. On his own he made model planes and flew them, all of which gave him a pretty good understanding of aircraft behavior.

He learned the other part of bush flying, too. He knew that the fog coming in from the sea closed in last right at the base of the mountains. He knew the routes I chose to get the best visibility when the clouds were low, and he was familiar with the places that I counted on for safe landings in an emergency. He knew how to land in strong winds and how to make a glassy-water landing. But the rules said he couldn't get a student license and fly solo until he was sixteen, and couldn't hold a private license until he was seventeen. He was eager, but we went by the rules.

I had my flight instructor's license, and when Allan was sixteen I bought a blue-and-silver Cub for him to learn with. Al Nogard flew it down to Portland Creek. As a teacher I put Allan through the same exercises that Lew Lavery had me practice. But perhaps because of the years my boy and I had flown together, the maneuvers were much easier for him than they had been for me. He wasn't upset by spins, and we both enjoyed those nose-down, rotating stalls in which you watch the world go round and round beneath you. Parachutes were no longer required for that maneuver, and we had none to use, anyway.

When I stood on the ramp and sent Allan out for his first solo flight, he had all of Portland Pond to land in. I realized after he'd taken off that I hadn't warned him the plane would fly differently without my weight in the front seat. But then, Lew Lavery hadn't warned me, either. While Lew's weight had been about two-thirds of mine, my weight was almost double Allan's. The effect of the lightness in increasing the length of the plane's glide was much greater for Allan than it had been for me. When he came down to land and just floated along for a time, he realized the difference and climbed a bit—without touching the water—to try once more. When he came down for a landing the next time he stretched out his glide long enough to make it a smooth one.

Allan then took off again and climbed high above the pond. As I watched, I saw a long streamer of white drifting earthward. He'd thrown a roll of toilet paper out the window, and it unrolled swiftly into a long vertical ribbon. Allan dove down to get below it and then come up under it in a vertical climb, his prop chewing up the paper for quite a distance before he leveled off to avoid a stall. That was his way of celebrating his first solo and telling me that he would have been capable of flying long before I let him. He'd been attentive to my techniques and had really worked with his radio-controlled model planes.

From then on Allan practiced the essential maneuvers. He could do things with the Cub that I couldn't. Because he was so much lighter he could lift off the water sooner and climb faster. When the water was calm he'd practice the single float maneuver until he could do it beautifully. As a culmination of his efforts—with me watching—he got up on one float in Daniel's Harbour pond, which has a diameter of a little over a thousand feet, and circled it on glassy water before lifting up into the sky. I was proud. His flying capability was excellent. So was his judgment. I knew he could safely fly wherever I could and that he'd have no trouble passing his pilot's test when we got back to the States and found an examiner.

For the rest of his sixteenth summer Allan—under my direction—flew needed supplies to the outlying camps or flew me on exploratory fishing trips. I was already looking forward to the following summer when, with his private license, he'd be able to carry passengers and would be one step closer to his commercial license.

# LABRADOR

❦

N ow that our operation had a second four-passenger plane
(the Stinson), another pilot to fly fishermen in and out
(Frank Frazee), and an airstrip that was large enough for
a DC3, I began to reach farther and farther "down" (north) into
Labrador in the Pacer. Part of the same province as Newfoundland,
this territory was almost entirely undeveloped. It had a hundred
and ten thousand square miles of land and thousands of miles of
coastline, stretching from the Strait of Belle Isle north to Cape Chi-
dley. There, the Atlantic spilled over into Ungava Bay which, in
turn, emptied into Hudson's Bay.

Bowater Paper Company had set up a small logging operation
at Port Hope Simpson, deep inland on the long indraft of the
Alexis River. Goose Bay, a military air base, was at the lower end of
Hamilton Sound, a hundred and eighty miles from the Atlantic
coastline and two hundred miles farther north. The Grenfell Missions were at Cartwright, on Sandwich Bay, and at Northwest River,
just thirty miles from Goose Bay. There was a Moravian Mission at
Nain for the Inuits. Beyond that a few small settlements were scattered along the coast. The rest of that great territory was empty except for the mining operation at Labrador City.

I was interested in Labrador's salmon rivers and wanted to explore the possibility of setting up fly-in camps in otherwise inac-
cessible areas. I knew that in Newfoundland, the roads would soon
be creeping north toward Portland Creek. Premier Joey Smallwood, clever politician that he was, had even built a fine concrete
bridge well over a hundred miles north of the existing road at

Bonne Bay. He just wanted to let the people of the whole north shore know that he would build a road to their little outport if he were reelected.

As we flew north on one particular exploratory trip, we saw a shining new Chevrolet—just unloaded by barge from a coastal vessel—in front of a lobsterman's house. The car stood beside his skiff and dories, and it was seventy miles farther away from the Bonne Bay road than the new bridge! That Chevy owner, miles beyond my most northerly cabins at Castor's River, was a true believer. He was sure Joey Smallwood would be reelected and, with money from the federal government, would build a road right to his house.

So was I. Either I had to somehow ensure continued good fishing on the rivers we now used or I had to move my operation to Labrador.

Labrador was much like Newfoundland, but the distances were much greater and civilization was much, much farther away. The country was forested with smaller trees of fewer varieties. There were more spruce than fir and fewer birches, alders, and tamaracks. The extreme cold and the short growing season seemed to dwarf everything there except the rocks and the icebergs. With settlers and settlements so few and far apart, there'd be no lonely, individual settlers to provide safe, easy havens every dozen miles or so along the coast, places that we could fly into in case of sudden storms or fog.

With their continental drainage, the rivers were much bigger than those of Newfoundland. They could carry much larger runs of salmon with a great potential for fishing camps. Working out a way to get supplies in would be a problem, however. Still, a government steamer, the S.S. *Kyle*, made a three-hundred-mile journey along the coast a few times each summer. Freight could be off-loaded into barges or small boats and taken ashore. It all could be arranged if I found the right places for fishing camps.

So it was that Allan and I began to explore in earnest, often using his Cub, which we called the *Silver Blue*, after a fine salmon fly made up of a silver body, bright blue hackles, and gray teal feather wings. Those colors matched the blue and silver of the J3's body and the gray of its aluminum floats. We called the plane by that name when we didn't just refer to it as "the Cub."

On one journey we headed north to Hawke River, farther down the shore than I had ever pushed before. Allan was flying the *Silver Blue* alone, with a load of gas either to cache or to use for the return trip if we needed it. I flew the Pacer, and in it with me—besides several gas cans—was Manuel Caines, whose cousin, Ase Wentzell, lived on an offshore island twenty miles from the river mouth. Deer Island was a tiny piece of land measuring less than a dozen acres. It was one in a long chain of similar islets that stretched across the mouth of Hawke Bay. We landed in the lee and taxied into Ase's tiny harbor to tie up at his pier. Ase and his family lived on this little speck of land, lonely as a lighthouse on an offshore rock.

They were twenty-five miles from the nearest settler. Ase was a crusty man, they'd told me at Daniel's Harbour, where he had lived for a time. By contrast, we found his welcome warm and friendly. After greetings and tea and quickly made sandwiches, we unloaded a pair of twenty-gallon cans of gas for Ase to hold for our future needs. Then the three of us flew to the river in the Pacer, to check its salmon-fishing potential. The weather at Portland Creek had been dry for more than a week, and the water was low everywhere in the vicinity. Salmon rivers are easiest to check when they're low because the fish are crowded into a relatively small number of pools. But Ase warned us that our trip to the Hawke would be a waste of time. They'd had a week of downpours, he said, and the river would be in flood.

It was. We had to tie up to the alders when we taxied to shore at the first pool. The beach was three feet underwater. We were barely able to get out far enough to cast without going over our waders, but we spread out and tried. The flooding waters were dark as bitter tea, and we couldn't see the bottom, which made wading treacherous. Back at the camps, my guides often said that when the water was heavily peat stained the salmon didn't like its taste and hated to open their mouths to take a fly. One salmon did make a pass at Manny's pattern but missed. That was the only action in two hours. We gave up and flew back to Ase's.

He and his family put us up for the night. For dinner there was caribou meat that his wife had canned in jars the winter before. There were new potatoes under gravy, some turnip greens and carrots from his garden, and the same wonderful, homemade bread we loved at Portland Creek. At the end of the meal we had preserves made from the bakeapples they'd picked and put up the year before, along with raspberries fresh from the bushes on the island. Over everything was cream from the cow they kept.

Lying in bed that night under a warm down comforter I thought long on the Newfoundlanders who live in these lonely places. Ase had never learned to read and write. Chances were his kids wouldn't either unless he gave up his life of isolation and moved to one of the missions or to a place like Goose Bay to work in construction. But Ase had a wonderful world all his own. He knew what he needed to know in order to live in it and enjoy it. He had his nets and his boat and his guns. During the summer the pickup steamers came by to buy his catches of cod and salmon, and to bring news of interest.

In his boat Ase could travel to nearby settlements like the cluster of five houses at Square Island, forty miles distant, or the three at Holloway's Bight, thirty miles away. When weather was good he could reach Cartwright Mission, with its store and supplies. In the winter, using his dogs and sled, he could go over the ice into the back country to trap or to hunt caribou. They had said at Daniel's Harbour that when Ase went into the mountains with a group to hunt, he'd start out with the few things he needed in a light pack. But apparently before the trip was over he'd be helping out others with their loads and carrying the heaviest pack of all. Ase was a man of accomplishment and pride. I'm sure he envied no one.

For his children life would be different—just as it would be for him if he lived long enough. There would be other seaplanes coming along behind ours. There would be mining and logging, even though the trees of Labrador grew more slowly and were smaller. There would be large, efficient ships coming to reduce the rich bounty of cod in his little part of the sea. Ase's world, like that of the mountain men of the Rockies, would pass, and he and his wife—and all the isolated settlers like them—would pass with it. Joey Smallwood was already working on a decree that would force all those like Ase to move to towns where there were schools for their children. Then they would live in housing developments and buy aluminum skiffs instead of making their own cabins and boats from the roots and logs of their forests. They'd buy food instead of growing it or taking it from the sea, and they would eat store-bought bread instead of baking it. They'd move into the modern world, and this would be called progress.

The following day dawned bright and clear, with an August sun that warmed up the air. There was a light breeze coming in from the sea, and it was a beautiful day to fly. Ase said the other rivers in the area would be similarly high and difficult to judge for fishing. We were soon on our way back to Portland Creek.

There was a little haze far out to sea, and it gave a softness to the scene. There were icebergs drifting all along the shore. Inland the mountains were soft and green. I flew along the outer islands or followed the coast. It had become my pattern to stay within gliding range of land whenever possible.

The Pacer was faster than Allan's Cub, but if I throttled back we could fly along at almost the same speed. He ranged farther out from shore to see the icebergs better as we traveled. They were snow white with green fringes at the waterline in a sea of cool, arctic blue. I thought how beautiful his plane was, out over the iceberg-dotted sea that faded away to an almost indiscernible horizon. The Cub's color scheme fitted so well with the blue, blue sea. Having been an artist, I looked hard and long, etching the scene into my memory. Sometime, I thought, I will paint a picture of each of my airplanes, and this is the picture I want of Allan's. I took a few shots with the Leica.

As it always did when I flew, the thought came to me: What happens if I go down? Or Allan? On my first sea crossing I naively believed the Cub would survive any water landing. I knew now, however, that to go down in even a moderate sea meant almost certain doom for the plane and, most likely, for the pilot, too. I remembered again what Billy Bruce had said about those engines running forever. I was sure Allan felt that way, as well. But I knew they didn't.

Suppose the motor in the *Silver Blue* did stop, and he had to land in the sea. Could he ditch safely? If he got down and—as was likely—his floats crumpled under him, how long would he last? For me to go in beside him would be foolish. Allan's plane could land in a heavier sea than mine but not in the waves I saw below us. How long would it take for me to fly to Square Island and get a boat to come out? And how long would I be in the air guiding it to Allan? I wouldn't have gas enough. It would take too long. Allan would freeze in that icy water in short order. He was staying off-shore too far, too long.

Because Allan had no radio, I flew out beside him and motioned him to follow me back to my path, closer to shore. He did, and we flew on together. I knew it would be better to land on shore—even in the trees—than to go down in the cold sea with a breeze blowing the wreckage into the North Atlantic. I'd grown cautious and I wanted that caution in Allan, too.

We landed next in a pond in the flow of the Pinware River, near the Strait of Belle Isle. That might be where we'd need gas most if we were coming home from a long trip farther north. We hid a ten-gallon drum in the bushes on a narrow point, where we could both easily remember it and easily bring a plane ashore to pick it up.

We flew on southward toward Flower's Cove and its readily available gas, some forty miles away. We hadn't found a new site for a camp, but our fuel caches would make future trips a lot easier. We'd be able to range farther inland and worry less about head-winds on the way home. Twilight was coming, but we'd be back at Portland Creek before it was full dark. Barry would be waiting with eager eyes for the sight of the planes, and—as always—he'd be the first to hear us approach. We would tell him about the trip, and he'd give us a report on the doings at the camps and at Daniel's Harbour.

# THE FINAL SEASONS

∼

Our operation was progressing. A few planes were coming into the airstrip with fishermen. The catch-and-release program was working pretty well, and our fishing was holding up. Joey Smallwood had been reelected premier and had more money coming down from Ottawa. Memorial University, Newfoundland's first, was open in St. John's. The province needed roads, and Joey was obliging. One of them was under construction on the north side of Bonne Bay and was due to come north. When completed, it would bring an army of cars and trucks and people into my world and that of the hardy settlers who had previously known only ships and dog teams.

I made one last, desperate effort to save the fishing. I flew to St. John's and had a meeting with the top officials of the Department of Natural Resources, the Tourist Board, and the St. John's Sportsman's Club. My case was simple: Of the roughly two hundred salmon rivers on the island, only a few—those in the roadless areas—offered more than a ghost of their former fishing. The waters that were accessible by road or railroad had been devastated. It was obvious, I pointed out, that the present laws and enforcement did not preserve the salmon runs and only allowed anglers to finish off the great damage done by nets offshore. But at least when those diminished runs reached the rivers, they could be protected enough to be built back up when the commercial fishing on the high seas could be limited to a reasonable take.

But would officials change the old, failing rules and set up a better system? Would they even put catch-and-release restrictions on the rivers where the runs were barely surviving to make sure there were fish in those rivers for Newfoundlanders to catch? Would they try to save the remaining good rivers to ensure a continuance and an expansion of the flow of tourist dollars that I was bringing in?

The answer was—unequivocally—that they would not. I knew then that I had better sell my camps rather than watch their slow but inevitable deterioration. Perhaps a new owner would have more political clout than I did, and maybe he could gradually shift to Labrador, which had years and years of roadlessness ahead of it.

I knew the fishing in my corner of Newfoundland would remain fairly good for a few years. Salmon now swimming in the sea would be coming back to the rivers the next year and the year following. Parr now in the stream would be going to sea for the next three years and coming back a year or two or three later. There was still time to save the rivers we fished, and my heart was with them. My head, however, told me the operation had become a very poor gamble.

In 1954 the Great Lakes Carbon Company bought the camps. I stayed on to manage them for a while. The sixteen-fisherman capacity of the main camp at Portland Creek had to be boosted to thirty. We built a larger cookhouse right around the older one, demolishing the lesser building but keeping everything going as the new one went up around it. More cabins were built, and the outlying camps were expanded. The old icehouse was replaced by a walk-in cold room and generator-powered refrigerators.

There was also a major change in the flying. Great Lakes Carbon brought in two of the new Cessna 180 seaplanes, which surpassed all the other four-place ships in performance. The company had its own aviation department and its own pilots to fly the Cessnas. To bring in anglers, they had two DC3s and a PBY Catalina flying boat, which they piled up on the rocks in Big Pond at River of Ponds and left there for the insurance company. Two of the men who came down with the Cessnas had been test pilots for a major aviation company, and the third had just returned from a stint in Korea. They were fine when flying conventional aircraft under normal conditions, but in the bush they were like babes.

The Cessnas had radios, which—by that time—had become small enough and light enough to be carried in a four-place plane. The pilots could talk to each other, but there were no ground stations they could call for weather information or instructions in case of trouble. They had instruments that might have helped them fly in the clouds or in fog, but because there were no instruments on the ground to lead them in safely, these devices were useless in the bush. These pilots hadn't learned to sense when low clouds would develop by the look of the sky or the strength and direction of the winds to come. One of them had a problem getting back from the camp on the Main River—only twenty-five miles away—because he either didn't believe his compass or hadn't checked the landmarks on the way in. He came back long overdue and would never fly into that camp again.

The company's aviation division was under the supervision of a wartime navy pilot who instituted some special rules, such as insisting that everyone who got into a seaplane had to wear a Mae West life vest. He enforced this policy even when the plane was not flying over open sea but over land, with lots of lakes and ponds for safe landings, and even though the floats themselves were the best and most durable of life preservers imaginable. In fact, the Mae West rule led to an amusing incident when one of the pilots—getting out of his Cessna with a heavy duffel bag—accidentally pulled the string on his vest's $CO_2$ cartridge, inadvertently expanding it. He was stuck in the doorway until he could get help from inside the plane.

The Great Lakes pilots didn't like the bush and really didn't want to fly in it. Although, technically, they worked for me they continued to take orders from the top, and soon word came that they were only to fly between established camps and Lomond, Deer Lake, and Corner Brook. Even the Main River camp—only a hippity-hop away—was off limits for them. Between the accepted places, they would fly only when they thought the weather was good, which was entirely proper because a pilot must be responsible for his ship and its destiny. But that meant that the transportation of supplies and the mercy flights fell to Allan or me.

Since I was involved more and more with camp management due to the increased number of cabins and guests, Allan, who was then seventeen, had to do a lot of that flying. He was my mainstay and my best bush pilot. Most of the time he flew the Pacer, and I flew *Silver Blue*. Often, when I needed a pilot to fly to one of the permitted places, I'd turn first to the Great Lakes pilots, and they would refuse because of possible bad weather. Then I would ask Allan, and he would always go.

They would say, "Lee, this is no weather to fly in. You're sending that kid out to die."

I'd just smile. Allan would take off and come back. I never asked him to make a flight that I, myself, would not have undertaken.

On one occasion when a single guest wanted to go out by rail from Deer Lake to deal with sickness in his family, I turned first to the company pilots. The weather was fair, but deterioration was predicted. They refused to fly and, as usual, I turned to Allan. The guest had no qualms about flying with the skinny teenager, and the two of them took off in the Pacer.

Throughout the afternoon the weather did worsen. As we sat down to dinner I asked one of the fishermen who had been down near the mouth of the river how high the ceiling was. He replied that it had sort of settled in at about fifty feet. Where the camp was—at the running out—it was no higher than that. Over at their table the company pilots were speculating that "the kid had stayed over in Deer Lake" and were wishing that they could have been there for the dance that night. Then Barry shouted, "I hear him. That's Allan."

The fog was down to the tops of the spruces on the far side of the Home Pool. The motor sound intensified, then the red-and-yellow Pacer flashed by us, low over the water. Seconds later we heard the splash of his landing. One of the pilots said, "I'll be God damned!"

This was Allan's story of the flight: "When I left Deer Lake for the return, the ceiling was about a thousand feet, and the drizzle had started. It was getting toward evening, but I figured I could get home before dark or at least to some safe place along the way. I got to Rocky Harbor and then it began to close down, lower and lower. The ceiling was about four hundred feet at Cow Head, and I thought I could get on to Parson's Pond and stay overnight with the plane in the brackish water. When I got there, the ceiling was about a hundred feet high, but it didn't seem to be changing too fast and there was still light. I was fairly sure I could get right on through to Portland Creek. With a little luck I would see the telegraph wire at the mouth of the river and go under it.

"I knew that the shoreline was straight and that if I hung right over it I wouldn't hit Portland Head. It was tight, but the sea was smooth enough to land on and I could have taxied to the cove or the river mouth in a pinch. When I reached the cove, the ceiling went up a bit and at the tidal pool I could see the wire. I lifted over it, dropped low to the river, and knew that I was home."

# Taming the Wild Land

 ‿

That was my last year at the camps, and I had to figure out what to do with my life. Like everyone else, I guess, I thought of teaching school. I was fifty and hadn't had a steady job since working for Dupont Cellophane in 1933. When Charlie Cole, the president of Amherst College, was fishing at Portland Creek I'd talked to him about teaching, and he had advised against it. "The kids would love you, but your engineering degree wouldn't stack up against the degrees you'd need to get ahead and really enjoy it."

Then the Newfoundland Tourist Board asked me to make a film for them on bow hunting for moose and caribou. I jumped at the chance and decided, as I shot the footage, that I'd give up my writing and most of my lectures to concentrate on making the best outdoor films ever.

But in 1957 provincial officials skipped a year in their film program. And my former sponsor, Piper Aircraft, claimed hard times and had no budget for films. Without that sort of work I took on the task of selecting the best sites for the establishment of recreational fishing camps for military personnel near the Goose Bay Air Base in Labrador. It would be challenging work, with a lot of flying and exploration involved. I had the right plane, a new 150-horsepower Piper Super Cub, which I called *Lima Whiskey*—the call words for the letters at the end of my license number. I was sure, too, that I had the right experience for the job.

Flying down I had to cross a four-hundred-mile stretch of empty land that lies between Sept Isles on the north shore of the gulf, where the St. Lawrence River widens, and Goose Bay, on Hamilton Sound. Not a soul lived in that country except at Lake Eon, a radio beam station that sent out a signal I could not receive on my VHF set, which was designed for U.S. frequencies. Most of the land was far enough north to be beyond the timberline. It was made up of rocks and bogs and barrens, save for a few deep valleys where the big rivers flowed southward to the gulf. Flying across it I'd encountered strong headwinds from the east and had not been able to keep on course. I was burning up my limited but normally adequate supply of gas faster than I liked.

Looking down on each lake and run and matching it with the sketchy information on the maps I carried proved impossible. I was lost. There was an overcast, so I could not fly high enough to get a broad view of the land below me. The lakes I looked down on did not resemble any of the shapes I saw on the map. I could have set down on any pond and waited out the weather, but I had filed a flight plan. If I didn't show up at Goose on time they'd start looking for me, and I didn't want that. It wouldn't look good if the man coming down to find the best fishing couldn't even locate his home base!

After half an hour's uncertainty as to my position, I came to a major river and, following it, identified my position when it flowed into a large, long lake. I altered my course and made it to Goose before they started a search-and-rescue effort.

Goose Air Force Base sits on a great, level spread of gravel—the delta of the Hamilton River (now renamed the Churchill). Stationed there were some ten thousand U.S. troops, along with two thousand Canadians. Goose had all the radio frequencies—including VHF—and I could talk to them when I got within range. The tower directed me to the seaplane base on the Goose River, and I landed.

Bush flying was becoming much less hazardous than when I'd first arrived in Newfoundland in the *Yellow Bird*. Weather forecasts were improving in accuracy and availability. Radios were getting better, and there were more of them both in planes and at ground stations. The planes were getting better, too. The Super Cub I flew in was far superior to the old J3 Cub. The dependable old Norseman was being replaced by the DeHavilland Beaver, which came on the scene in 1950, and by the same company's new Otter, which could carry a dozen or more passengers. In fact, the air force had several Beavers and a shining new Otter moored at the seaplane base. A lone Norseman rode there, too, a charter ship for Wheeler Airlines. All of them were heavy, powerful planes that could easily weather high waves and northern gales.

My Super Cub seemed like a sparrow in a flock of eagles, and the pilots at Goose looked at it askance. Perhaps they'd all had bad bouts with the winds and were sure no such light plane could take what they'd been through. There was a sort of disbelief, a resistance to my being there. True, the base was the middle of a great, bleak wilderness area, but I'd already penetrated to within less than a hundred miles of it in the Pacer. So had Allan in his J3. My Super Cub 102LW was far tougher than either of those two ships.

This was wild country, but it was beautiful, too. Even in late summer there was snow on the Mealy Mountains just south of Lake Melville, which led to the open Atlantic. There was more bare rock showing than in Newfoundland and many more marks of recent glaciation. Among these were the eskers, those long, wormlike boulder ridges created when the water drained off in great veins beneath the deep layers of ice, piling up gravel and rocks—some of them as big as houses—along the deep glacial channels.

There were miles and miles of sparse spruce forests, where slender trees rose up in scattered patterns over the blanket of white reindeer lichen that covered the land wherever it was dry enough. Great areas of bog would turn a bright, new green in the spring, then a deeper green mixed with many colored flowers in the summer, and finally, red and gold with the arrival of fall. Icebergs sparkled like bright snowy jewels, sometimes kissing the dark green shores, sometimes stretching away in great white blankets over the wide, open North Atlantic.

The lakes could throw the sky's bright blue back from below more brilliantly, it seemed, than anywhere else because the air was so clear. Sometimes the fog crept in like the softest of blankets, covering everything with gray. Sometimes, too, the world was so dark in midafternoon that all one could see was dull and damp, and the wind spoke shrilly of Nature's power.

By contrast, the base was pure civilization. The officer's club and the noncom clubs were elegant. Famous entertainers were flown in frequently, and every effort was made to provide recreation for the otherwise unhappy personnel forced to be there. The nightclub acts were fine for the spectator types. But for the hunters there was nothing, because the Newfoundland-Labrador government allowed no hunting except by residents. For the fishermen, there were no opportunities close at hand.

The Hamilton River was big and muddy, and it discolored a great area where it spilled into the brackish water of Hamilton Sound. The Goose River, a small one, was usually muddy, too. The fishing in both was poor. To experience decent angling—the one good sport this bleak but sometimes beautiful country had to offer—one had to travel at least thirty miles from the base, and all of the productive water lay an airplane flight away. The Canadians had arrived in Labrador first, early in the war, and had staked out the premier fishing sites within easy flying range. I had to pick the best of what was left. Like the civilian scouts of the Western cavalry—men who knew the country and the Indians—I knew fishing and that type of country, so I'd been chosen for the job.

The air force already had one camp at No Name Lake, thirty-odd miles away. It was a good location on a narrow neck of land between two lakes. (I called them lakes although, of course, the Newfoundlanders called them ponds.) The trout there tended to drift into the short flows or "thoroughfares" between two bodies of water, in a concentration that made them much easier to catch than would have been the case out in the open water. The trout being caught at No Name were averaging about three pounds in weight.

Three-pounders are big brook trout, and I knew that the conditions under which they lived were well suited to good growth. That was an indication that the whole drainage should hold fish of a similar size. So I explored it and found another larger thoroughfare between two very big, shallow lakes. I dubbed it No-No Name and took the base's recreation officer there. The fishing was fantastic. The same big brook trout were present in even greater numbers.

Because of the tendency of this species to concentrate in such runs between lakes, they are very vulnerable. Consistent, heavy fishing in the thoroughfares will eliminate almost all the brook trout from the lakes. Those fish were wild and unsophisticated and easy to catch with the spinning gear the air force provided. I suggested to the recreation officer that he establish a two-fish-per-day limit on individual catches—even though the official government limit was fifteen fish. If hundreds of troops came through the camps in a season, even two trout a day for each of them could seriously cut down those magnificent stocks. I recommended that the men go further and release any fish they didn't actually need for food at the camp. I feared, however, that this was a forlorn hope and that most of the trout caught would go back to Goose for bragging or eating purposes.

A few days after I took the recreation officer into No-No Name, a general came through the base and wanted to fish for a day. The air force took him to the new spot, and he had superb fishing. When it was over, he took about *two hundred and fifty* of those big, beautiful trout back to Washington to make a splash with his fishing friends. Half a dozen catches like that, and there'd be few fish left for the troops. I appealed directly to the chief of staff, General Tommy White, who was an amateur ichthyologist and a fly fisherman. Fortunately, after that, the two-fish rule was enforced fairly well, and there were no more big killings. Still, I knew that I needed to find other productive waters.

One can tell a lot about the trout fishing in a given flow by observing its color from the air. I'd learned long before that where the water is very clear the trout will grow as large as anywhere else, but there won't be too many of them. The clear waters, usually flowing over granitic formations, are somewhat acidic and don't support the usual amount of trout food.

When the flow is very dark it carries too much peat and is far too acid to support the insect life and minnows that trout need for growth. By contrast, when the water is a certain pale brown the aquatic life flourishes, and so do the trout. Sixty miles west of Goose Bay there were two big, forested basins that were drained by flows that ran through a lot of relatively shallow lakes. I could see lily pads scattered in clusters all across the surface of those lakes and knew there would be a lot of trout food there. At this latitude the sun did not penetrate waters of much more than twelve feet deep and, so, was unable to give energy to bottom-growing plants which, in turn would have provided hiding places and food for trout.

*Lima Whiskey* purred smoothly as I flew over those pale brown ponds. After a good look for submerged rocks that might lie in my landing path I nosed down, knowing that I would cast the first fly ever to land on the waters of that valley. I came to shore at the outlet of one of the lakes.

Rod in hand I stood on the shore and looked over the water. Some big mayflies were coming to the surface in nymphal form, breaking free of their cases, drifting onward while their wings dried out, then flying away. That is, if the trout didn't eat them first. The fish were actively rising—every trout fisherman's dream. I had flown in with a streamer fly—a minnow imitation—tied to the end of my leader, but I took it off and replaced it with a Gray Wulff tied on a #8 hook. It was about the size and color of the hatching mayflies. I dressed it with line grease to ensure its floating performance and cast it out to one of the rising trout. He came up immediately but took a natural insect right beside the fly. I cast it back, and on that drift he rose and was hooked.

This trout was a solid fish and fought well. On my little spring scale he weighed just an ounce under five pounds. I decided to show that brookie to the recreation officer. I caught more, putting back all the smaller ones but keeping two that were more than six pounds apiece. Taking off and landing at two other lake outlets in those valleys, I found the trout in both of them to be about the same size. And I discovered something else: there were northern pike in most of those northern lakes. I moved away from one outlet, walked along the shore, and caught several pike on a streamer fly with a wire trace ahead of it to withstand the northerns' sharp teeth. There were lots of small minnows for the pike to feed on close to shore and clouds of scuds and other aquatic insects for the trout.

When I was ready to leave, the sun was low, and the wind had dropped out completely. My 150 horses lifted me swiftly from the glassy water. A great wild area lay below me. No one was within fifty miles of where I sat in the sky and looked down on those fabulous ponds, as still as mirrors in the evening light. Their surfaces were broken here and there by a swimming loon or a beaver or a flock of mergansers. Everywhere trout were rising and making tiny dimples. I'd flown over this phenomenon before, but this time the trout were huge. I had a full five-pound average in the fish I'd caught, and that—for brook trout—was phenomenal. I had discovered a trout fisherman's paradise, a place with clouds of mayflies and big, hungry brookies to feed on them. It deserved to be ranked as one of the finest trout fishing areas of all time.

I soon went back to the valley, taking with me the recreational officer. He decided, however, that it would be simpler to put more air force camps in the galaxy of lakes in the upper Eagle River drainage (where No Name and No-No Name were) than to operate a more distant camp in one of these Minipi valleys. I knew that I, for one, would later return with both fishing tackle and movie cameras. I wanted to get these great places on film, even though—at the time—there was no real market for fishing movies.

Years afterward I would find an angel, Bob Albee, who—with one of my guides—set up a fishing camp at Minipi when the U.S. forces were pulling out. He instituted a rule of only one fish per week per angler, a trout to be taken home and mounted. That stiff restriction broke with the local tradition of taking all the fish you could before someone else got there to catch them. It started a trend because Bob's customers were so well pleased while the other camps with diminishing runs were having problems getting customers. As I write this in 1990, I've had word that a friend, Dave Brandt, went to Minipi last year and came back with photos to prove that he'd caught a trout of eight and a half pounds and that his companion had taken one of more than nine pounds.

Such foresight and its attendant results were rare in Labrador and Newfoundland. I knew from the outset that the camps set up for the troops in the Upper Eagle drainage would produce lots of trout for quite a while. Then, when the anglers from the base reduced the stocks of brookies, they'd turn to pike. Because the northerns were spread out all over the lakes, I was sure that they would survive the fishing pressure for a long, long time.

I turned my attention to finding a place where the air force brass and their guests could be certain of catching salmon.

# SEARCHING FOR SALMON

⁓

In establishing a salmon camp for the VIPs and officers I'd need a place like the falls of the Eagle River, down near its mouth at Sandwich Bay. The Canadian camp there, a hundred miles away to the east, was on a unique and magnificent salmon pool. Thousands of fish came to lie in the quarter-mile stretch below the falls in that great river. Because it was just across the bay from the Cartwright Grenfell Mission, it had enjoyed more protection from poaching than the other, more remote rivers. The fishing was done mainly from boats, and there was room for as many as twelve anglers at one time. Each of them might catch as many as a dozen salmon or more in a day. Most would be four- to five-pounders, with a few ten- to fifteen-pounders thrown in.

There was no other such concentration of salmon anywhere else in Labrador. The best I could hope to do was find a lesser river where perhaps eight or ten anglers could find fishing from a single camp. It would have to be farther away from the base because the flows that still had good runs terminated in the Atlantic Ocean. I had a lot of country to cover.

Cover it I did, and the flying was a never-ending source of pleasure. I wanted to be so good at it that I could draw from *Lima Whiskey* every bit of performance she could give. I would just brush the trees coming in to land on the small ponds. I would try to touch the water precisely at a particular spot near a water lily or floating log. I would fly the shores of the lakes in river drainages as I had in learning to fly over Saratoga Lake, bending my course to match the contours of the shore and staying equidistant as I looked for the inlets and outlets. I did all these things for fun when I was flying alone on scouting trips.

Most of all I loved to fly low over the rivers. They offered wonderful, twisting air lanes that hugged the ground, were nearly level, and remained open ended, with never a telephone or telegraph line to worry about. If I came to a sudden turn that was too sharp for *Lima Whiskey* to follow, I always had the speed and climb potential to lift up over the trees until the course of the flow straightened out again. This was wonderful wilderness and, more than anyone else's, it was mine.

The rivers along the Labrador coast had long been abused. Some enterprising but shortsighted individuals had long since discovered each of them and, during the two-week peak of the salmon runs, had stretched a net across the river mouth from one bank to the other. Such netting took practically every fish that entered the river. The fisherman could then take them out to the S.S. *Blue Peter,* the vessel that would ice them down and carry them away to market. Of course all this was illegal, but with only two Newfoundland rangers to police and manage 110,000 square miles of territory, the law relied on the honor system, and enforcement was just about nonexistent.

The size of the mesh of the gillnets the poachers used determined the size of the salmon they'd catch. If the mesh opening was too small a big salmon, driving into it, would not penetrate far enough to have the twine catch in his gills and hold him securely, thus preventing him from backing out and swimming away. On the other hand, if the mesh was big enough to catch the largest salmon then many of the small fish—those with just one year of feeding at sea—could pass through the nets and swim on to the spawning grounds. Since the big fish brought a better price pound for pound, the poachers used large mesh. As a result of this artificial selection the small fish that reached the spawning grounds created more small fish, and eventually most of the large salmon were eliminated from the runs.

With the arrival of airplanes at Goose Bay—and pilots who could look down on the illegal netters from the sky—the poaching became more discreet and was reduced for the most part to a nighttime operation. The runs that had been devastated were slowly coming back, but they were still made up almost entirely of small salmon.

As a first step in my efforts to establish a salmon camp for the U.S. Air Force, I wanted the recreation officer at the base to know just how good the Canadian facility on the Eagle River really was. I thought that he should understand what sort of facility they had because some of our future U.S. guests would have visited Eagle River, too. So, I wangled an invitation from the Canadians to come and fish at the falls. I carried my usual more-than-adequate anchor ready below my seat in case the plane's motor failed. I picked out a stretch of water between the rocks and the main salmon runs in the flow just below the falls but above the rocky white-water chute that drained the pool. To the amazement of those on shore I landed safely and taxied to the dock. The camp's larger Beavers had to land two miles upstream, where their passengers were picked up in a carryall and driven to the camp.

I wanted to make sure my hosts knew that my landing hadn't scared all the salmon out of the pool, so as soon as I could we took a boat to the area I'd landed on and caught some salmon. In fact, we hooked and released more than twenty fish before the lunch gong rang. The recreation officer wasn't a salmon fisherman, but because those fish were fresh-run and unwary, he caught his share.

The Canadian VIP camp was simple, a relic of its beginnings in the war days. The cabins were nowhere near as plush as the trailerlike buildings the U. S. government was putting up for its troops. We lunched with two Canadian generals and then, at their urging, went out again to catch another bunch of fish, most of them four- to five-pounders. The recreation officer was beginning to like salmon fishing.

In the weeks following our visit, I found one promising wild river, which ran into the Atlantic some thirty miles beyond the Eagle. There were two good-sized lakes in its flow for Beavers or Otters to land in, along with four or five smaller "steadies" that I could get into and out of with my Super Cub. Near one of the lakes there were a dozen pools where anglers could fish. As in the Eagle, the salmon ran small, with very few in the ten-pound class or over. This fishing couldn't compare with that just over the mountains at the Canadian camp with its far greater flow and thousands more fish. Where was the supreme salmon fishing spot that continued to elude us?

As I moved north along the Atlantic coast in my search I discovered that the fish were of slightly larger average size. I found the biggest ones of all in the most northerly rivers, just before the water became too cold for salmon and was taken over by the Arctic char—a fish better able to stand the cold. At the northern end of salmon territory there were fewer "foreign" fish, individuals that were bound for rivers in other provinces. There were also fewer nets set to catch them. That gave the big fish native to these far northern rivers a better chance to survive. Ase's nets, for example, were set to catch the salmon that were merely passing by his house—not those of the Hawke, just twenty miles away. Someone had probably all but eliminated that run long before.

I found the Adlatok to be the best of the northern rivers. It had a majestic flow for its last mile and a half, and there were some good pools throughout that stretch. It was an unusual river in that it forked just before it reached the salt water. The largest flow in the fork, called the Ujitok, had a twenty-eight-foot falls just before the river emptied into the sea, cataracts the salmon could not climb. The lesser branch, still called the Adlatok, dropped to the sea through a mile-and-a-half-long gorge. At the very head of this canyon, there was a falls that the salmon *could* swim through under certain low-water conditions.

Throughout the river's swift flow from there to the sea were deep, dramatic, rock-faced pools. They were filled with salmon from the time the run entered in late July until the water dropped to the critical level that let the salmon worm their way up through the white-foamed falls, a time that came in early September. Once above the falls the fish spread out in a lazy flow of 130 miles that terminated at the river's source. Nowhere in that long stretch could I find any pools that would make setting up a camp worthwhile.

Air Force Chief of Staff Thomas White, himself a fly fisherman, came to Goose before the final VIP camp decision was made. He wanted to see the Adlatok, so our little group flew up in two planes—an air force Beaver and mine. General White elected to fly with me, and it was a signal honor to have him riding in the back seat of *Lima Whiskey.* There had been the usual remarks about sudden gales blowing me over, but by that time it was more in good humor since the winds hadn't yet flipped my plane in two months of flying in Labrador.

There were salmon in all the pools along that mile and a half of the Adlatok. I took the general to the place I liked best, where the river poured over a narrow lip into a big basin and swung around in a great, slow eddy before emptying into a hundred-foot race of fast water and flowing on into another pool. It was there on one of my exploratory trips that I watched the biggest salmon I'd seen that summer follow my fly on a long retrieve. He was clearly visible forty feet away in the transparent water, inches behind my fly but not making a move to take it. As I brought it closer and closer I was sure he'd see me and turn away. Should I speed up the fly? Slow it down? The fish just continued its slow swim, following the fly toward me. I had to stop the retrieve at the rock ledge beneath my feet. At that point the great salmon turned leisurely away to disappear in the deep, curling waters. I continued fishing for an hour and a half until approaching darkness sent me back to my plane for the return flight to Goose. Two other, lesser salmon had taken my fly, but that big one never showed again.

On the day the general fished that pool, some salmon were leaping in the wide, slow sweep, a few big ones among them. He caught two, one a twenty-pounder. As we worked our way down the river toward the bay he caught another we judged to weigh nineteen pounds. Then it was time to move on. I knew the river had impressed him and, later on, it was the one chosen for the Top Brass Camp.

Flying back in clear skies, General White studied the map and the land under us. Over the Makkovic River he leaned forward to touch my shoulder and ask, pointing down, "Are there any salmon there?" I nodded. Then he asked if we could land there and when I nodded again, he pointed a finger downward. I put down in a long, slow pool not far above tide head, a place where I'd caught fish in my earlier scouting. Because of my plane's shallow draft I landed without trouble, but the Beaver had to go on to the bay and wait for us there.

The general caught a beautiful, twelve-pound male and lost another salmon just as large. I suggested a snack and at his nod I brought out a can of peaches, some cookies, and a thermos of tea from one of the float compartments. We sat on the floats beside the pool and talked.

The name Makkovic was one the general knew, and he proceeded to tell me a story. During the war an air force C47 coming back from Europe had missed Goose Bay in a snowstorm and had run out of fuel. They ditched successfully in the snow about twenty miles from where we sat. It was midwinter. The crew's instructions were to stay with the ship in case of a forced landing because the search planes would find them; they were told not to go barging off into a hostile environment. The men were beyond radio contact but kept believing the search planes would find them. Sadly, they weren't discovered until several years later, when a group of local hunters going into the hills for caribou stumbled across the plane.

The crew had kept a diary. It had taken more than a month for the last of the men to die. Had one of them climbed the highest hilltop a few miles to the east, he could have seen the lights of Makkovic.

The weather must have been bitter cold. The airmen were probably city boys, fearful of the wilderness. The crew wouldn't have known how to fashion makeshift snowshoes. They wouldn't have realized that they should send two men out while they still had supplies, to follow the nearest flow of water to a settlement or to the sea. It was a sad story, and I pondered it as we flew back to Goose. How lucky I was to love that wild land and feel at home in it.

It wasn't until I had completed my work and flown home to Shushan that I heard another, similarly sad story. A good many air force bases have flying clubs. In the beginning, Goose did not because the large seaplanes they felt necessary for safety in their area were too expensive for a flying club to manage. But a plane like mine, bought secondhand, would cost only a few thousand dollars. After I left Labrador that summer—and perhaps because of my safety record in a light plane—a flying club was formed at the base. They bought an Aeronca C7 with a sixty-five-horsepower motor, a float plane much like my first J3 Cub. It was back in the States, and a Lieutenant Caton went out to fly it back to Goose.

Caton took off from Sept Isles on the four-hundred-mile flight to Goose with enough gas to get him through. He was alone. The weather was good, but he failed to complete his flight plan. The search that was started immediately was soon hindered by rain and low clouds. A few days later rescuers found the plane, intact, where he had landed it in the St. Augustine River, almost out of gas. The distance from Sept Isles to that spot was almost the same as that from Sept Isles to Goose. On the day of Caton's flight, there were no strong winds that could have blown him so far off course. In that area of Labrador, near the Earth's magnetic pole, the compass variation is about thirty degrees westerly. Failing to allow for that would have put Caton somewhere near the spot where he landed the plane. Had he failed to set up the proper course?

Ironically, he landed the plane safely in the river and moored it there. Caton then found a canoe and started down the river in it when he capsized and drowned. His body and the banged-up canoe were eventually found downstream.

It would be three years before a local contractor named Miller—from Northwest River, site of the Grenfell Mission close to Goose Bay—bought a Super Cub float plane like mine and flew it safely in the area. And it was two more years before Gordon Rezac, who was a teenager that year, got a Cessna on floats and based it at Goose Bay. More light planes followed. The country was overdue to be opened up. Small, light radios and better weather forecasting would make everything easier. Trout and salmon camps would be established on the wild rivers. Labrador would not long remain the lonely country that I looked down on and felt was all mine, to land on and fish where no one else had ever fished before.

# THE TROUT FILM

❧

Not long afterward, a sportswear manufacturer approached me about making a film to show off his clothing line. He wanted a dramatic setting with action that would draw *oohs* and *ahs* from outdoor audiences. I convinced him that the big brookies of Labrador would do the job. I decided to shoot the footage in the upper Eagle River drainage, where it would be simple to set up a bush camp. When that promotion was finished I wanted to get over to Minipi to document that marvelous fishing in a film I hoped to sell to the Newfoundland Tourist Board.

John Crook of Allied Aviation had set up the camp for us on Double Eagle Lake. He had flown in the guides, the cook, the cameramen, and the sound man. It was a tent camp, but John had gone to great lengths to make it comfortable. He'd flown in some fine Alberta steaks, along with wines, cognac, and liqueurs to add sparkle to the meals. The star of the film, Jack Rose, flew in with me. Jack was a writer and occasional actor who loved trout fishing but had recently had a heart attack. He was a longtime friend of the sponsor and insisted that he could manage the rigors of outdoor camping. The sponsor, however, was worried and wanted to be sure Jack wasn't put under any stress. He gave me complete, detailed, written instructions on what to do if his star's heart acted up while on location. These dos and don'ts were complicated and at first reading left me quite confused. I planned to go over them again as soon as I had time. I'd had very little experience with sickness and medicines, and I dreaded the thought of Jack's having a second heart attack and depending on me to nurse him through it.

When he arrived at the Goose Bay seaplane dock, Jack appeared to be hale and hearty. He peered into my little Super Cub and smiled. His look took in my small fly rod—ready to go on its hangers on the left side of the tandem cabin—and the flies that were stuck in the fabric here and there. Jack said, "This plane smells of happiness." His bush clothes were beautiful, his eyes sparkled, and I liked him immediately. I knew that he'd be good in the film.

We were blessed with good weather, and the filming went well. In four days the job was just about finished. I had all the essentials but still needed to polish up the footage with "beauty shots" and fill last-minute gaps for one more day. The local cook from Goose Bay whom John had hired had turned out good, substantial meals. The sleeping bags, set on layers of springy spruce-bough tips, were comfortable and fragrant. We'd seen eagles and otters, and we had listened to loons. A bear had come to the garbage pit one night— but quietly—and we'd slept right through it. Everything went beautifully until that fifth afternoon when Jack walked back into the cook tent just before our evening meal.

What he saw there appalled him. There was a swarm of big, black flies buzzing around and occasionally landing on the food. He came back to the main tent pale and looking as if he needed to throw up. He said, "I've got to get out of here."

I looked at the sky and didn't like it. There were only a couple of hours of daylight left, and Goose was fifty miles away.

Jack just said, over and over, "I've got to get out of here."

Reluctantly I gave in. "Okay, but we'd better hurry."

I kept wishing he'd *really* hurry. But he didn't just grab things and stow them in a bag. He packed his fishing gear and clothes neatly. Then he put in the hairbrushes and pajamas. Finally the overnight case was ready, and Jack climbed into the back of *Lima Whiskey.* The clouds were lowering.

We were deep in the great, broad, Eagle River valley, and I had to fly back across some of the upper lakes to find the Kenamu River, which led down from the high ground to Hamilton Sound. Rain was starting. Passing over the last lake before flying on into the steep forested area I had a strong urge to turn back. Then, with early dark approaching swiftly, I realized that I might not be able to make it to the camp and would have to set the plane down on a lonely pond to spend the night, the two of us cooped up in a small tandem aircraft with no way to be comfortable and rain pouring down outside. How would we fare then? Goose Bay was closer. I went on over the forest and the height of land.

I found the brook that led down to the valley of the Kenamu, and with its white tumbling water under me I breathed a sigh of relief. Once I reached the main flow—even with the very low cloud ceiling—I would be able to fly just over the river and come out on Hamilton Sound, about fifteen miles from Goose. I stole a look at my star in the seat behind me. He looked okay. With the engine throttled back and half flaps I slowed to about fifty miles an hour and dropped low over the brook to follow its foam-covered boulders to the Kenamu. The water there would be just as rough as in the feeder stream, but I was sure the fog would not be right down to the rocks.

The first bolt of lightning sounded as if it had hit a tree just beside us. It blinded me momentarily, and I couldn't see what was ahead. My vision returned just in time to allow me to avoid the trees and follow the curving of the river. Heavy rain flashed down with the lightning. I put my head outside the window to see because the windshield was opaque with the battering rain. We barely missed trees, first on one side, then the other. My vision was blurred, but I thought, gratefully, thank God I don't wear glasses. Night was closing down prematurely, and the clouds were just above us. The trees were at our wingtips. I dared not look back at Jack, but I heard no sound to indicate a crisis.

Slowly the valley widened and leveled off. At last I could see the lights of Goose Bay shining to us from under the clouds, fifteen miles away. The thunderstorm was over, and the water beneath us was calm. We were minutes away from the Goose "Hilton" and a good, warm meal.

As we got out of the plane Jack said, "That was damn touchy back there, wasn't it?"

I felt like saying, "Oh no. Just routine." Instead I nodded and replied, "Sure was," as I turned to walk into the flight office to call a cab.

I had figured it wouldn't be worthwhile to tell Jack that, while the flies in civilization are likely to carry the germs of all the world's ills, those in the wilderness have nothing on them but the pollen and sterile dust from the leaves, flowers, rocks, and branches they lit on. They couldn't have given him any diseases, but Jack wouldn't have believed me. I hoped he wouldn't walk into the kitchen of the "Hilton," where there might be some flies, too, and the danger of contaminated food had to be far greater. The dinner and the overnight went well. Next morning Jack flew happily home, and I returned to the camp to pick up my cameraman and head for the Minipi.

The film was a great success.

# A Last Long Look

In 1959 I had six weeks of free time in the summer. The New-foundland Tourist Board commissioned me to survey all of the trout and salmon rivers in Labrador and then to make recommendations on how they could best be used in developing tourism. It would give me one more long look at the wild country before the rest of the world moved in.

I based at Goose again. From there I ranged as far south as the Pinware, at the Strait of Belle Isle, and north to the char and Inuit country at Nain. There were still very few other light planes in the area, and I could still fly into river pools and small, shallow ponds where larger aircraft could not follow. I still had the wonderful feeling that this great area was mine more than anyone else's, that its secret places were mine alone to cherish and enjoy.

Something that had happened long before was a great help to me in my summer of work. On my first flight back to the States from Portland Creek in the *Yellow Bird* I'd flown over the Outer Bald Island Rip at Wedgeport, Nova Scotia, and looked down at the boats and the baits of the sportfishermen trolling for tuna. Since I recognized some of these vessels and knew their captains I waved to them even though they couldn't know who I was. Then I saw three big bluefin cruising along on the surface. I swung toward them for a closer look and, as I did, the shadow of the plane fell on those fish. Instantly there was a great splash, and the tuna dove out of sight.

Flying on to Maine, I thought about this incident. There was no reason why those monsters of the sea—weighing upward of five

219

hundred pounds apiece—should fear my shadow. No bird that ever lived could have lifted so large a fish from the water and carried it off. Yet, the tuna had been frightened—and badly. Perhaps it was an ingrained fear or a memory from their days as small fry, when a frigate bird or a gannet could have struck down and lifted them from the ocean.

This experience told me that salmon—still small enough to be preyed upon by eagles and fish hawks—would have an even greater fear of shadows from the sky.

Before I learned to fly, finding out about the salmon-fishing potential of a wilderness river meant hiking in overland, or going in by canoe and portaging to the pools. Then I had to spend days fishing there and—given the number of fish I raised and caught—writing a report on what I thought the angling potential was. It was a long and time-consuming process of limited accuracy. While I had certainly enjoyed it, from the moment I took to the air I was working more efficiently.

I could fly over the pools on a sunny afternoon at about two hundred feet or less and throw the shadow of the plane onto the water. Unless the flow was dark from the peat stain of recent rains I could look down and see every salmon in the pool because they'd move in fear and show themselves. I'd see either the fish or the shadows they made on the streambed and could get a rough count and make an estimate as to their general size.

When I first flew over the Big River on my survey that year, the sky was overcast. So I landed at the head of the long, narrow, salt-water channel to fish the sea pool. It was small, but just above it was a long, deep pool that looked like an excellent one to test out. Dave Burchinal was with me. We beached *Lima Whiskey* and started to cast, Dave at the spot where the water poured over some rocks to reach the sea and I in the deep, faster flow above him. This was a big river, true to its name. We could barely reach the deep, mysterious flow of the central channel where the fish should be lying. Soon Dave was fast to a salmon, and I reeled in and went down to watch. He brought in a bright twelve-pounder.

I went back to my spot farther up in the run and began to cast again. Suddenly, out of the corner of my eye, I saw a great, dark shape roll to the surface in a half leap, just above where I was casting my fly. It disappeared as swiftly as it had come. No salmon could be so enormous. No shark or tuna would swim up into a salmon river, and this animal was too big to be an otter. Finally I decided it must have been a seal that was catching a breath as it swam past us to reach the long, quiet pool above.

I knew how much the presence of seals could frighten salmon. Occasionally they had shown up in the Camp Pool at Portland Creek, for a pair of them raised a brood each year at the outlet of the deep inner pond. When they came to our pool they terrified the salmon. The fish would almost beach themselves to avoid being caught and eaten. They'd lie alongside rocks with the tips of their tails and dorsal fins showing.

I signaled to Dave, and we walked upstream.

As we approached the long, still pool we saw seals splashing into the water from the shore. They swam with their eyes just above the surface—like periscopes— for a short run before submerging again. I knew any fish in that pool would be badly frightened. I realized, too, that we were a long way from any settlement, or someone would have come over to shoot them and send their noses to St. John's for the fifteen-dollar bounty each one would bring. The Big River had to be one of the last salmon rivers to be seriously bothered by seals. As soon as someone from along that shore discovered them, they'd die.

The animals were wary and kept their heads up for only the briefest of looks. They may have been shot at in some other rivers or bays along the coast. They slipped out through the fast water without showing themselves. Soon there were no more black heads popping up for quick looks at us.

To pass a little time we walked back to the plane to get lunch. It was cool under the overcast. I built a fire, and we had hot soup and hot coffee along with the other things I carried in the floats. A flock of sea ducks flew by. A mother mink came along over the rocks, dove into the pool, and—coming out with a parr in her mouth—disappeared into the alders. A Canada jay sat on a nearby branch, waiting for us to leave so he could pick up the crumbs. I tossed him some pieces of bread, and he ate them but wouldn't take one from my hand.

When we returned to the upper run where the seals had been, it was quiet. We cast our flies and, with the danger gone, began catching sea trout. A big run of fish had just come in, probably drawing the seals behind them. They were a pearly gray and silver instead of having the usual green tone to their backs. These trout were strong, beautiful fish that averaged about four pounds. We caught and released them till we were tired of it. We neither raised nor saw any salmon, and I knew I'd have to come back again on a sunny day when I could look over not only that pool but the pools above, where the seals would not have driven the salmon out.

I covered all the Labrador rivers of any real potential that summer—a much wider survey than I'd made for the air force. It meant some lonely nights in a sleeping bag beside whispering rivers and lots of notes on how best to draw in tourists. Along with the other recommendations in my report I suggested that the Newfoundland government set aside a ten-square-mile section of Labrador's 110,000 square miles—in one of the fine trout areas like Minipi—as a sanctuary that would remain forever wild. Then it would show how well Nature, when left alone, can provide waters filled with big trout. It would always be there as a comparison for present management and would provide a challenge for all future managers of similar waters. Perhaps that's one of the reasons why the proposal wasn't accepted. If there were no such comparison, officials could always say they were doing a superb job.

My second suggestion was that the government take some of the best big breeding stock and transfer the trout to some of the small, spring-fed ponds in the city of St. John's. Under a catch-and-release program in those waters the people of the provincial capital would come to realize that catching big fish would be possible for everyone if they'd only keep putting them back. That idea, too, failed to gain serious consideration.

By 1962 I no longer had any time to fly in the bush. I'd made a film at Minipi called *Three Trout to Dream About,* in which I put three flies on my leader and in a single cast caught three big brook trout that had a total weight of about seventeen pounds. In 1960 this footage was aired on *CBS Sports Spectacular* and became the first fishing film ever to appear on network television. From that time on I was busy producing outdoor films, work that took me to many wonderful places like Africa and South America, with stars like Jack Nicklaus, Peter Duchin, and Cale Yarborough. It was an exciting life.

My wild, northern world was no longer wild. It was being tamed, never to be the same again. Fishing camps were being set up in all the good places, and they were being equipped with radios to contact the outside world and the ever-growing fleet of seaplanes ferrying in adventurous anglers. Gas was available a short flight from anywhere. Soon there would be no place in the whole region where another float plane or helicopter might not drop in to share your fishing.

The memories of the *Yellow Bird* and the era of my life she ushered in will always be with me, for it was a time when my plane and I were one, when the world I flew over seemed to belong to me. I still remember the beauty of that wild flying: the early spring, when the cold-footed gulls stood on pans of ice and watched my plane go by, and the color of fall, when the ice threw back diamonds of light from the freshets in bogs that were gold with marsh grass, red with the leaves of the blueberry bushes, and still green from the mossy eyelids of the tiny bits of water. I remember, too, the heavy-antlered moose and graceful caribou, trotting along their trails.

I have endless recollections of a world of air and sea, of evergreen forests and blue lakes lying quietly in the sun. It was a place that had beckoned with beauty and promise, but also challenged with unsuspected dangers. This world had led me into the filmmaking that finally took me away from it, a world that no longer existed. Yet it is still there with me when I walk down to the meadow just below our house and climb into *Lima Whiskey,* warm her up, then lift up into the Catskill skies. There I fly again and dream of the Adlatok and the Minipi and all the other rivers my plane and I once knew so well.

# Epilogue

∾

The year was 1983. It had been a long time since I'd been back to Newfoundland and even longer since I'd gone there in the winter to work on the films for the Signal Corps and the Bowater Pulp and Paper Company. Over the years my work in conservation had continued. One of my titles was chairman of the board, Atlantic Salmon Federation of Canada—a signal honor for an American at a time when Canadian nationalism was running strong.

We, the anglers, needed to organize for our fight to secure the future of the Atlantic salmon. Only fragmented groups existed, and they had not started to work in unison. No representatives from other clubs had ever come to our annual meetings in Montreal. I decided to remedy that by donating my time for a lecture trip through the maritime provinces, where most of the unorganized clubs were. Joan, my wife of sixteen years, a former longtime fly-casting champion, and a leading American woman angler, gave her time, too. On that cold February trip we donated performances for which the local clubs charged admission. After each of the shows I went to the club officers and suggested that, in as much as we'd helped them make some money, we expected them to do something for salmon conservation. We wanted them to send a representative to our Montreal dinner meeting and join us in a federation council that would include all the salmon fishermen on the North American continent.

When April and the Montreal meeting rolled around there were delegates from other salmon organizations for the first time—

thirteen of them. A council was, in fact, formed and within a year its membership—counting all the clubs—numbered some ninety thousand. A year later, when more fishing groups and the Canadian Wildlife Federation joined, our total membership jumped to roughly half a million. We were on the way to political clout in Canada, which holds 99 percent of the continent's remaining salmon stocks.

The First Federation Field Conclave was held at Corner Brook in July 1985. Joan and I were the sponsors. The event was a success, bringing hundreds of salmon fishermen together and highlighting—through the publicity it generated—both the salmon's problems and some of the possible solutions.

When the meeting was over we stayed on for a few days to fish at the invitation of old friends, Arthur and Ida Lundrigan. I knew that Newfoundland's salmon stocks had deteriorated almost beyond belief and that there was no hope of finding anything like the fishing of the "old days." However, Arthur had a helicopter, and he planned to fly us to my former home waters. He wanted to show me one of the old cabins he'd bought from the owners of my former camp when they sold out. "Just a brief visit," he said. "I know you'll love to see it."

For three days we fished those wonderful, well-remembered pools. Under very low clouds we reached Big Bluie and landed at the inlet pool, where—long ago—I'd seen that long, black ledge disintegrate into hundreds of living, moving salmon. We spotted only two small fish. There was a warden in a shack on the beach beside the flow. There were also three fishermen, and that morning had brought them only one small grilse. The warden reported that not one salmon of more than five pounds had been caught in the upper river for the past five years. Logging roads crisscrossed the area, and there were lots of anglers. Unemployment was around 40 percent.

We fished and fished. We drifted flies where Allan had caught his twenty-three-pounder. We worked the Infant's Pool and didn't get a rise. In all of our time Joan caught two small grilse, and Arthur and I each took one. None of these fish weighed as much as four pounds. Each evening we returned to the old cabin. There, on the old plank door, were the outlines of two great fish, one weighing thirty-three pounds, the other slightly less.

How could it have happened? I used to tell the Newfoundlanders they had a gold mine in the salmon rivers but that they wouldn't pay a pittance to have a watchman save any of that gold for their kids. Once, in 1970, when I went down to work on a hunting film with Jacques Bergerac for ABC's *American Sportsman,* I ran into Hal House, a merchant I'd known from the early days. He shook his head and said, "The salmon are going fast, Lee. You were ahead of your time."

My reply was, "It's your country, not mine, Hal. It's your people that were behind the times. I was only trying to help us all."

Finally, though, good things were beginning to happen, albeit slowly. The kind of catch-and-release program I'd pioneered and been ridiculed for in Newfoundland was put into use by the Nova Scotia Fish and Game Department on the Margaree River—the first official admission that putting back salmon made sense. Next the program of releasing all large, angler-caught salmon was instituted in New Brunswick, then in Nova Scotia, and, finally, in Newfoundland. Although they were the main cause of the problem all along, commercial nets were still killing all the big salmon they captured.

As I write this, the Atlantic salmon are on the verge of salvation. Like the wild turkeys and the antelopes and all the living things that sportsmen love, they will—in a final effort—be saved and brought back. Although my own efforts were a record of failure, I am glad to have helped and to have lived long enough to know that someday, perhaps many years away, there will be great salmon swimming again in those beautiful pools of the upper River of Ponds and in all the waters I loved. Though they are now devastated and barren, these rivers still run reasonably cool and clean. The work of those who care will one day restore their Atlantic salmon.

# LEE'S LEGACY

*by Joan Salvato Wulff*

IN 1990, FOR HIS BOOK *SALMON ON A FLY*, LEE WROTE a first chapter in which he presented the "God of Angling's" thoughts on the Atlantic salmon. An excerpt:

> *He'll be my masterpiece among all sporting fish, this Atlantic salmon of mine. I hope the anglers of the world will love him above all others, cherish him, and challenge him but never forsake him, using all their powers to save him from any and all other predators in sea and stream, and to keep his spawning rivers ever bright and clean.*

Until the day he died in April of 1991, Lee fought valiantly to have the Atlantic salmon of the North American continent designated as "game fish," seemingly to no avail. However, in 1992, then Federal Minister of Fisheries John C. Crosby, declared a moratorium on Newfoundland's commercial salmon fishery. Canada closed its last remaining commercial fisheries at Quebec and Labrador in 1998, under the leadership of Minister David Anderson.

This action has led to the North Atlantic Salmon Conservation Organization's (NASCO's) success in negotiating lower quotas for the subsistence fishery in Greenland. It is in those waters that most North American salmon spend their ocean feeding time. The Atlantic Salmon Federation (ASF) reports that the overall commercial kill of North American salmon is down from a peak of more than 1.5 million fish annually in the mid-1970s, to fewer than 10,000 fish today.

Even with the dramatic cutback in commercial netting, there are further problems in the ocean, indicated by the plummeting number of Atlantic salmon returning to spawn in their native streams. These problems may include the melting of icebergs, with a resulting critical change in water temperatures; the overfishing of food-chain species such as krill, sand lance, herring, and capelin; the taking of salmon as a by-catch in fisheries for other species; and the expanding seal population.

Closer to home, the aquaculture industry, which was originally seen as a solution to commercial harvesting, is having a negative impact on wild salmon. Situated in the estuaries of the Atlantic provinces, these fish-farming operations give rise to continuing problems including new diseases (such as the deadly Infectious Salmon Anemia), parasites, and escapement. Escapees, with the ability to dilute the wild salmon's gene pool, have taken over at least two rivers in New Brunswick.

A series of Canadian supreme court decisions on aboriginal rights to harvest salmon is causing more concern in the conservation field.

On the positive side, the Department of Fisheries and Oceans (DFO) has announced a three-year salmon management plan (1999–2001) for Newfoundland and Labrador, based on a river classification system. Seasonal retention limits have been determined for each river individually. Anglers will be required to use barbless hooks for all angling, and the rivers will be closed when low water levels and high water temperatures reach the critical point. Autumn catch-and-release fisheries will be permitted on the Gander and Humber Rivers.

ASF, whose mission is to promote the conservation and wise management of the Atlantic salmon and its environment, continues to be thoroughly involved in all of these problems, seeking solutions both nationally and internationally. Under this organization's leadership, we may one day have an answer to a most troubling question:

Can we yet save what Lee called "this most magnificent fish"?